STARGAZING *for* BEGINNERS

A USER-FRIENDLY GUIDE FOR LOCATING AND UNDERSTANDING CONSTELLATIONS, THE SUN, THE MOON, ECLIPSES, AND MORE

John Mosley

A ROXBURY PARK BOOK

LOWELL HOUSE

LOS ANGELES

CONTEMPORY BOOKS

CHICAGO

MONTHLY AND SOUTHERN SKY CHARTS CREATED WITH
STARRY NIGHT BY
SIENNA SOFTWARE
105 PEARS AVENUE
TORONTO, ONTARIO, CANADA
HTTP://WWW.SIENNASOFT.COM/SIENNA

Library of Congress Cataloging-in-Publication Data

Mosley, John.
    Stargazing for beginners : a user-friendly guide for locating and understanding constellations, planets, comets, meteors, and more / by John Mosley
      p.   cm.
    "Roxbury Park book"
    Includes bibliographical references and index.
    ISBN 1-56565-821-3
    1. Astronomy—Observers' manuals. 2. Constellations—Observers' manuals. I. Title.
QB64.M68 1997
522—dc21

Requests for such permissions should be addressed to:

Lowell House
2020 Avenue of the Stars, Suite 300
Los Angeles, CA 90067

Lowell House books can be purchased at special discounts when ordered in bulk for premiums and special sales. Contact Department TC at the above address.

Publisher: Jack Artenstein
Editor in Chief, Roxbury Park Books: Michael Artenstein
Director of Publishing Services: Rena Copperman
Managing Editor: Lindsey Hay
Text Design: Carolyn Wendt

Roxbury Park is an imprint of Lowell House,
A Division of the RGA Publishing Group, Inc.

Manufactured in the United States of America
10 9 8 7 6 5 4 3 2

To my parents, John and Edna,
for 50 years of love

Contents

Introduction

✧

"The sky is accessible" is the theme of this book. Although perhaps confusing at first, finding order in the patterns formed by the stars and in the motions of the sun, moon, and planets is not difficult. Learning to find your way around the sky and understanding the changes that happen in it are, in fact, surprisingly easy. And that knowledge is lifelong. Studies show that once you've learned to recognize the constellations, you do not forget them. Like learning to ride a bicycle, learning the constellations remains with you.

Another interesting aspect of the sky is that we see the genuine thing. This may sound trivial, but it is actually profound. We have all heard of the Eiffel Tower, Mount Everest, and the Great Wall of China, but to see them in person is difficult, and we don't often return to them. Usually, we experience the world's greatest attractions through pictures. Yet when we look at the star Betelgeuse, the constellation Leo, or the Milky Way, we are seeing the original article. We see what all the peoples around the world see and what generations before us saw and wondered over. The sky binds cultures across space and time; it is one of the few things we all have in common, no matter when or where we live.

This book assumes that you want to know more about the things you see in the sky. It is targeted toward armchair and amateur astronomers who would like greater familiarity with the sky. The book is essentially for naked-eye viewers and emphasizes the constellations and motions in the sky. Included are notes on the brighter objects you can see with binoculars.

Not only is the sky accessible, but watching it is a lot of fun.

Chapter One

✴

WHAT IS A CONSTELLATION?

A constellation is a pattern of stars, but it is also more than that: It is a specific area of the sky and everything that lies within this area. There are billions of stars in the sky, and every one of them belongs to one of the eighty-eight official constellations. Think of a state (or province, if you are in Canada). Each state has a shape or outline, but everything within its boundaries is part of that state.

At one time, constellations were thought of as patterns of major stars only, while in between were "no-man's lands" where ownership was in dispute. The boundaries of the constellations were decided by a committee of astronomers in 1928, and these boundaries are shown on some star charts. Everything in the sky is in one constellation or another.

Antique star charts show fancy figures, such as ladies in flowing robes and an animal that is half goat and half fish. These colorful figures appeared during the Renaissance, when all charts—both terrestrial and celestial—were decorative as well as functional and when it was considered a sin to leave margins unadorned. You will not find (and should not look for) such fancy figures in the sky. Look instead for simple patterns such as crosses, squares, triangles, and bent lines. These unofficial lines and patterns will vary from chart to chart, but using them makes it easier to learn the constellations. You can even make up your own to help you.

A few constellations, for example, Scorpius and Orion, do look like what they are named after, but these are exceptions. Others were named in honor of heroes and objects, but not because of any resemblance to them. We do similar things today. The state of

Washington, for example, does not look like George—and it was never intended to. It is the same with the constellations.

Many constellations seem to have been named for symbolic reasons. Libra, for example, is a set of balance scales. Perhaps it was so named because the sun appeared here on the first day of autumn, when day and night are equal (balanced) in length. It is thought that the Great Bear (Ursa Major) reminded people of the seasonal behavior of hibernating bears. It is likely that the *positions* of the stars were more important than their *patterns* when it came to naming them—a celestial example of *location* being more important than appearance. Why each ancient constellation was given its name has a good cultural reason, but in general, that reason has been lost in prehistory.

> ## ✦ GREEK LETTERS ✦
>
> *The brightest stars in a constellation are named with letters of the Greek alphabet. The first five letters, in order, are alpha, beta, gamma, delta, and epsilon. Usually, the brightest star in a constellation is named alpha. For example, Vega is known as Alpha in Lyra (or Alpha Lyrae for short).*

Learning the constellations is not hard. It's certainly not necessary to learn all eighty-eight. Many contain only faint stars and are unimportant, and some cannot be seen from North America. If you learn about thirty major constellations, you will know the sky very well. You can learn the others later if you wish.

The constellations change with the seasons, so it takes most of one year to learn them all. When you start doesn't matter. At any instant, you can see half the sky, and if you watch all night you will see roughly two-thirds of the sky. However, you cannot see stars in the part of the sky that is presently behind the sun. To see those stars, you must wait until the sun has moved out of the way, which takes a few months. Take one year to learn the constellations. During the following year, they will become old friends you will remember for the rest of your life.

✳ MAGNITUDE SYSTEM ✳

Since the time of Hipparchus in the second century B.C., stars have been ranked by brightness according to their magnitude. *The magnitude of a star expresses its apparent brightness as seen from Earth; it tells us nothing about the star's intrinsic luminosity. Hipparchus divided all naked-eye stars into six magnitudes, assigning a magnitude of 1 to the brightest and 6 to the faintest. His system has since been put on a firm mathematical footing and has been extended to both brighter and fainter objects. The very brightest objects have negative magnitudes (Sirius is magnitude –1.5; Venus can be magnitude –4; the full moon is magnitude –12). The faintest stars you will see from a city are magnitude 4 or 5. On a clear night you can see magnitude 6; with binoculars or a small telescope, 9; with a good amateur telescope, about 14; and with the Hubble Space Telescope, 30. The progression from one magnitude to the next represents a change of 2.5 times (a third-magnitude star is 2.5 times brighter than a fourth-magnitude star), so a first magnitude star is one hundred times brighter than a sixth-magnitude star.*

✦

Chapter Two

HISTORY OF
THE CONSTELLATIONS

The constellations were invented. They are imaginary, and someone had to think them up. A few were invented in modern times, but most are thousands of years old. Some are even prehistoric. Discovering the origins of the constellations requires detective work in which historians and astronomers piece together the few existing clues to attempt to work out a story. The task is far from complete. Today we know very little about the origins of many of the most famous constellations.

The oldest constellation may be the Great Bear. People in widely separated lands such as Siberia and North America see a Great Bear near the sky's north pole. It is possible that these people independently thought these stars acted like a hibernating bear, disappearing in the autumn and reappearing in the spring. It is also possible that one group of people began calling these stars a bear and carried this idea with them as they migrated. If so, people have been calling these stars a bear for more than ten thousand years—since the last ice age—and perhaps even longer. The Great Bear may be the oldest human invention that has kept its identity continuously throughout the millennia.

Many of the most familiar constellations were invented by the Sumerians, who lived in what is now Iraq. The Sumerians were the first systematic stargazers that we know of. More than five thousand years ago (before the invention of writing), they invented the idea of dividing the sky into the familiar patterns we still see today, like Leo, Scorpius, and Orion. In trying to understand the changes in the sky that accompany the changes in the seasons, they charted the path of the sun and planets among the stars. The first catalog of constellations appears as cuneiform inscriptions on clay tablets dating to around 1000 B.C. Called the *mul-Apin* ("Constellations of the Plow"), this work describes the relationships among about thirty constellations.

The Babylonians, who followed the Sumerians, kept this information alive until it was borrowed by the Greeks much later. Other constellations may have come from peoples in the Mediterranean region, but the details have been lost and we may never know their histories. It is certain, however, that many of our familiar constellations are Mesopotamian in origin and some are even prehistoric.

The ancient Greeks added to the Babylonian collection. By the beginning of the Christian era, forty-eight constellations had been named and recognized. These were summarized in the *Syntaxis (System)* by Ptolemy, written around A.D. 150 in Alexandria, Egypt. The *Syntaxis* contains a catalog of 1,022 stars and descriptions of the forty-eight "Ptolemaic" constellations. His main source was a long poem called *Phaenomena*, composed about 275 B.C. by Aratus of Soli but based on an earlier (and now lost) work from around 350 B.C. by the Greek astronomer Eudoxos. Only scattered references to stars and constellations appear in earlier Greek literature.

✦ THE ORIGIN OF MODERN CONSTELLATIONS ✦

ANON. (about 1500): Crux

BAYER (1603)*: Apus, Chamaeleon, Dorado, Grus, Hydrus, Indus, Musca, Pavo, Phoenix, Triangulum Australe, Tucana, Volans

PLANCIUS (1613): Camelopardalis, Columba, Monoceros

HEVELIUS (1690): Canes Venatici, Lacerta, Leo Minor, Lynx, Scutum, Sextans, Vulpecula

LACAILLE (1752): Antlia, Caelum, Circinus, Fornax, Horologium, Mensa, Microscopium, Norma, Octans, Pictor, Pyxis, Reticulum, Sculptor, Telescopium (Lacaille also divided Argo Navis into Carina, Puppis, and Vela)

* Bayer's constellations originally came from Keyser and Houtman.

During the Dark Ages in Europe, learning was kept alive by the Arabs, who copied and preserved Greek and Roman learning. Ptolemy's work was called *The Greatest Book,* or *Almagest,* and it is known through Arabic translations. The Ptolemaic constellations remained unmodified for fourteen centuries, and the Arabs gave most of the stars the common names by which we know them today. These names are usually simply Arabic translations of descriptions of the stars' positions as given by Ptolemy, but those unfamiliar with Arabic often find the strange-sounding names beautiful. For example, Rigel (in Orion) means "foot"—which is exactly where the star is in the constellation.

Ptolemy's *Almagest* was translated into Latin (the universal language of the Christian world) and reintroduced into Europe around the year A.D. 1000, after an absence of nearly a millennium. The constellations acquired their familiar Latin names at this time.

The remaining forty constellations were added relatively recently. When European navigators sailed far south of the equator, they saw for the first time stars that previously had been hidden below their southern horizon. Several new constellations, such as the Southern Triangle, were invented in the late 1500s and early 1600s.

The German lawyer and astronomer Johannes Bayer is generally credited with adding twelve new constellations, including the Peacock (Pavo) and the Flying Fish (Volans), in 1603. He used reports and maps of the southern seas made by explorers and navigators but did not personally see these stars. They were first charted by, and should be credited to, the nearly forgotten Dutchmen Pieter Keyser and Cornelis de Houtman. Keyser navigated a trading ship to Java in 1596, where he cataloged 135 "new" southern stars and arranged them in twelve new constellations he invented. His constellations first appeared on Dutch celestial globes in 1598 and 1600. His countryman, Houtman, who was on the same expedition, later extended the catalog to 303 stars, which appeared in the same twelve constellations on a celestial globe by Dutch cartographer Willem Blau in 1603. Not until they were included in Bayer's great *Uranometria* that same year, however, did they achieve legitimacy and permanency. Bayer also introduced the idea of using Greek letters to name the brighter stars.

Petrus Plancius, a Dutch cartographer who worked with Pieter Keyser, added several constellations of his own. Most have been discarded, but the Giraffe (Camelopardalis), the Dove (Columba), and the Unicorn (Monoceros) survive today.

Almost a century later, seven additional constellations were invented by the Polish astronomer Johannes Hevelius, who used them to fill in places on his star atlas that to him looked too empty. His aim was to make his charts more attractive and to "use up" faint stars that were located between major constellations. These new northern constellations, including the Lizard (Lacerta) and the Fox (Vulpecula), are made up of faint stars and are not easy to see. Hevelius is remembered today for being the last astronomer to observe with the naked eye, despite the invention of the telescope two generations earlier (he did not trust the poor-quality lenses common in early telescopes). His new constellations appeared in his great atlas, *Firmamentum Sobiescianum,* which was printed posthumously by his wife in 1690.

Nicolas Louis de Lacaille, a French astronomer who lived in Cape Town, South Africa, from 1750 to 1752, created fourteen new constellations from the southern stars. He named them after scientific and artistic inventions and tools he thought important. Among them are the Telescope (Telescopium), the Microscope (Microscopium), the Air Pump (Antlia), and the Compass (Circinus). These constellations are faint, but they honor the achievements of the age that saw them named. Lacaille's unromantic inventions are quite a contrast to the gods and heroes of the classical northern sky, and he has been accused of turning the sky into someone's attic. Although they cannot be seen from North America or Europe, the southern constellations are described briefly in this book for completeness.

Through the centuries, other astronomers and mapmakers added new star figures to their charts or renamed old ones, often to flatter a patron. At one time, there were a Battery, a Cat, and a Flying Squirrel in the sky. One astronomer Christianized the sky, renaming the constellations of the zodiac after the twelve Apostles. Many constellations appeared briefly before being rejected by the astronomical community and are no longer used; you can see them only on antique star charts, where they are curiosities from a bygone age. Others have evolved; Apis, the Bee, became Musca, the Fly, for example. The modern constellations were finalized by a committee of the International Astronomical Union in 1928 and presumably will not change again.

Although we use the Latinized name of the constellations, some have common names that come from northern Europe that do not reflect a Greek or Middle Eastern origin. The seven bright stars of Ursa Major, for example, which we call the Big Dipper in North America, are called the Plough in England and the Wagon in Germany.

Our familiar constellations are called "Western" because they are part of the heritage of our Western civilization. Other people in other lands divided the sky in their own way and saw entirely different groups of stars. The ancient Chinese, for example, divided the sky into about three hundred small constellations of only several stars each. The ancient Egyptians saw crocodiles and hippopotamuses. In general, people discarded their own constellations—along with much of the rest of their culture—when they came in contact with westerners. The Western constellations are now recognized around the world and have become truly universal.

Chapter Three

✦

THE CHANGING SKY

The sky is in constant motion relative to observers on the earth. The sky itself is not something that can move, but the earth's motions cause the sky to appear to change its position hourly and monthly. While we "stand still" and look at the stars overhead, the earth is carrying us in two directions at once: It is spinning on its axis (once a day) and orbiting the sun (once a year). Although we do not feel these motions, we see their results in the sky, because they cause us to see different constellations at different times of the night and at different times of the year.

HOURLY CHANGES

The easiest motion to see and to understand is the daily rotation of the earth. The earth spins on its axis, rotating counterclockwise as seen from above the North Pole. As we turn toward the east, the sky seems to turn toward the west, carrying with it the stars, sun, moon, and planets. We say that the stars "rise" in the east and "set" in the west even though we know that what is really happening is that the earth is turning. The earth's spinning causes us to face different parts of the universe at different times of the night.

During the course of a night, the stars rotate around the sky's north pole, called the North Celestial Pole. The North Celestial Pole is the point in the sky that lies directly above the earth's North Pole and is the point where the earth's axis, projected into space, meets the sky. Polaris, the North Star, is very close to the North Celestial Pole.

The path an object takes across the sky depends on its distance from the North Celestial Pole. Polaris, which is so close to the pole that it moves very little, remains in virtually the same spot all night long and is the pivot around which the rest of the sky turns. Stars near Polaris make small circles around the pole each night, while stars farther away make ever larger circles. Stars far enough from the pole to make circles that intersect the horizon rise and set each night. Stars close enough to the pole to remain above the horizon are called "circumpolar." Far to the south and centered on the spot opposite the North Celestial Pole is an area of the sky, equal in size to the circumpolar stars, that forever remains below the horizon as seen from the Northern Hemisphere. These southern stars were unknown to Europeans until the Age of Exploration took sailors south to new lands—and to a new sky.

MONTHLY CHANGES

At the same time that the earth is spinning on its axis, it also orbits the sun. It takes the earth 365 times longer to orbit the sun than to rotate once on its axis, and the change in the sky is correspondingly slow. We see the effect of the earth's rotation in just a few minutes if we are watching the sun set, but we notice the effect of the earth's orbital motion around the sun only after several nights have passed.

We do not feel the spinning of the earth, yet we see its effect in the nightly turning of the sky overhead. In the same way, we do not feel the orbital motion of the earth around the sun, yet we see its effect in the seasonal change of the constellations. The stars we see at night lie in the direction opposite the sun. (The stars that lie in the same direction as the sun are in the daytime sky—and we cannot see them.) As the earth orbits the sun, the part of the sky that lies opposite the sun changes week by week and month by month. Thus the constellations we see at night change with the seasons.

As the earth moves around the sun, the sun appears to move around the sky. It is no wonder that until the fifteenth century it was universally assumed that the earth is stationary and the sun goes around the earth once a year. It certainly does seem that way. Although we cannot see the sun and the stars at the same time, we can keep track of the sun's location and know its position against the background constellations.

Face the noontime sun and imagine the earth's orbit as a circle with the sun at the center. We are moving to the *right* around the sun; consequently, the sun appears to move to the *left* around the earth. Each day we move 1/365 of the way westward around the sun, and each day the sun appears to move 1/365 of the way eastward around the sky. This 1/365 of a circle is almost exactly 1 degree. (This is no coincidence. Babylonian astronomers originally divided the circle into 360 parts instead of, say, one hundred because they were plotting the annual motion of the sun; we still use their system today.) Each night, the sun is 1 degree to the left, or east, of where it was the night before.

We keep time by the sun, not the stars, and each night's observing begins when the sun sets. The sun's daily 1-degree eastward shift against the stars seems to cause the stars to shift 1 degree to the west each night. Tonight the stars will be 1 degree west of where they were at the same time last night, 7 degrees west of where they were last week, and about 30 degrees (about one-twelfth of 365) west of where they were last month. After a year, they will have returned to their original positions. Thus, we see the stars in the same place in the sky on the same date each year.

Because each night the stars appear to the west of where they were the previous night, they set earlier each night. A star that sets due west will set four minutes earlier tonight than last night (four minutes = 1/365 of twenty-four hours), it sets eight minutes earlier than two nights ago, a half-hour earlier than a week ago, an hour earlier than two weeks ago, and two hours earlier than a month ago. Likewise, a star that rises due east will rise four minutes earlier each night. For example, if Regulus rises at 11:00 P.M. tonight, it will rise at 10:56 P.M. tomorrow night, a half-hour earlier (10:30 P.M.) after a week, an hour earlier (10:00 P.M.) after two weeks, and two hours earlier (9:00 P.M.) after a month. You can wait up to see stars that rise in the early morning hours tomorrow morning—or you can wait a few months until those same stars have shifted their rising to the evening sky.

Stars that rise in the northeast and set in the northwest show a smaller hourly and nightly change in position than stars that rise due east and set due west. The closer a star is to the North Celestial Pole, the smaller its shift in position each hour and each night. The North Star itself does not change position at all.

If you could make a time-lapse movie of the sky in which one frame equals one night (which is possible in a planetarium theater or with planetarium software on a home computer), you would see the stars rotating from east to west as they do during the course of one night. Not only do we face different parts of the sky each hour as the earth turns, but we also face different parts of the sky each month as the earth orbits the sun. The constellations change both hourly and seasonally. It is difficult for descriptions alone to explain these movements. To understand them, you should actually go outside and watch the sky for a few hours and over a few weeks—then it will all become clear.

In addition to the two motions of the earth, our moon and the planets also move around the sky. Their endlessly changing configurations provide much of the entertainment in sky-watching.

THE MOON'S MOTION

The most rapid change we see in the sky—other than the daily rotation of the earth—is the motion of the moon. The moon orbits the earth once a month, traveling completely around the sky in just under thirty days.

There are actually two kinds of "month." The time it takes the moon to circle the earth and return to its original position with respect to the stars is a *sidereal* month (sidereal means stellar). It is equal to 27.322 days. If the moon is near the star Regulus, 27.322 days later it will be near Regulus again. However, this is not the time it takes the moon to go through a cycle of phases. The moon's phases are determined by the moon's position relative to the sun, not to the stars. During those 27.322 days, the earth has moved almost a twelfth of the way around the sun, causing the sun to move almost a twelfth of the way around the sky; therefore, the moon needs an extra two days to regain its position relative to the sun. The *synodic* month—the time from new moon to new moon—is 29.531 days and is the "month" that we usually use (called a lunar month).

The most obvious aspect of the moon is its changing phases. One side of the moon is illuminated by the sun while the other side is in darkness (this is true for any globe in full sunlight), but the half that is lit and the half that is dark change in a monthly cycle as the moon orbits the earth. The phases of the moon were probably the first astronomical cycle noticed—many thousands of years ago—yet they are still confusing people today. One complication is that the moon keeps one face permanently turned toward the earth. How the angle of sunlight changes on the moon through the month while the moon keeps one face toward the earth is a difficult concept to grasp. A simple analogy may help.

Place a chair outside in the sun. Imagine that the sun is low in the sky (unless it actually is). The chair represents the earth; you are the moon, and the sun is the sun. Move sidestep counterclockwise in a large circle around the chair, always facing it, and notice what happens to the sunlight striking your head. At one point in your "orbit," you are facing the chair with the sun behind you; the back of your head is illuminated, while your face is dark. A person sitting in the chair would see no light on your face; you are at "new moon" (which is "no moon" as seen from the earth). After you take a few steps to the right, the left part of your face becomes illuminated, and a person sitting in the chair would see a crescent of light on your face. One quarter of an orbit after "new moon," the left half of your face is lit while the right half is dark. Your face is half lit, but you are a "first-quarter moon" because you have traveled the first quarter of the way around the earth/chair. One-quarter of an orbit later, you are facing both the chair and the sun; your face is fully illuminated, and a person sitting in the chair would see a "full moon." One-quarter of an orbit later, the sun shines on the right side of your face. You now appear as a half-moon, but you are at "three-quarters" phase because you have gone three-quarters of the way around the earth/chair. After a final-quarter orbit, you have returned to "new." One cycle takes just over twenty-nine days, or one lunar month.

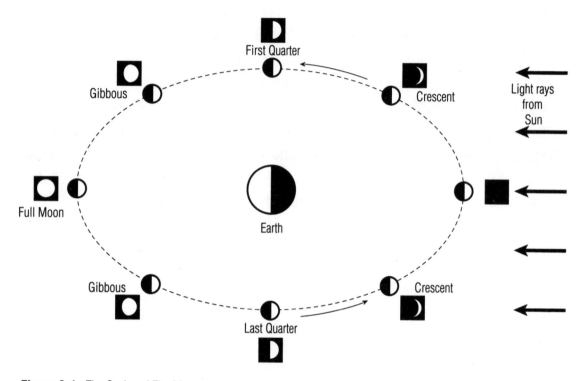

Figure 3.1 *The Cycles of The Moon*

During a month, the moon makes a complete circuit of the sky. Our calendar month approximates the lunar month, and our week approximates a quarter of a month.

THE PLANETS' MOTIONS AND THE ZODIAC

The earth moves around the sun in one earth year (365¼ days). Each planet orbits the sun in its period of time, which ranges from 88 earth days for Mercury to 248 earth years for Pluto. We can watch the planets move around the sky at various speeds, moving from constellation to constellation.

Because the solar system is nearly flat and the planets' orbits all lie in nearly the same plane, we see their orbits essentially edge-on. If we were to look down on the solar system from above, we would see the planets move around the sun in nearly circular orbits. From our vantage point *within* the solar system and in the plane of the orbits, we see the planets move back and forth along the line that marks the plane of the solar system. That line, called the *ecliptic*, is the orbit of the earth projected into space. It is identical to the apparent path of the sun through the sky. The important point is that, because the solar system is flat, the planets and our moon stay close to the path of the sun.

The ecliptic is a line that encircles the sky. The sun remains on it, as do the moon and the planets. The constellations through which the sun passes are known as the constellations of the *zodiac*. Although they are well known, many of them are inconspicuous and contain no bright stars. For example, Aquarius has no bright stars; it is famous because of *where* it is rather than *what* it is (which is a bunch of faint stars with no easily recognizable shape).

The zodiac, invented in Babylon about 2,600 years ago, was divided into the twelve traditional constellations. But the sun actually passes through thirteen constellations using modern constellation boundaries, and the astronomical zodiac has thirteen constellations: Capricornus, Aquarius, Pisces, Aries, Taurus, Gemini, Cancer, Leo, Virgo, Libra, Scorpius, Ophiuchus, and Sagittarius. The amount of time the sun spends in each depends upon the constellation's width, which is different for each constellation.

The planets orbit the sun in the same direction as the earth (counterclockwise as seen from above the solar system's north pole) and would move from west to east in the sky, as the moon does, if our view of the sky were not complicated by our earth's own motion. To understand the planets' apparent motion in the sky, we divide them into two groups: those that orbit inside Earth's orbit (Mercury and Venus) and those that orbit outside Earth's orbit (all the rest). Planets in the first group are called "inferior planets," and the others "superior planets."

Inferior planets remain in the vicinity of the sun and are either in front of the sun, behind it, or a short distance to the east or west. We cannot see them when they are in front of or behind the sun, of course. When they are to one side of the sun, they are in the morning sky or the evening sky. Mercury remains so close to the sun (no more than 28 degrees from the sun) that it is visible only in twilight, and even then it is never far from the horizon. The challenge in observing Mercury is simply to find it. Venus, poetically called the "morning star" and the "evening star," can stray up to 47 degrees from the sun and can be seen against a dark sky, but it too is usually visible in twilight.

Both Mercury and Venus go through cycles that begin when they are between Earth and the sun, at which time they are invisible. They then move westward and to the right of the sun, rise before the sun, and appear in the morning sky. Their visibility improves as their angular distance from the sun increases, until they reach their maximum angular separation from the sun (called "maximum elongation" in almanacs). Then, receding from Earth, they swing around to the far side of the sun, disappearing from view before aligning behind the sun and again become invisible (when directly behind the sun, they are said to be at "superior conjunction"). They then move eastward and to the left of the sun, appearing in the evening sky. Because they are on the far side of the sun when they begin their evening appearance, their relative motion in the sky is slow and they reappear gradually. Their visibility in the evening sky improves daily until they eventually reach their maximum eastward angular separation from the sun. The cycle is complete when they move back in front of the sun. Because they are close to Earth when they are in front of the sun and their apparent motion is greatest then, they disappear from the evening sky relatively rapidly.

The outer, superior planets cannot move between Earth and the sun, but they can position themselves on the far side of the sun. A planet on the far side of the sun, at "superior conjunction," cannot be seen. It is *Earth* that moves between the sun and a superior planet; when it does, that planet lies opposite the sun and is said to be at "opposition." A planet at opposition is at its closest to Earth and at its brightest and largest. Because it is opposite the sun, it rises at sunset and is visible all night long.

Superior planets would move only eastward around the sun and against the background of stars if Earth did not move faster on an inside orbit. Our speedier motion, however, causes us to catch and pass each outer planet, and for a few months Earth's more rapid motion makes it appear as if the planet we are passing were moving backward against the stars. This westward or "retrograde" motion is an illusion; the outer planets do not actually back up in their orbits; they simply appear to do so as seen from Earth. You see the same effect when you pass a slower moving car on the freeway—it *appears* to move backward as seen against distant trees and hills, but you simply are moving forward at a greater speed. Each planet is in retrograde motion as we pass it, and after we have moved on the planet resumes its normal eastward motion. Hence, each outer planet appears to make a backward loop in the sky each year as we overtake it and move on.

The planets look like bright stars and are easy to recognize. Mercury is visible only near the horizon during morning or evening twilight, and it takes special knowledge to find it. Uranus, Neptune, and Pluto are too faint to be seen without the help of a telescope and detailed charts.

Chapter Four

✴

MONTHLY STAR CHARTS

JANUARY

The new year begins with a shower. The short-lived Quadrantid meteor shower peaks on or near January 3, and the best time to watch these meteors is before dawn on the morning of the peak. Far fewer meteors are visible the morning before and after. These meteors appear to radiate from the northern part of the constellation Boötes (formerly part of a larger but now obsolete constellation, Quadrans Muralis, the "Wall Quadrant"; hence the name). Under ideal dark-sky conditions, a single observer may see one meteor each minute after midnight. The Quadrantid meteors travel across the sky at medium speed (25 miles per second), and few leave smoke trails.

Although this is the coldest time of the year—to the discomfort of stargazers—the earth is actually nearer to the sun in January and February than in July and August. The seasons are caused by the tilt of the earth's axis, not by the earth's changing distance from the sun. The earth is at *perihelion,* its point closest to the sun, on or near January 1. On that date, the sun is about three million miles or 3 percent, closer to the earth than when it is at its farthest point, or *aphelion,* on or near July 4. (Thus, the earth's perihelion and aphelion both occur on or near national holidays—in the United States, which is as it should be.) We are cold in January because our Northern Hemisphere is tilted away from the sun and thus the days are short, not because we are far from the sun. The seasons are reversed in the Southern Hemisphere.

Orion dominates the southern sky this month. The most conspicuous part of Orion, the Hunter—and the part people notice first—is the short string of three equally bright stars that form his belt. Nowhere else in the sky are three bright stars so close together. These stars—Mintaka, Alnilam, and Alnitak, from west to east—span 3 degrees and are a convenient way of visualizing 3 degrees as measured in the sky. Hanging from Orion's belt is his great sword, and in the sword is a "jewel" known as the Orion Nebula. This enormous cloud of gas some 1,600 light-years from Earth is the best-known stellar nursery. A group of brand new stars within it is lighting up the gaseous material out of which they are forming. Without optical aid, the Orion Nebula appears as a slightly nebulous faint star, but even a small telescope shows its true nature. It is one of the showpieces of the sky.

Orion's shoulders are marked by the red star Betelgeuse and Bellatrix, his knees by Saiph and the blue star Rigel. Rigel and Betelgeuse display a nice contrast in star colors.

The Hunter is raising his shield to defend himself from Taurus, the Bull. Trace a line along Orion's belt and extend it westward until you come to the orange star Aldebaran—the eye of the Bull. The face of the Bull is marked by a large cluster of stars known as the Hyades. The Bull's horns arch menacingly over Orion. The Bull has no back, but where his back would be we find the Pleiades, the prettiest star cluster of all and a delight when viewed through binoculars. These two star clusters in Taurus are the loveliest in the entire sky. Do not use a telescope to view them. Doing so will restrict your sight to only a few stars at a time. The best views of such large star clusters are with the naked eye or binoculars.

In line with the stars of Orion's belt but in the opposite direction from the Bull is Sirius, the Dog Star—the brightest star in the sky. It is also the brightest star in Canis Major, the Large Dog. Canis Minor, the Small Dog, is north of the Large Dog. Canis Minor is made up of only two stars and looks more like a hot dog than a hunting dog, but if you have only two stars to make a dog, it will always look like a hot dog.

Below the Hunter's feet is Lepus, the Hare—a more realistic adversary for Orion than the Bull.

Note how devoid of bright and even medium-bright stars the southwestern sky is. Here, the constellations Eridanus, Cetus, and Pisces lie away from the Milky Way in an underpopulated part of the sky.

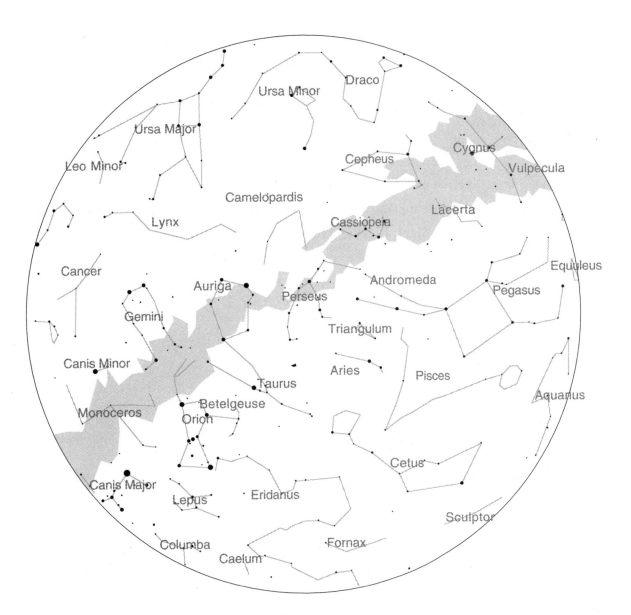

The Sky in January

Feb. 15	*6 P.M.*	*ST*
Feb. 1	*7 P.M.*	*ST*
Jan. 15	*8 P.M.*	*ST*
Jan. 1	*9 P.M.*	*ST*
Dec. 15	*10 P.M.*	*ST*
Dec. 1	*11 P.M.*	*ST*
Nov. 15	*midnight*	*ST*

FEBRUARY

There are more bright stars visible in the south and overhead during early February evenings than at any other time of the year. Nowhere else do we see so many brilliant stars concentrated in such a small area. Aldebaran in Taurus, Capella in Auriga, Castor and Pollux in Gemini, Procyon in Canis Minor, Sirius in Canis Major, and the seven brightest stars of Orion all fall within an oval about 65 by 45 degrees in extent. Many other parts of the sky that are equal in size (for example, Eridanus and Cetus to the west or Hydra to the east) have *no* bright stars. Why are so many very bright stars grouped together in this one small area?

When we face these stars, we are facing the closest arm of our Milky Way Galaxy. All the stars in the sky are part of an enormous flattened system of stars we call our galaxy. We live within it, and we see it as the band of light called the Milky Way. Stars are not spread uniformly throughout the Milky Way but instead are concentrated in long, winding spiral arms. Our sun lies on the inside edge of the Orion Arm, and when we face Orion we are facing the nearest concentration of stars. Several of these thirteen bright stars are relatively near to us, but the bright stars of Orion and many of the fainter ones that make up these constellations are in fact part of that arm. The Orion Arm lies in the direction *away* from the center of the Milky Way.

If you could memorize the appearance of the winter Milky Way near Orion and later look at the summer Milky Way near Sagittarius and Scorpius, you would notice that the winter part of the Milky Way is only one-third as thick and bright as the summer part. (You can actually do this experiment in a planetarium theater, where you can rotate the sky through half a year in a moment.) However, because we are nearer to the Orion Arm than to the Sagittarius-Scorpius Arm, we see more bright stars in the winter than in the summer.

In both cases, the Milky Way is filled with star clusters and nebulae of great delight to observers with telescopes. More star clusters are visible through a telescope in the band of the Milky Way that stretches from Cassiopeia in the northwest through Perseus, Auriga, Gemini, and Monoceros in the south than are visible in any other part of the sky except the summer Milky Way. A good star atlas will show their locations in the sky.

One other very bright star (Canopus, the second brightest after Sirius) is visible from the southernmost part of the United States. If you live south of a line that runs from Atlanta to Dallas to Los Angeles, you can catch a glimpse of Canopus as it skirts the southern horizon.

With so many bright stars so close to each other, this is a good time to notice their contrasting colors. Sirius and Castor are about as white as stars can be. (When Sirius is near the horizon, it appears to change colors rapidly and dramatically because of atmospheric turbulence, but this twinkling comes from our atmosphere, not the star.) Rigel is distinctly blue and in fact is the bluest bright star in the sky. Procyon, Pollux, and Capella are yellowish and more closely resemble our sun. Betelgeuse and Aldebaran, often described as red, are really orangish-white. (Which looks redder to you?) All these colors are subtle, but you can recognize them if you look closely. Use binoculars that are slightly out of focus to enhance the color.

In the northeast, the Great Bear (Ursa Major) is beginning to rise, announcing that spring is coming soon.

The Sky in Februrary

The sky also appears as shown on the following dates:		
Mar. 1	*7 P.M.*	*ST*
Feb. 15	*8 P.M.*	*ST*
Feb. 1	*9 P.M.*	*ST*
Jan. 15	*10 P.M.*	*ST*
Jan. 1	*11 P.M.*	*ST*
Dec. 15	*midnight*	*ST*

MARCH

March is the transition from winter to spring, and in the sky we see the transition from the bright area containing the Milky Way in the west to the comparatively empty part of the sky outside the Milky Way's boundaries to the east. The many bright stars in and around Orion dominate the western sky, while the eastern sky is much blander, with Regulus as its sole bright star. This contrast is most apparent on March evenings. In April, May, and June, the Milky Way is at its poorest angle for viewing.

To the northeast, notice the Great Bear, Ursa Major, which comes out of hibernation by rising during the early evening as spring arrives. The Great Bear behaves like its terrestrial counterpart. In late fall, it retreats low in the northern sky, and during the winter it is at its lowest, under the North Star and largely hidden from view. It returns to the sky as life returns to the land in spring. Today we accept this as a simple coincidence, but apparently it had significance to people who lived as long ago as the Ice Age. Scholars are fairly certain that the celestial Great Bear was originally associated with bears because it *behaves* like bears, not because of any physical resemblance in its pattern of stars. Cave bears were worshiped during the Ice Age in Europe and Asia, and it is quite likely that the celestial Bear was worshiped too. The idea of the celestial Bear may have originated more than ten thousand years ago in the Old World and been carried to the New World during the migrations that peopled North America. Calling these stars a Bear may be the oldest intellectual idea that survives. In comparison, calling the seven brightest stars of the Bear a Dipper seems to date back no more than about two hundred years (see Ursa Major, page 107).

Spring begins in the earth's Northern Hemisphere on or near March 20. Autumn begins in the Southern Hemisphere. On this date, called the vernal equinox, the sun rises due east and sets due west, and the days and nights are equal in length all over the earth. This is the day when the sun, in its apparent annual path around the sky, crosses the celestial equator from south to north. For the next six months the sun rises in the northeast and sets in the northwest, and the days are longer than the nights. The full moon—which lies opposite the sun—also rises in the east and sets in the west this month.

The winter constellations Orion, Taurus, Auriga, Gemini, and Canis Major and Minor still dominate the western sky. Sirius is actually at its highest soon after sunset in March. This is a good month to try to see Puppis, Vela, and other parts of the former constellation Argo Navis that lie below it. These constellations are glorious when viewed from the Southern Hemisphere, where they are high overhead.

Cancer is a curious constellation. It consists of almost empty space, with no bright stars, and few people would have heard of it if it lay in another direction. It is known only because the sun moves through it. It does, however, have a star cluster—the Beehive—at its center. Seen through binoculars on a dark night, the Beehive is one of the nicest star clusters of the sky. It is also one of the few bright star clusters that planets move in front of, and you will occasionally see Mars or Venus among its stars. (Slower-moving Jupiter will move very near to or in front of the Beehive in the years 2002, 2003, and 2014, Saturn in 2005 and 2006, but not again in our lifetimes.)

The head of Hydra is under Cancer, a good example of the faint leading the faint. To the north of Cancer is the even fainter Lynx. Only Ursa Major, Leo, and Virgo when it rises provide something interesting to look at in the eastern sky in March.

The Sky in March

The sky also appears as shown on the following dates:		
Mar. 1	7 P.M.	ST
Feb. 15	8 P.M.	ST
Feb. 1	9 P.M.	ST
Jan. 15	10 P.M.	ST
Jan. 1	11 p.m	ST
Dec. 15	midnight	ST

APRIL

It seems to get dark late at night in April not only because the sun sets almost a minute later each day, but also because in the United States (except in Arizona and Hawaii) the government implements daylight saving time. Set your clock ahead one hour (for example, from 2:00 A.M. to 3:00 A.M.) on the first Sunday in April, and lose an hour of sleep. Remember, "spring forward, fall back." Daylight time runs from the first Sunday in April to the last Sunday in October. Children enjoy playing outside later—but stargazing, like bedtime, is delayed by an hour. Calendar times in this book—on the star chart on the facing page, for example—are adjusted for daylight time. Daylight saving time was introduced during World War I to assist war production by making it easier for people to work an hour later in dimly lit buildings. It was discontinued in 1919, revived in 1942, discontinued again in 1945, and revived once more in 1967. Many countries go on daylight time during the summer, although the starting and ending dates are not synchronized.

When the sky becomes dark, we see the winter constellations Orion, Auriga, Gemini, and Canis Major and Minor in the west, but they set early in the evening. The part of the sky that replaces them has so few bright stars that you can count them on the fingers of one hand: Regulus in Leo, Spica in Virgo, and Arcturus in Boötes. Leo and Virgo are recognizable patterns, but to the south are the sparsely populated constellations Hydra and Vela and a sprinkling of small, obscure constellations that almost nobody knows, such as Leo Minor, Sextans, and Antlia. They make one think that if the constellations were created afresh today, astronomers would find a better way to arrange the sky.

The sun lies very close to Regulus on August 22 each year. The nightly path of Regulus across the sky is the same as the path of the sun across the sky on that date. No other bright star lies as close to the ecliptic, the sun's annual path around the sky.

To the north lie the two Bears. These two constellations have been called many things through the years, but calling them the Bears is an old custom that crosses many cultural boundaries. Boötes herds or guards the Bears. In 1690, Johannes Hevelius created a new constellation called the Hunting Dogs (Canes Venatici) to accompany Boötes in his duties.

Vela and Puppis are part of a huge constellation of former times that was called Argo Navis—the ship of Jason and the Argonauts. The "ship" was reduced to several smaller constellations by Lacaille in the 1750s. The top part of the ancient ship is visible from the southern United States as a sprinkling of medium-bright stars along the southern horizon.

Hydra, the Snake, is the largest and one of the longest constellations. It takes practice to trace the long string of faint stars, which are not closely grouped, and to connect them to form a snakelike pattern. Her head is a little circle of stars south of Cancer.

Hydra's one medium-bright star, Alphard, is the only notable star in a huge area of the sky. The constellations Crater and Corvus are associated with Hydra and rest on her back.

The Lyrid meteor shower is active from approximately April 18 through April 25, with the greatest activity on April 21 and 22. This is a minor shower with only about a dozen meteors per hour at maximum. Observe during the early morning hours.

The Sky in April

The sky also appears as shown on the following dates:		
Apr. 15	9 P.M.	DT
Apr. 1	9 P.M.	ST
Mar. 15	10 P.M.	ST
Mar. 1	11 P.M.	ST
Feb. 15	midnight	ST

MAY

In May and June, the Milky Way lies flat along the horizon during the early evening. If you can see stars near the horizon, you can see the Milky Way ringing the earth and can easily imagine it as a flat plane with the earth at its center. In a planetarium theater, where the sky can be positioned precisely where you want it and the sky is always perfectly clear, the effect is striking. The Milky Way surrounds the earth, but the part toward Scorpius, which is rising in the southeast, is much brighter than the part toward Orion, which is setting in the southwest.

The sun, carrying the earth with it, orbits around the center of the Milky Way. It takes the sun 230 million earth years, or one "galactic year," to complete one orbit. This is the longest period of time found in nature. The sun is heading toward Cygnus, which lies in the northeast.

When the Milky Way lies along the horizon, its north pole is overhead. The Milky Way's north pole, called the North Galactic Pole, is simply a point in space—there is nothing there to be seen. It lies within the constellation Coma Berenices, the only constellation that is a cluster of stars. Coma Berenices is the second-closest cluster of stars, after the Hyades in Taurus. It spans such a large area of the sky (equal in size to the bowl of the Big Dipper) that it is too big to be seen with a telescope or even binoculars and must be looked at with the naked eye under a very dark sky to be appreciated. Binoculars will bring out the fainter stars, but only wide-angle binoculars will show the whole cluster at once. Beyond the star cluster, which lies nearby in our galaxy, is a faint but famous cluster of distant galaxies known simply as the Coma cluster.

The richest concentration of galaxies in the sky extends from Ursa Major south through Coma and into Virgo and Leo. This is the direction of the famous Virgo cluster of galaxies—the closest large cluster of galaxies to the Milky Way. Amateur astronomers viewing through large telescopes enjoy exploring the many galaxies visible here. Professional astronomers, too, are intensely interested in this part of the sky, because the Virgo cluster holds the key to understanding the size and age of the universe. If astronomers knew the precise distance to this cluster of thousands of galaxies, they could calibrate distances to the remotest objects in the universe. Beginning with Edwin Hubble decades ago, astronomers have concentrated on Virgo's cluster of galaxies, and understanding it is the major project of the Hubble Space Telescope today.

North of overhead is the Big Dipper, which is at its highest in May. Merak and Dubhe, two stars in the bowl, are called the Pointer Stars because they point to Polaris, the North

Star. The Pointer Stars are separated by 5 degrees—a convenient model for visualizing the span of 5 degrees in the sky. Polaris is at a distance equal to five times the separation of the Pointer Stars.

The Eta Aquarid meteor shower peaks on or about May 5, although activity is high for several days before and after. These swift meteors (their velocity is 41 miles per second) come from Halley's Comet, and they appear to radiate from the direction of the constellation Aquarius. The shower's radiant point does not rise until almost 3:00 A.M., and the best time to observe is shortly before dawn.

The Sky in May

The sky also appears as shown on the following dates:		
Jun. 1	8 P.M.	DT
May. 15	9 P.M.	DT
May. 1	10 P.M.	DT
Apr. 15	11 P.M.	DT
Apr. 1	11 P.M.	ST
Mar. 15	midnight	ST

JUNE

Summer's long days and late sunsets are a pleasure to vacationers as well as to anyone who needs to work outside late into the evening, but they are a liability to stargazers, who cannot begin to enjoy the heavens until the late evening. The short nights also put an end to stargazing relatively early in the morning. June is not a productive month for astronomers.

Summer begins officially in the earth's Northern Hemisphere on or near June 20, the date of the summer solstice—the moment when the sun, in its apparent annual path around the sky, reaches its farthest point north of the celestial equator. On this date, which is the longest day in the Northern Hemisphere, the sun rises as far north of east (and sets as far north of west) as it will during the year. At the same moment, winter begins in the earth's Southern Hemisphere. Summer ends in September at the autumn equinox.

Arcturus is June's dominant star. Viewed from much of the United States, it passes nearly overhead. Arcturus is now considered the brightest star in the constellation Boötes, the Herdsman, but in Greek times the star *was* the herdsman. He herds bears, not sheep or cows—the Great Bear and the Small Bear in their nightly journey around the pole.

Use the Big Dipper to find Arcturus. The last five stars in the bowl and handle of the Dipper form an arc of a wheel. Continue the "arc to Arcturus," and you will have found the star and remembered its name. Continue southward and "speed on to Spica," the brightest star in Virgo. Virgo is at its best in June; look for a large letter Y on its side, with a few fainter stars to the east. Trace the full length of Hydra, the Snake, in the southwestern sky. The head is low in the west when the tail is low in the south.

Far to the south of Virgo lies Centaurus, the half-man, half-horse centaur. Although it is one of the dominant constellations of the Southern Hemisphere, little of it can be seen from the United States. The Milky Way passes through Centaurus, and the constellation contains many interesting star clusters and nebulae.

Libra, the Scales, the only constellation of the zodiac named after an inanimate object, is a diamond-shaped pattern of four stars in the southeast that represents an old-fashioned set of balance scales. Libra is midway between the bright stars Spica in Virgo and Antares in Scorpius.

To the north, the Little Dipper is at its highest and best in June, although it is visible every clear night of the year. Draco also is highest in June and July. Like Hydra, Draco is a long string of faint stars. It curves between the Dippers, which define its position. (Hydra, in contrast, has few bright stars nearby to guide you to it and is much more difficult to pick out.) Draco is circumpolar and never sets when viewed from most of the United States, but its stars are too faint to be seen when it is under Polaris.

Scorpius, which is best visible at the end of summer, rises late in the evening in June. Scorpius brings with it the summer Milky Way.

The Sky in June

The sky also appears as shown on the following dates:		
Jun. 15	9 P.M.	DT
Jun. 1	10 P.M.	DT
May. 15	11 P.M.	DT
Mar. 1	midnight	DT

JULY

Although July is noticeably warm, the earth is actually at its farthest point from the sun on or near July 4. Then the sun is about three million miles farther from the earth than it was at its closest point, early in January. It is warm in the summer because then the earth's Northern Hemisphere is tilted toward the sun and the sun shines down on us more directly and from a higher angle than in the winter, when the Northern Hemisphere is tilted away from the sun and the sun is low in the sky. Also, the longer summer days have more hours of sunlight.

In the west, Leo is about to set, soon to be followed by Virgo. The brightest star in the western half of the sky is Arcturus, a yellow giant star some thirty-six light-years from the earth. The two Dippers are to the north, accompanied by Draco, the Dragon.

In the south, we see the full extent of Scorpius—a magnificent constellation under dark skies, especially when viewed from the southern United States. Because it is so far to the south, Scorpius is clearly visible in the evening only during July and August. Antares, in Scorpius, is the reddest bright star in the southern sky, and when Mars is near it you can see why it was given the name Antares, which means "rival of Mars." Because Antares is always low in the sky, atmospheric turbulence often causes it to twinkle fiercely, especially as seen through a telescope. Antares is one of only three bright red stars in the entire sky. The other two, Betelgeuse and Aldebaran, are visible in the winter.

Immediately to the right of Scorpius is Libra. Libra was formerly the claws of the Scorpion, and it makes sense to see it as such, but in ancient times it was separated from the Scorpion and given independence.

Below Libra is the top part of Lupus, which from the southern United States looks like two rings of faint stars a short distance above the southern horizon.

Above Scorpius is Ophiuchus, the Serpent Handler, and Serpens, his Serpent. Ophiuchus is a huge constellation with no exceptionally bright stars, and its shape is not apparent at first glance. After a little practice, you can spot it easily. He is holding a serpent that seems to cross in front of his body. Since one constellation cannot be in front of another, Serpens is divided in two: Serpens Caput, the head, and Serpens Cauda, the tail. Both, however, are parts of the same constellation. Ophiuchus and Serpens are the best example of constellations whose identities are commingled.

Hercules is near its highest position in the sky. This ancient constellation has no bright stars and can be found only after you have found nearby stars to guide you to it. Look one-third of the way between Vega and Arcturus. The full extent of Hercules, the original Superman, can be traced only with practice. The four stars that mark the Keystone are the most recognizable part of the Strongman (or Kneeler, as he was called in former times). Amateur astronomers know Hercules as the site of the great globular cluster M13, a glowing mass of hundreds of thousands of stars. Although there are brighter globular clusters in the southern Milky Way, none are as well placed as M13, which passes nearly overhead for the United States. M13 is the star attraction of many summer "star parties."

Notice the Summer Triangle, formed by three stars, Vega, Deneb, and Altair, to the east. The Summer Triangle is high in the east on July evenings and nearly overhead at the end of summer and in early fall.

The long Delta Aquarid meteor shower peaks during the last week of July, but meteors streak across the sky from the middle of the month well into August, overlapping the better-known Perseid shower. In terms of the total number of meteors, the Delta Aquarid is the greatest shower of all, but because its meteors are spread over so many weeks it is not as intense as shorter showers with sharper peaks. The meteors radiate from the constellation Aquarius, which is in the south most of the night, and meteors can be spotted all night long.

The Sky in July

The sky also appears as shown on the following dates:		
Jul. 15	9 P.M.	DT
Jul. 1	10 P.M.	DT
Jun. 15	11 P.M.	DT
Jun. 1	midnight	DT

AUGUST

August is the month of meteors. The Perseid meteor shower, traditionally the best shower of the year, is active for several days on and around August 12. Look from a dark location during the early morning hours on August 11 through 13, and you might see up to one meteor per minute, including faint meteors. Fewer meteors are seen during the evening hours. People in urban locations see only the brightest. Some people plan their vacations so that they will be in a dark location, such as a national park, during the shower. The Delta Aquarid meteors, which peak in late July, continue to fall through the first half of August; they can be distinguished from the Perseids by their slower speed and different direction of travel. The Perseid meteors, which radiate from the direction of the constellation Perseus, approach the earth nearly head-on and are relatively swift. The Perseid meteors derive from Comet Swift-Tuttle, which last passed through the inner solar system in 1992.

The Summer Triangle is the dominant star pattern of the summer sky. It is made up of three first-magnitude stars: Vega in Lyra, Deneb in Cygnus, and Altair in Aquila. These are the only first-magnitude stars in the summer sky other than Arcturus, Spica, and Antares, and the eye is immediately drawn to them. The Summer Triangle is a wonderful starting point that can guide you to other constellations around the sky. Hercules is immediately to the west of Vega, Sagittarius is to the south of Altair, and the comparatively empty part of the sky containing Aquarius and Pegasus is rising east of Deneb. Ophiuchus is to the southwest of Vega and Deneb. Although it is not an official constellation, the Summer Triangle is one of the best-known groups of stars in the sky.

In the south, Sagittarius and Scorpius are at their best this month. They never rise very high, so they are visible in the sky for a relatively brief time. Scorpius actually looks like a Scorpion. It has three stars for truncated claws and a long string of medium-bright stars that wind down and to the left to form the body, finally curving up to end at the bent stinger in the tail. The red star Antares is the Scorpion's red heart. Sagittarius is another matter; you'll have little luck seeing it as an Archer who is half man, half horse. The stars do outline a nice teapot—a kitchen device unknown in ancient times. After you trace the teapot, notice the "teaspoon" made up of a small group of stars to the upper left of the lid and the lemon conveniently placed below (the ring of stars of Corona Australis).

The summer Milky Way is at its best in August and September. Face south and look about one-quarter of the way up the sky, and you will be facing the center of our Milky Way Galaxy. Stars are packed much more closely at the center than they are in our neighborhood, where stars are more thinly scattered. The absolute center of the Milky Way lies about 5 degrees northwest of the tip of the spout of the "teapot" that outlines Sagittarius. The center itself is invisible from the earth except with the aid of a radio telescope, which picks up radio emissions from it, but the vast swarm of stars that make up the central bulge peeks out from behind interstellar clouds of gas and dust and appears as the Great Sagittarius Star Cloud. On a clear night, it is easily visible without optical aid as an elliptical thickening of the Milky Way immediately above the teapot's spout.

The summer Milky Way in the direction of Sagittarius and Scorpius is several times thicker and brighter than the winter part we see near Orion. The most majestic part of the Milky Way is low in the south as seen from the United States, but to observers in the Southern Hemisphere it is high overhead during July and August.

If you have binoculars, notice the pair of pretty star clusters in the tail of Scorpius. Many star clusters and nebulae are present in this rich part of the sky, but the two named M6 and M7 are bright enough to be seen without a telescope.

The Sky in August

The sky also appears as shown on the following dates:		
Sep. 1	8 P.M.	DT
Aug. 15	9 P.M.	DT
Aug. 1	10 P.M.	DT
Jul. 15	11 P.M.	DT
Jul. 1	midnight	DT

SEPTEMBER

The Summer Triangle is at its highest position in the sky early on September evenings. These three bright stars are good examples of the fact that the apparent brightness of a star as seen from the earth tells us little about its true brightness. Altair appears to be almost twice as bright as Deneb, but your eye cannot tell you that Altair is a hundred times closer. Altair, ten times more luminous than our sun, is nearby at a distance of a scant 17 light-years. Deneb, a whopping fifty thousand times more luminous than our sun, is 1,600 light-years distant. It is a true giant and one of the intrinsically brightest stars of all. If Altair were the same distance from the earth as Deneb, it would be invisible; if Deneb were as close as Altair, you could see it during the daytime. Vega is fifty times more luminous than our sun and 25 light-years distant.

Nearby are the tiny but easily recognizable constellations Delphinus, the Dolphin, and Sagitta, the Arrow. Most very small constellations are relatively recent inventions, but these two are ancient. Dolphins were familiar companions to Greek sailors, and it is easy to imagine Sagitta as an arrow fired by Sagittarius toward the Eagle and the Swan. He seems to have missed both.

The Milky Way crosses the sky diagonally on September evenings, stretching from the southwest to the northeast. Sagittarius and Scorpius are toward the southern horizon, the Summer Triangle is overhead, and the familiar W of Cassiopeia is in the northeast. As the Milky Way rotates on its axis, it carries the stars in the vicinity of the sun toward Cygnus. The stars of Cygnus are also being carried forward by this rotation, and we will not catch them.

The sun has a small amount of individual "proper motion" that causes it to deviate slightly from the overall motion of our part of the Milky Way. Our solar system is actually heading toward a point in space roughly in the direction of Vega, at a speed of 43,000 miles per hour. Thus, if you've ever wondered where we're going on the grandest scale, it is toward Vega.

On a dark night, notice that the Milky Way appears to be split from Deneb in Cygnus south past Serpens. Our galaxy is not divided in two; rather, dense clouds of dust that lie in its equatorial plane block light from distant stars and create the dark Great Rift. This split is striking once your attention is called to it.

The ecliptic is low in the sky. Trace it from the southwest to the east as it passes through Libra, Scorpius, Sagittarius, Capricornus, and Aquarius. The sun will be in these constellations in November through March, respectively, when its path is low in the winter sky. The sun is at its lowest point—about 7 degrees above the top of the spout of Sagittarius—

on or near December 21. Trace the movement of this point across the sky on a September night to visualize the path of the sun across the daytime sky at the winter solstice.

In September, the sun is midway between the solstices. Autumn begins in the earth's Northern Hemisphere on or near September 22—the autumn equinox. Spring begins in the Southern Hemisphere at the same time (there it is the spring equinox). The equinoxes are the *moments* when the sun crosses the celestial equator, the projection of the earth's equator into space. Beginning on the equinox and for the next six months, the sun is south of the equator, shining down on the earth's Southern Hemisphere. The equinoxes are also the days when the sun rises due east and sets due west.

The Harvest Moon is the full moon closest to the autumn equinox; it falls in late September or early October. The Harvest Moon's bright light helps farmers harvest their crops late into the night. Many people comment on the orange hue of the Harvest Moon when it is near the horizon, but the moon is always reddened by our atmosphere when it is low in the sky.

The Sky in September

The sky also appears as shown on the following dates:		
Oct. 1	8 P.M.	DT
Sep. 15	9 P.M.	DT
Sep. 1	10 P.M.	DT
Aug. 15	11 P.M.	DT
Aug. 1	midnight	DT

OCTOBER

The southern part of the early autumn sky is filled with "water constellations": Pisces, the Fishes; Delphinus, the Dolphin; Cetus, the Whale; Aquarius, the Water-Carrier; Capricornus, the Sea Goat (or Goat-Fish); Piscis Austrinus, the Southern Fish; and Eridanus, the River. These constellations all date to Sumerian times. Perhaps this section of the sky became associated with water when the Sumerians noticed that the sun was located here during the rainy season. It takes practice to see most of these constellations. Capricornus is a simple triangle, but neighboring Aquarius is essentially a shapeless bunch of stars. The little Water Jar in Aquarius is a recognizable pattern of five stars that becomes the starting point for finding the rest of the constellation. The easiest-to-recognize part of Pisces is the Circlet, a small ring of faint stars immediately south of Pegasus. Find the rest of the Fishes by drawing a line southeastward from the Circlet and then northward to the second fish, which is south of Andromeda. Cetus sprawls below Pisces and contains little of interest other than the star Mira. Mira is a "miraculous star" (the name Mira comes from the root word for *miracle*) because it changes its brightness dramatically over the course of a year. Although this variable star is usually too faint to see, several times a century it becomes one of the brightest stars in its part of the sky.

Grus, the Crane, is easy to see from the southern United States because it is made up of relatively bright stars arranged in a simple cross pattern. Look for it directly below Fomalhaut, the only bright star in an immense area of the sky. Fomalhaut is the eighteenth brightest star. It marks the mouth of the Southern Fish (Picis Austrinus).

The southern part of the sky is devoid of bright stars because it lies away from the Milky Way, which stretches diagonally across the sky from southwest to northeast, passing north of straight overhead. The part that crosses Cassiopeia and Perseus is much thinner than the part you see tonight in Sagittarius or the part you will see in the winter in and near Orion.

You can see *two* galaxies in the autumn sky: our very own Milky Way and the Great Galaxy in Andromeda. The Andromeda Galaxy is similar to our own, but because we see Andromeda from the outside, it shows what our galaxy would look like from a distance. On a dark night it is visible without a telescope if you know precisely where to look, but even a telescope shows it as a nearly shapeless smudge. Only long time-exposures show its structure. The Andromeda Galaxy is 2.9 million light-years away and is the most distant object you can see with your unaided eyes. Another, slightly fainter galaxy in Triangulum is a similar distance away.

The Orionid meteor shower peaks on or near October 21. This is a broad shower, and the meteors fall at nearly maximum intensity for approximately a week. During this week, a single observer in a dark location may see as many as twenty-five meteors per hour, most of them faint; from brightly lit cities, few meteors can be seen. The Orionids come from Halley's Comet, and they occur when dust shed long ago enters the earth's atmosphere at the high speed of 150,000 miles per hour. The meteors radiate from the constellation Orion. More meteors are seen during the early morning hours, when Orion is visible.

Daylight saving time ends at 2:00 A.M. on the last Sunday in October in most of the United States. Set your clocks back one hour before going to bed on Saturday night and enjoy the extra hour of sleep you lost in April. Notice that the next day the sun sets surprisingly early—to the joy of stargazers, who can begin watching the sky an hour earlier. Daylight time resumes on the first Sunday in April.

The appearance of the Pleiades low in the east signals the approach of winter.

The Sky in October

The sky also appears as shown on the following dates:		
Nov. 1	7 P.M.	ST
Oct. 15	9 P.M.	DT
Oct. 1	10 P.M.	DT
Sep. 15	11 P.M.	DT
Sep. 1	midnight	DT

NOVEMBER

Cassiopeia, which lies on the opposite side of the Pole Star from the Big Dipper, is at its highest point in the sky. The Queen is surrounded by her family. Cepheus, the King, is to the northwest. Cepheus is difficult to pick out, because it has neither bright stars nor a clear pattern. Andromeda is Cassiopeia's daughter. Perseus rescues and marries Andromeda in an enduring Greek myth, riding off into the sunset on Pegasus, the flying horse.

November is the worst time of the year to see the Big Dipper, which lies at its lowest on the northern horizon. If you live in the northern United States, the Dipper is circumpolar and does not set. Seen from the southern states, at least part of it dips below the horizon, and it is invisible for a few hours each night.

Much of the sky is occupied by constellations that are largely shapeless, and the fall constellations are often the last to be learned. Some of them cannot be seen from urban areas. Pegasus dominates the high southern sky, and people use it as a guide to find other constellations. Pegasus is usually thought of as a square of stars, but the star in the northeast corner is actually in Andromeda. The Great Square of Pegasus is not a constellation but a convenient pattern of stars that is useful for finding other constellations. Andromeda extends away from the Great Square's northeastern star. Pisces is below and to the east (the Circlet is directly below the center of the Great Square). Aquarius is south of the Great Square's west side, and Fomalhaut is farther south, in line with the two westernmost stars of the Great Square.

Far to the south, Phoenix is a challenging constellation to spot from the southern United States but is invisible from the Canadian border north.

Although winter is fast approaching, the Summer Triangle remains a major star pattern in the western sky. Vega and Altair are at a similar height, while Deneb stands above them. The Northern Cross, which rose on its side in the late spring, sets standing vertically in the late fall.

Notice the contrast of the many bright stars in and around Orion to the paucity of stars in the southern part of the sky. Fomalhaut is the only bright star in a broad area that spans half the sky. October and November evenings are the best time to see this lonely star. The fairly bright star east of Fomalhaut, lying at approximately the same altitude, is Diphda, the brightest star in Cetus (unless Mira has become exceptionally bright). Second-magnitude Diphda, also known as Beta Ceti, would go unnoticed in any major constellation, but here the competition is so poor it stands out.

The Milky Way stretches from west to east, passing north of overhead. This is a thin part of the Milky Way, and its star clusters (visible with binoculars or a telescope) are more distant and fainter than those in Scorpius or near Orion.

The position of the sun on the vernal equinox lies a short distance east of the Circlet that forms the westernmost fish in Pisces. Spring begins the moment the sun reaches this point on its annual trip around the sky. This point lay in Aries thousands of years ago, but it has regressed westward through the constellations of the zodiac. It is still often called the First Point of Aries in memory of its former position. The point regresses because the earth's axis wobbles slowly in a 26,000-year cycle called the Precession of the Equinoxes; the wobble is ultimately caused by the moon's and sun's gravitational pull on the earth.

The Leonid meteor shower peaks on or near November 17. In most years, observers see about a dozen meteors per hour, but every thirty-three years (centered around 1999) it can produce a super shower of thousands of meteors per hour over a restricted part of the earth. Because the shower's sharp peak lasts only a few hours, some locations on the earth are more favored than others. Leonid meteors come from Comet Tempel-Tuttle, and they are the fastest meteors known, with speeds of 44 miles per second (160,000 miles per hour). They approach the earth head-on from the direction of the constellation Leo, which rises late at night, and they frequently leave bright smoke trails.

The Sky in November

The sky also appears as shown on the following dates:		
Dec. 15	6 P.M.	ST
Dec. 1	7 P.M.	ST
Nov. 1	8 P.M.	ST
Nov. 15	9 P.M.	ST
Oct. 15	10 P.M.	DT
Oct. 1	11 P.M.	DT
Sep. 15	midnight	DT

53

DECEMBER

Days are short and nights are long in December—a perfect situation for stargazing if it were not so cold. At mid-latitudes, the sun sets at approximately 5:00 P.M. and rises at about 7:00 A.M., and during the fourteen hours of darkness you can see three-fifths of the sky. Contrast this with June, when the sky is truly dark for less than ten hours, and the advantages of December stargazing become clear.

Winter begins in the Northern Hemisphere at the winter solstice, on or near December 21. The solstice is the moment when the sun, in its apparent path around the earth, reaches its southernmost point in the sky. The solstice is the shortest day of the year, although the length of the day actually changes little from late November through mid-January. Summer begins in the Southern Hemisphere at the same moment.

Notice the path of the sun across the sky during the days near the solstice. The sun rises in the southeast, is at its highest at noon, and sets in the southwest. This is the southernmost daily path of the sun for the entire year. It is cold in winter because the days are short and because the sun's light strikes the earth at a low, oblique angle and spreads its rays over a larger area of ground.

The sun is at its lowest in December, but the full moon is at its highest. The full moon always lies directly opposite the sun in the sky. Observe the nightly path of December's full moon. It rises in the northeast, is very high in the south at midnight (nearly overhead from the southern United States), and then sets in the northwest approximately fourteen hours later. The winter moon follows the path of the summer sun. The moon follows its northernmost path and is at its highest point when it is in Taurus.

The evening sky in December is characterized by a large area in the south and west devoid of bright stars, a scattering of stars along the Milky Way overhead and to the northwest, and a major group of very bright stars to the east. Our eyes are drawn to these stars and the winter constellations they mark: Orion, Taurus, Auriga, Gemini, and Canis Major and Minor.

The brightest of all the stars, Sirius, often twinkles madly as it rises, changing colors and flashing wildly. This light show is caused by temperature variations within the earth's atmosphere; the effect is most noticeable with Sirius because it is the brightest star.

Pegasus and Taurus are two animals shown without backs. Taurus is represented by his head and horns, and Pegasus is represented by his front half.

Cassiopeia, Perseus, and Andromeda are at their highest early on December evenings. The Andromeda Galaxy—the closest and brightest galaxy visible from the Northern Hemisphere—is nearly overhead.

Try to trace the faint line of stars that forms Eridanus, the River. Begin near the bright blue star Rigel in Orion, and look for a long riverlike stream of faint stars that stretches westward and then loops down and back to the east. The stars are grouped relatively close together, and on a dark night you can trace the constellation to the southern horizon. Nearby Cetus is another challenging object that is not obvious at first glance. Look to see if Mira, the "wonderful" variable star, is near maximum. It is usually too faint to be seen without a telescope, but for about a month every year it becomes the second brightest star in Cetus.

The Geminid meteor shower, one of the year's best, has a sharp peak that lasts for only one morning (usually December 13 or 14), when meteors fall at a rate of up to one per minute as seen from dark locations. Fewer meteors are seen the nights before and after. The Geminid shower is known for its many bright meteors, which leave few smoke trails. The meteors radiate from the direction of the constellation Gemini but appear all over the sky. It is one of the few showers that offers good viewing before midnight as well as after. Dress warmly (some veterans choose a sleeping bag in a lawn chair).

Cygnus, also known as the Northern Cross, sets in an upright position in the northwest on Christmas Eve.

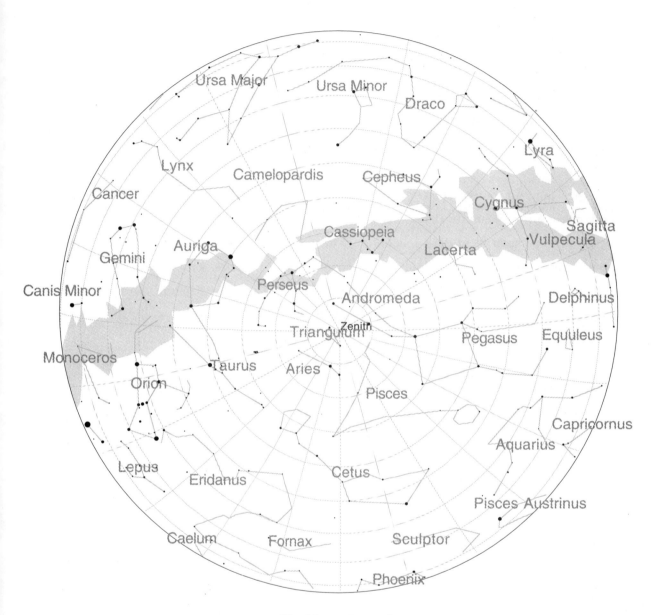

The Sky in December

The sky also appears as shown on the following dates:		
Jan. 15	6 P.M.	ST
Jan. 1	7 P.M.	ST
Dec. 1	8 P.M.	ST
Dec. 15	9 P.M.	ST
Nov. 15	10 P.M.	ST
Nov. 1	11 P.M.	ST

SOUTHERN SKY

A large but important part of the sky is never visible from midnorthern latitudes. This final chart shows the constellations that remain below our southern horizon in relation both to one another and to the familiar northern constellations. It is included for completeness. Use it to find what is below the other twelve charts. If you ever travel to the equator or farther south, it will come in handy.

Unlike the preceding twelve monthly charts, this chart is centered on the South Celestial Pole. You will see the sky in this orientation only from the earth's South Pole.

Many southern constellations have odd names. The far southern part of the sky is not visible from Europe or the Middle East, and the ancient peoples who named our familiar northern classical constellations did not know about the southern stars. The ancient constellations they invented in the northern sky have beautiful names such as Centaurus, Capricornus, and Canis Major. Those in the south are hardware store items, such as the Air Pump and the Carpenter's Square, that sound as if they belong in someone's attic, and minor animals such as the Fly and the Peacock. This part of the sky was divided and named by European sailors in the fifteenth century, and later by astronomers who apparently did not feel bound by tradition. Many other constellations were proposed for the southern sky in a naming frenzy; those that remain are the survivors.

Of course, these southern stars were divided into groups and named by local peoples long before Europeans ever saw them. But, as is true around the world, indigenous constellations have not survived. Field researchers are reconstructing this lost lore.

One of the more interesting native South American systems for dividing the sky comes from Peru. The most spectacular feature of the southern sky is not the Southern Cross but the Milky Way, which is much brighter and wider than the part we see from northern latitudes. The Milky Way's bright areas are made up of countless stars; in the dark areas (such as the Great Rift in and south of Cygnus), enormous clouds of dust hide the stars beyond. The most famous of these dark clouds is the Coal Sack, near the Southern Cross. Ancient Peruvians recognized patterns of bright stars just as we do—for example, they called the small circle of stars in the Scorpion's tail a "storehouse"—but they also named the Milky Way's dark clouds, seeing in them what we might call "dark constellations." They saw Yacana, the Llama; Atoq, the fox; Yutu, the bird; and Hanp'átu, the Toad, among others.

It is not surprising that ancient Peruvians focused on the Milky Way. The center of the Milky Way is in the southern sky (in Sagittarius), and the center is its richest part. Although we can see it from the United States, it is low in the south at best, so we miss its full glory. From Peru it passes overhead—and ancient Peruvians were rightly impressed! There is more than one way to divide the sky; the ancient Peruvians would find it curious that our familiar Western constellations ignore the bright and dark areas of the Milky Way.

This chart of the southern sky also proves that the Milky Way makes a complete loop around the sky. From North America, we see it disappear below Sagittarius and Scorpius in the summer and below Canis Major in the winter, and we must take it on faith that it connects to itself.

Perhaps the most famous constellation of the southern sky is Crux, the Southern Cross. This compact constellation is featured on the flag and stamps of several southern countries, including Australia and New Zealand, and it symbolizes the exotic southern sky. A feature of Crux is the Coal Sack, a dark cloud that blocks light from stars beyond and creates a dark "hole" in the Milky Way. Nearby is the classical constellation Centaurus, with its bright stars Alpha and Beta. Alpha Centauri is the closest bright star to Earth (Proxima Centauri is slightly nearer, but it is very faint). It is half as distant as Sirius, the closest bright star visible from northern latitudes.

Looking like two detached portions of the Milky Way are the two Magellanic Clouds, named by Ferdinand Magellan in his first around-the-world voyage. They are small irregular satellite galaxies that slowly orbit our Milky Way and may eventually collide with it. The Large and Small Magellanic Clouds are about 165,000 and 190,000 light-years from Earth, respectively, and are the nearest galaxies to our own. The Large Magellanic Cloud is shared between Dorado and Mensa, and the Small Magellanic Cloud is in Tucana.

In classical times, people visualized a huge ship south of Hydra known as Argo Navis—the Ship of the Argonauts. It was an enormous constellation that commemorated the Greek legends of Jason and the Argonauts. Lacaille broke it up 250 years ago into the more manageable constellations of the Sails (Vela), the Poop Deck (Puppis), and the Keel (Carina)—and then added a Magnetic Compass (Pyxis), which no Greek ever saw!

The southern sky has no recognized "South Star." There is no reason it should; it is only lucky chance that the northern sky has a North Star. The South Celestial Pole (the sky's south pole) is in the constellation Octans, and only faint stars mark the southern sky's pivot point. Before the advent of global positioning satellites, navigators traced a line through the Southern Cross and continued four cross-lengths (27 degrees) to find the South Celestial Pole.

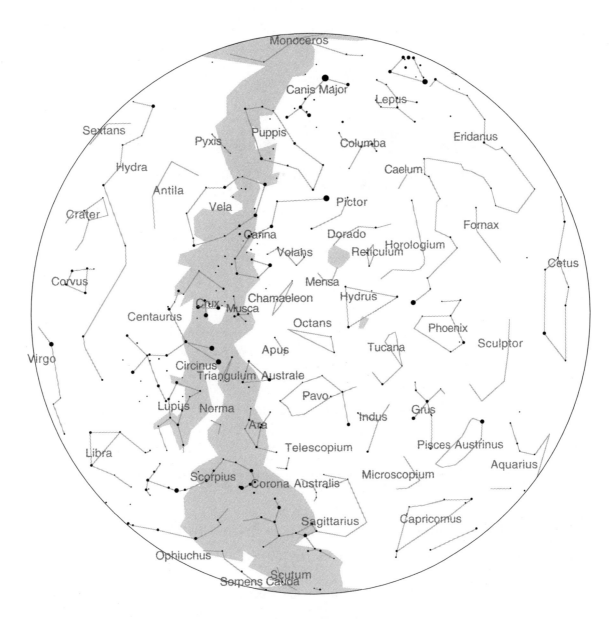

The Southern Sky

✦

Chapter Five

THE EIGHTY-EIGHT CONSTELLATIONS

The constellations have no order in the sky; in this section they appear alphabetically.

THE CONSTELLATIONS

ANDROMEDA—Princess Andromeda (an-**drom**-eh-da)

(see September through January monthly charts)

Andromeda is a major constellation in the eastern sky early on autumn evenings. It is a line of three equally spaced bright stars and a second line of fainter stars that diverges from Alpha to form a large V, with the eastern side much brighter than the western. The southernmost bright star of Andromeda (Alpha) is used to complete the Great Square of Pegasus. This star was once considered part of Pegasus; because no star can be in two constellations, however, it was officially assigned to Andromeda.

Andromeda is famous for housing the Andromeda Galaxy, the closest large galaxy to our own Milky Way. It is important to our understanding of galaxies, and photographs of it appear in many books and magazines.

Andromeda figures prominently in perhaps the most familiar Greek myth. According to the famous ancient story, Queen Cassiopeia of Ethiopia was a vain woman who boasted that she was more beautiful than even the sea nymphs. The nymphs—themselves vain—complained to Neptune, god of the sea, who angrily sent the sea monster Cetus to punish Cassiopeia. Neptune decreed that Cassiopeia's daughter, the Princess Andromeda, be chained to the rocks by the sea, where Cetus would devour her. Poor Andromeda, who has since been known as the Chained Lady, was fastened to the rocks and left to her fate. As Cetus approached, the hero Perseus arrived. He happened to be passing by, carrying in a leather bag a souvenir of a previous adventure, the head of Medusa, a head so ugly that it turned to stone anyone who gazed upon it. Perseus flashed the head at Cetus, who turned to stone and sank into the sea. Perseus was given Andromeda's hand in marriage, and they flew away on the flying horse Pegasus. (If this sounds familiar, it might be because the story was made into the movie *Clash of the Titans*.) All of these constellations are found together in the autumn sky.

The Brightest Galaxy

The brightest galaxy (other than our own Milky Way!) visible in the northern sky is the fifth-magnitude Andromeda Galaxy, also known as M31. You can barely see it without a telescope on a dark night if you know where to look, but it is easily seen through binoculars. Telescopically, it is a bright but essentially shapeless glob of light without clearly defined boundaries—we see only the inner, bright part of it, which appears nearly as large as our moon. Its outer regions extend to a distance of 3 degrees from the center, but these dim regions are visible only on time-exposure photographs.

The Andromeda Galaxy is a system of hundreds of billions of stars more than 2.9 billion light-years away. It is the most distant object you can see with your naked eye. Our Milky Way Galaxy would look similar if viewed from the Andromeda Galaxy. Edwin Hubble's discovery of Cepheid variable stars (see Cepheus) within what he called the "Andromeda Nebula" in 1923 proved that what was formerly thought to be only a cloud of gas within our Milky Way is actually a distant and huge galaxy—and the study of galaxies beyond our own began.

The Andromeda Galaxy was known as long ago as the tenth century, although people then had no idea what it was.

ANTLIA—the Air Pump (ant-lee-a)

(see Southern Sky chart)

Antlia is too far south to be visible from the United States. It is barely visible even from the Southern Hemisphere, since it consists of only very faint stars. Lacaille invented it in the eighteenth century, when the air pump was seen as a remarkable invention.

APUS—the Bird of Paradise (ay-pus)

(see Southern Sky chart)

Apus, a colorful tropical bird, lies near the South Celestial Pole—much too far south to be seen from the United States. It first appeared on Bayer's star atlas in 1603.

AQUARIUS—the Water Carrier (a-kware-ee-us)

(see August through December monthly charts)

Before the advent of indoor plumbing, water was delivered door to door by water carriers like Aquarius. On antique star charts, Aquarius is shown as a man on his knees pouring from a jug of water. In the sky, Aquarius is a large, shapeless group of faint stars lying south and west of Pegasus.

Aquarius is one of the "water constellations," part of a "celestial sea" that includes nearby Cetus, the Whale; Pisces, the Fish; and Capricornus, the Sea Goat. The sun was in front of these constellations during the rainy season when these constellations were named in Sumeria about five thousand years ago. Aquarius seems to be associated with the "great flood" that we are told once inundated the entire world—a story that had its origin in Sumeria and later appeared in the Old Testament, among other places.

Aquarius is a member of the zodiac, and the sun is within its boundaries from February 16 through March 11.

Although large, Aquarius lies away from the Milky Way and contains little of interest for people equipped with binoculars or small telescopes, other than the Helix and Saturn nebulae.

The Aquarid meteors radiate from the direction of Aquarius in May (see May star chart).

The "Age of Aquarius"

An "age" takes its name from the position of the sun on the first day of spring (the sun's position on that date is called the vernal equinox). Presently, the sun is within Pisces on that day, and we are in the "Age of Pisces." The vernal equinox very slowly drifts westward through the constellations of the zodiac in a cycle that lasts 25,800 years; this happens because the earth's axis is wobbling (precessing) as the earth spins. The sun remains in each constellation for an average of 2000 years before regressing to the next one to the right; thus, each "age" lasts roughly 2000 years. Using modern constellation boundaries, astronomers calculate that the vernal equinox will enter the constellation Aquarius in about six hundred years—and that will be the dawning of the "Age of Aquarius." (That's quite a while to wait for universal peace and brotherhood.)

AQUILA—the Eagle (ah-kwee-la)
(see July through November monthly charts)

The Eagle is a pretty constellation that lies in the Milky Way and is best seen during the summer. Today we visualize the star Altair as being at the Eagle's head, Epsilon and Theta at the wing tips, and Lambda at the tip of the tail, but the ancient Greeks imagined it as flying southeast, with Altair only a wing tip.

Altair, Aquila's brightest star, is the southernmost star of the Summer Triangle (see July and August monthly charts), which it forms with Deneb and Vega. Altair looks similar to Deneb in brightness, but Deneb is one hundred times more distant and ten thousand times more luminous, proving that you cannot tell much about a star by just looking at it.

Aquila has been identified with eagles since Sumerian times. In Greek mythology, Aquila carried the thunderbolts of Zeus, king of the gods.

Although Aquila is in the Milky Way, it contains surprisingly few objects for viewing through binoculars or a telescope. The Great Rift, which splits the Milky Way (see page 00 and the September monthly chart), is especially conspicuous in Aquila.

The Eagle Star

Altair appears so bright because it is so close to the earth. It is seventeen light-years distant, magnitude 1, and about ten times more luminous than our sun. Two slightly fainter stars lie an equal distance on either side of it, and the three form a nice but short straight line in the sky.

ARA—the Altar (air-ra)

(see July and August monthly charts and Southern Sky chart)

Ara, a southern constellation, does not rise high enough to be seen from the northern United States. Seen from the southern states, it rises only a short distance above the southern horizon, and only briefly. Look for it below the tail of Scorpius, the Scorpion, at about 10:00 P.M. in July. Ara is both small and faint, and it looks like two parallel strings of faint stars.

In mythology, Ara was an altar used for sacrifices in pagan times.

ARIES—the Ram (air-eez)

(see October through February monthly charts)

Aries is a large constellation with three medium-bright stars that form a simple, easily recognizable pattern. However, the rest of Aries is relatively empty sky. Aries is in the east in the autumn and high overhead in the early winter.

In Sumerian times, these stars were a "day laborer" who plowed a field to plant grain; the celestial ox who pulled the plow may have been Taurus, the Bull. The constellation has been called a ram at least since Greek times. In Greek mythology, the adventurers Jason and the Argonauts sailed far to find the ram's fleece. Part of the process of gold mining was to capture flecks of gold in a coat of wool (fleece), which when full became a valuable "golden fleece."

The sun is within the boundaries of Aries from approximately April 19 through May 13. Four thousand years ago, the earth was oriented so that the sun was in Aries on the first day of spring (March 21), a day that was then generally considered the first day of the year. At that time, the sun's position was called "the first point of Aries." The sun is now in Pisces on the first day of spring, but Aries is still called the first constellation of the zodiac in memory of this ancient alignment.

AURIGA—the Charioteer (aw-ree-ga)

(see November through April monthly charts)

Auriga is a large pentagon-shaped figure with many bright stars. It is visible most of the year, but few people are familiar with it—probably because it is far from the path of the moon and planets and is at its best in the winter, when people spend less time stargazing. It is also overshadowed by even grander constellations nearby.

The star farthest from Capella in the pentagon (Beta Tauri) is actually in Taurus, but it is needed to complete the shape.

Because it is so far to the north, Auriga is visible most of the night throughout most of the year. It is straight overhead in January and February but is not visible on summer evenings. You can often see Auriga (or at least Capella) low in the northeast or low in the northwest.

In Greek mythology, Auriga was a chariot driver or charioteer, but he is shown without the chariot. On old star charts, he is holding one goat (the star Capella) over his shoulder and a group of small goats, called the Kids, in his arms. He may originally have been seen as a shepherd.

The Milky Way runs through Auriga.

A Bright Yellow Star

Capella (ka-**pel**-ah), which means "the little she-goat," is the sixth-brightest star in the sky and has a magnitude of 0. Lying midway between Orion and the North Star, it is the northernmost bright star and is important to celestial navigators because it is above the horizon most of the year. Above latitude 44 degrees north, Capella is circumpolar and never sets. It is a yellow giant star—the kind of swollen star our own sun will become as it nears the end of its life. Capella is forty-two light-years from the earth.

The Giant

The third-magnitude star Epsilon Aurigae is one of the largest and most complex stars known. It is a binary star (two stars in orbit around a common center of gravity) oriented such that every twenty-seven years (next in 2010) the huge but relatively dim star hides its smaller but brighter companion in an eclipse that lasts a year. At a distance of over 4,000 light-years, it is one of the most distant stars you can see without optical assistance.

Clusters for Binoculars

Several star clusters in Auriga (M36, M37, and M38) are bright enough to be seen with binoculars. They are about 4200 light-years distant in an outer arm of the Milky Way. Many more are visible in small telescopes.

BOÖTES—the Herdsman (bo-**oh**-teez)

(see March through September monthly charts)

Boötes is nearly overhead during the early evening in late spring and early summer. Because Boötes follows the Great Bear around the sky, he is called the Bear Driver or Bear Herder, and this is how he is shown on antique star maps. In England, where the bear is seen as a plow, Boötes is called the Plowman. The constellation's shape is often compared to that of a kite. Children see Boötes as an ice-cream cone.

Boötes is mentioned as long ago as the *Odyssey*. To the ancient Egyptians, the stars of Boötes represented a hippopotamus.

A Speedy Yellow Giant

Arktos is Greek for "bear," and Arcturus (ark-**too**-rus) means "bear watcher" because it chases the Great Bear around the pole. It is the second-brightest star visible from most of the United States (magnitude 0) and the brightest star north of the celestial equator. Arcturus is a giant orange-yellow star, 20 times the diameter and 110 times the luminosity of our sun. Compare its color with other bright stars (Vega to the east is blue-white, and Spica to the south is white). At a distance of only thirty-seven light-years, it is the closest giant star to the earth. Its unusual orbit around the center of our galaxy takes it high above the equator of the Milky Way. (Its orbit around the Milky Way is similar to a comet's highly elongated, inclined orbit around the sun.) Arcturus moves through space at 300,000 miles per hour, much faster than any other bright star, and it moves from one constellation to another relatively quickly (in astronomical terms). It was in the middle of Boötes six thousand years ago, and in a few tens of thousands of years it will be in Virgo. By then, however, it will be a very distant, faint star. Arcturus is one of the few stars mentioned in the Bible (Job 38:32: ". . . or canst thou guide Arcturus with his sons?").

CAELUM—the Chisel (**see**-lum)

(see January through March monthly charts and Southern Sky chart)

Caelum is one of the smallest constellations. Because it is made up of only very faint stars, it is difficult to see. It lies south of Orion and barely rises above the horizon as seen from the United States.

Caelum, a sculptor's engraving chisel, was invented by Lacaille in the 1750s; it has no mythology associated with it.

CAMELOPARDALIS—the Giraffe (ka-**mel**-o-par-da-liss)
(see October through April monthly charts)

The Giraffe is a scraggly string of faint stars that occupies a basically empty area of the sky between the North Star and Perseus. It is high overhead in the winter, at the same time as Orion and Auriga. As seen from most of the United States, it never sets.

To the Greeks, a camelopardalis was a creature with the body of a giraffe, the head of a camel, and the spots of a leopard. The constellation itself, however, is not Greek. It was invented by the Dutchman Petrus Plancius in 1613.

CANCER—the Crab (**can**-sir)
(see January through June monthly charts)

Cancer is the faintest constellation of the zodiac. People know it only because the sun, moon, and planets pass through it; otherwise, few people would have heard of it. It has no bright stars, but its upside-down Y pattern of medium-faint stars can be made out on a dark night.

Cancer is midway between the major constellations Leo and Gemini. It is visible in the early evening sky from February through spring.

In Greek mythology, Cancer was the crab who was sent to bite Hercules. Hercules squashed it easily. Today we think of cancer as a dreaded disease, and the name might have come from the tendency of some skin cancers to develop long, thin extensions that resemble the legs of a crab. Ancient Egyptians saw this constellation as a scarab beetle, the Babylonians may have seen it as a turtle, and on some old star maps it was depicted as a lobster.

The sun is within the boundaries of Cancer from approximately July 21 to August 9. The tropic of Cancer marks the latitude at which the sun appears overhead at noon on the summer solstice (the first day of summer). The sun used to be in Cancer on the solstice, but its position on that date has precessed to a point on the Taurus/Gemini boundary.

The Beehive

Although Cancer has no bright stars, it does have one of the brightest and prettiest open star clusters. Today known as the Beehive or M44, in classical times it was called Praesepe (Latin for "manger"). Smack in the middle of Cancer, the fourth-magnitude Beehive is barely visible without binoculars on the darkest of nights, when it looks like a little small, fuzzy patch of light about a degree in diameter. Good binoculars or a small telescope will show several dozen faint stars. The Beehive is 580 light-years away and about 13 light-years in diameter.

Another binocular star cluster, seventh-magnitude M67, is almost 10 degrees to the south of M44.

CANES VENATICI—the Hunting Dogs (kay-nis vay-nat-i-see)
(see February through September monthly charts)

There are three dogs in the sky: the Large Dog, the Small Dog, and the Hunting Dogs. The Large and Small Dogs are prominent ancient constellations, but the Hunting Dogs are faint and were invented only in 1690 by Johannes Hevelius. They are the hunting dogs of nearby Boötes, and they accompany him as he follows the Great Bear around the celestial pole.

The Hunting Dogs are immediately south of the handle of the Big Dipper and are visible at the same time as the Dipper (best in spring and early summer). The only star within them that is even medium-bright is third-magnitude Cor Caroli (Latin for "the Heart of Charles," in honor of King Charles I of England; the star was named by the king's physician). Cor Caroli is below the center of the arc formed by the five stars in the handle and back of the bowl of the Big Dipper.

The Whirlpool Galaxy

The first galaxy whose spiral shape was recognized is the Whirlpool Galaxy or M51, in Canes Venatici. The galaxy is visible in any amateur telescope, but only a telescope about 18 inches in diameter or larger will show its spiral structure. M51 is a short distance southwest of Alkaid, the end star in the handle of the Big Dipper. It is about twenty million light-years from the earth.

CANIS MAJOR—the Large Dog (kay-nis may-jor)
(see January through April monthly charts)

Canis Major is the larger hunting dog accompanying the giant hunter Orion in his nightly journey across the sky (the other is Canis Minor). It follows Orion, rising in the southeast after his master and remaining to the lower left of the giant. Because it contains Sirius, the brightest star in the sky, it is very easy to find.

Sirius is in line with Orion's belt of three bright stars. It can be imagined as the jewel in the Large Dog's collar or as the tip of its nose. Orion's two companions are visible in the evening sky from the first of the year until May.

The Milky Way flows immediately to the east of Canis Major. Look with binoculars for the bright open star cluster M41, about 4 degrees south of Sirius. It is about 2,500 light-years distant in the Milky Way's Orion Arm.

The Dog Star

Sirius (**sear**-e-us), also called the Dog Star, is the brightest star in the nighttime sky, with a magnitude of −1.5. It is also the closest star visible from the United States (8.6 light-years distant). It is twice the diameter and twenty-three times the luminosity of our sun. Brilliant white with a touch of blue, it can twinkle wildly and flash with all the colors of the rainbow when it shines through turbulent layers of air near the horizon.

Sirius means "scorcher" in Greek. In ancient Greek times, it rose with the sun in summer. The "Dog Days" are summer's hottest days, when Sirius supposedly adds to the sun's heat.

The ancient Egyptians associated Sirius with life and with the goddess Hathor. When the ancient Egyptians saw Sirius rise before the sun, they knew the annual life-giving flood of the Nile River would soon follow. They may have thought that Sirius caused the flood. The first appearance of Sirius in the morning sky marked the beginning of their year (the ancient Egyptian New Year's Day).

Sirius has a companion star, discovered in 1862 and visible in a good amateur telescope. Called Sirius B or the Pup, it is the first and best-known *white dwarf* star—an evolved "dead" star no longer generating energy or light by converting hydrogen into helium. White dwarfs have collapsed upon themselves. Sirius B is not much larger than the earth, but it still has as much mass as our sun. Consequently its density is so high that a tablespoon of its material would weigh a ton. It orbits Sirius every fifty years.

CANIS MINOR—the Small Dog (kay-nis my-nor)
(see January through May monthly charts)

Canis Minor is the small hunting dog who follows his larger canine companion and Orion, the Hunter, across the sky. It is most visible in winter.

Canis Minor is essentially a two-star constellation, and it looks like a short straight line in the sky. Procyon is magnitude 0.5 and easy to find; the second star, third-magnitude Gomeisa (go-**my**-za), is a short distance to the northwest.

Procyon is left of Orion and north of Sirius. It forms an equilateral triangle with Betelgeuse and Sirius. This group of three stars is sometimes called the Winter Triangle. Gomeisa is a short distance (about 1½ times the width of Orion's belt) northwest of Procyon, in the direction of Gemini's feet.

To see these two stars as a small dog, imagine one (usually Procyon) as his tail and the other (therefore Gomeisa) as his head. It looks more like a hot dog than a hunting dog.

The Milky Way passes between Procyon and Sirius.

The Star Before the Dog

Procyon (**pro**-see-on) is Greek for "before the dog"—a descriptive name for a star that used to rise before the Dog Star, Sirius. This name is very old. In the twentieth century Procyon rises within a few minutes of Sirius, but three thousand years ago, when the earth's axis was tilted in a different direction, Procyon rose more than a half-hour before Sirius. In the distant future, Procyon will *follow* Sirius across the sky.

Procyon is a cosmic next-door neighbor only 11⅓ light-years distant. The only closer bright star you can see from the United States is Sirius. Notice that Procyon has a slight yellowish hue and is not as white as Sirius.

CAPRICORNUS—the Sea Goat (cap-re-**korn**-us)
(see August through November monthly charts)

The sun, moon, and planets pass through Capricornus as they travel around the sky, and it is a member of the zodiac. The sun is within its boundaries from approximately January 19 to February 15. Capricornus is most visible in the early autumn. It looks somewhat like the hull of a boat or an upside-down paper hat.

A sea goat is an odd creature not found at the zoo. It is a goat with a fish's tail, and it could also be called a goat-fish. About five thousand years ago, the Sumerians invented such imaginary composite creatures by combining familiar animals in strange ways. Sagittarius, half man and half horse, and Pegasus, a horse with wings, are two other examples.

The Greeks identified these stars with Pan, the goat-footed, flute-playing god who loved to chase women. They called the constellation Aegoceros ("goat-horned").

Capricornus has no bright stars.

CARINA—the ship's Keel (ka-ree-na)
(see Southern Sky chart)

One of the forty-eight ancient Greek constellations was an enormous ship in the southern sky called Argo Navis. It was the ship of Jason, a mythical hero of ancient times who led the Argonauts in adventures such as the search for the Golden Fleece (see Aries). The astronomer Lacaille broke it up in the eighteenth century, dividing it into Puppis, the Stern; Vela, the Sails; Pyxis, the Nautical Compass; and Carina, the Keel. (Pyxis was originally the Mast, but Lacaille transformed it into a compass.) You will see Argo on some star charts, but it is no longer an official constellation.

The Stern, the Sails, and the Compass are barely visible low in the southern sky in winter from much of the United States, but Carina—the lowest part of the ship—is too far to the south to be seen. All that can be seen of Carina from the southernmost United States is the very bright star Canopus.

The Second Brightest Star

Canopus (ka-**nope**-is) is the second-brightest star in the sky (after Sirius, in the Large Dog). Seen from the latitude of Los Angeles, Dallas, and Charleston, it is only a few degrees above the southern horizon when it is at its highest, at about 9 P.M. in mid-February. To find Canopus, trace a line from Gomeisa—the second-brightest star in Canis Minor—to Sirius, then continue in the same direction for a little more than the same distance.

Canopus is a giant star about a hundred light-years from the earth. It is magnitude −0.7.

The star is named after the pilot of the fleet of Spartan ships that sailed to Troy to recover Queen Helen (whose "face launched a thousand ships").

Today, Canopus helps pilot spaceships. A bright star out of the ecliptic plane, it is an important navigational star, used to determine the orientation of spacecraft.

CASSIOPEIA—Queen Cassiopeia (kass-ee-oh-**pee**-ya)

(see August through March monthly charts)

Cassiopeia is one of the prettiest of the winter constellations. After the Big Dipper, it is the best-known star pattern in the northern sky. People who know only a few constellations know the five-star W shape of Cassiopeia.

The main part of Cassiopeia lies 30 degrees from the North Celestial Pole, and the constellation is circumpolar from the United States and Canada. It is visible all night throughout the year, but the best time to see it is when it is at its highest—during the early evening from August through February, more than half the year. Cassiopeia rises in the northeast as a letter W and sets in the northwest as a sideways letter M.

Cassiopeia sits opposite the Big Dipper, with the North Star between them, so as one rises the other sets and when one is high the other is low. The Big Dipper is a spring constellation, and Cassiopeia is an autumn constellation.

In Greek mythology, Cassiopeia is a queen seated on her throne, and she is often called the Seated Lady. She was a queen of Ethiopia; her husband was King Cepheus. See Andromeda for a description of the popular Greek myth that links them. These three constellations are grouped together in the fall sky.

The Milky Way passes through Cassiopeia, and the constellation has several star clusters visible through binoculars and small telescopes. A supernova, or exploding star, that appeared in Cassiopeia in 1572 is still remembered today.

CENTAURUS—the Centaur (sen-**tor**-us)

(see May through July monthly charts and Southern Sky chart)

Centaurus is an ancient constellation that lies far to the south. Its northern part can be seen from the southern part of the United States, but the lowest part of the centaur cannot be seen from anyplace north of the southernmost tip of Florida and Hawaii.

A centaur is a composite beast who is half man and half horse. (Fortunately, the half-man part is the top part!) Centaurs were common in Greek mythology; they combined the skill of men with the speed of horses. Most were thugs, but this Centaur was different. His name was Chiron (**ky**-run), and he was kind and gentle and a wise teacher. The other centaur in the sky is Sagittarius.

Look for the top part of Centaurus as an indistinct group of faint stars below Virgo and just above the southern horizon in May and June.

The wonderful globular star cluster Omega Centauri is the sky's largest, brightest, and best.

The Closest Star(s)

Which is the closest star? That simple question turns out to have a tricky answer. Of course, our sun is the closest star to the earth, but the closest star in the *nighttime* sky is actually a group of three stars that lie at almost exactly the same distance. These three stars are held to one another gravitationally. The brightest of the three is Alpha Centauri, which is 4.4 light-years from the earth. Alpha has a companion star in orbit around it that is the same distance from the earth. Many trillions of miles away is a third, much fainter star that also orbits around Alpha; it is 0.2 light-year closer to the earth. This star is called Proxima Centauri, for "nearest in the Centaur," but, at magnitude 11, it is visible only in a telescope. Besides our sun, then, Proxima Centauri is the closest star, even though the honor is sometimes given to the much brighter Alpha (and Proxima is considered Alpha's fainter companion).

Alpha Centauri is the third-brightest star in the sky (after Sirius and Canopus), with a magnitude of −0.3. Curiously, this extremely bright star has no common name. It is also called Rigel Kentaurus, Arabic for "foot of the centaur."

CEPHEUS—King Cepheus (sef-ee-us or see-fus)
(see July through February monthly charts)

Cepheus is a large group of dim stars, and it takes some practice to learn to pick it out from among the many similar stars nearby. It lies in a basically empty part of the sky north of and between Cassiopeia and Cygnus. The Milky Way runs nearby.

Cepheus is a circumpolar constellation; it does not set as seen from the United States. It is high overhead during the autumn, but it can be seen in the evening sky from August through December.

Cepheus has the shape of a child's drawing of a house. The faint star halfway between the westernmost star of the W in Cassiopeia and the North Star marks the "top of the house." The other four corners of the house are equally spaced to the south and west and form a square of faint stars. The southernmost "star" of this square is actually three faint stars grouped together. Cephus is not an easy constellation to see.

Cepheus was a King of Ethiopia, the husband of Queen Cassiopeia and the father of Princess Andromeda (see Andromeda for associated mythology).

The Martian North Star

Mu in Cepheus is sometimes called the Garnet Star because of its redness. It is the reddest star visible without the aid of a telescope. Mu is the North Star for Mars, but at magnitude 3.6 to 5.1 (it is a variable star) it does not stand out as our Polaris does. Martians will have to make do with it.

The Distance to a Variable

Astronomers calculate the distances to faint galaxies by observing certain variable stars—stars that change their brightness in regular, predictable ways. Because we know the true, intrinsic brightness of such stars, when we identify one in a distant galaxy we can compute how far away that star must be to appear as bright as it does. The brightest of these variable stars—and the group's prototype—is fourth-magnitude Delta Cephei. Watch it carefully, and you will see that it grows brighter and then fainter by seven-tenths of a magnitude during a cycle that lasts just over five days. Although relatively faint, it is one of the most famous stars in the sky.

CETUS—the Whale (see-tus)
(see October through February monthly charts)

Cetus is the fourth largest constellation, but it has no truly bright stars and no particular shape. It lies south of Aries and Pisces, and like them it is in the evening sky during the autumn.

Cetus was the monster sent to devour Andromeda. It is depicted today as a whale, but in former times it was imagined as a variety of monsters, some with claws and scales.

The Wonderful Star

Although Cetus has no *bright* stars, it does have one *interesting* star. Mira, a red giant star, changes its brightness by more than a hundred times, from magnitude 3 to 9, during a cycle that lasts approximately eleven months. Most of the time it is too faint to be seen without a telescope, but at its brightest it is a medium-bright star. The star's variability was first noted in 1596, and it was named Mira (which means "wonderful" in Latin) by Hevelius in 1662.

CHAMAELEON—the Chameleon (ka-me-lee-un)
(see Southern Sky chart)

The Chameleon is a small constellation of faint stars near the South Celestial Pole. It was invented by Keyser and Houtman and included in Bayer's atlas in 1603. It has no mythology.

Chameleons are a type of lizard known for their ability to change color to match their background. There are two lizards in the sky; the other is Lacerta.

CIRCINUS—the Compasses (sir-se-nus)
(see Southern Sky chart)

Circinus is the fourth smallest constellation. Lacaille squeezed it in between Centaurus and Triangulum Australe—another drawing tool—in his effort to fill the sky with technical tools. It has only faint stars and is too far south to be visible from the United States.

There are two types of compasses: the kind you use to draw circles or measure distances, and the kind you use to find north. This is the drawing kind. It is often called a "pair of compasses," since properly speaking each side is a compass. The other type of compass is also in the sky, as Pyxis.

COLUMBA—the Dove (ko-lum-ba)
(see January through March monthly charts and Southern Sky chart)

Far south of Orion in the winter sky is Columba, the Dove. It has only a few medium-bright stars and is hard to see.

To find Columba, trace a line from Procyon (the brightest star in Canis Minor) to Sirius (the brightest star in Canis Major) and continue the same distance in the same direction. That will take you to the center of the Dove. The Dove is low in the south around 8:00 P.M. in February.

This is the dove released by Noah to find dry land following the biblical flood, and it was once called Columba Noae. It was invented by Petrus Plancius and first appeared on charts in the early 1600s.

COMA BERENICES—Berenice's Hair (ko-ma bear-ah-ni-sez)

(see March through August monthly charts)

This swarm of faint stars lies midway between Boötes and Leo and in classical Greek times was considered part of Leo. It is high in the sky all during spring and overhead in the early evening in May.

The constellation is named after a real person, and the story by a Roman poet of how the constellation got its name is more interesting than the stars themselves. Queen Berenice was wife of King Ptolemy III of Egypt in the third century B.C. She offered to cut off her beautiful hair if her husband returned safely from a military expedition, and when he did she cut her hair and placed it in a shrine in a temple. One day the hair was found missing, and the king threatened revenge on the temple guards. The court astronomer saved the day by showing the angry king and queen a faint group of stars and telling them that the gods were so impressed with her devotion they had placed her hair in the sky for all to see.

The stars of the constellation are actually a star cluster—a group of dozens of stars traveling together through space—called the Coma star cluster. It is about 250 light-years away. It is so large (about the size of the bowl of the Big Dipper) that it is best seen with the naked eye on a very dark night or with binoculars (a telescope shows only part of it at a time). The only closer bright cluster of stars is the Hyades in Taurus, which is about half as distant.

CORONA AUSTRALIS—the Southern Crown (ko-row-na os-tral-is)

(see August and September monthly charts and Southern Sky chart)

This constellation is a ring, or crown, of stars directly below Sagittarius and directly to the left of the tail of Scorpius. Although the stars are all faint, the ring is surprisingly easy to see from the southern United States when the sky is dark. The ring is, however, too far to the south to be seen well from the northern states or from Canada. It is just above the southern horizon early in the evening in August.

To the Greeks, the Corona was a laurel wreath worn at times of glory. Today it is shown as a crown.

If you see Sagittarius as a teapot, Corona Australis can be seen as the lemon that lies handily nearby.

CORONA BOREALIS—the Northern Crown (ko-row-na bore-ee-al-is)
(see April through September monthly charts)

This second crown in the sky is a ring of stars with one star much brighter than the others, and it looks like a diamond ring. It is a pretty constellation immediately east of Boötes. It is best seen in the spring and early summer, when it is nearly overhead.

Like Corona Australis, Corona Borealis is not a gold crown worn by kings, although it is sometimes shown this way on old illustrated star maps. A wreath of laurel leaves worn by victors of Greek athletic and poetry events and later by Roman emperors, it dates at least to classical Greek times.

If you think of Boötes as an ice-cream cone, you can think of Corona Borealis as a scoop of ice cream that fell off.

CORVUS—the Crow (kor-vis)
(see April through July monthly charts)

Corvus is a small constellation most visible in the spring from April through June. It rises in the southeast and sets in the southwest.

Look for Corvus as a battered box sitting below and to the right of the bright star Spica in Virgo. It is easily recognizable even though its stars are not bright.

Corvus is a crow (or sometimes a raven) who was associated with the god Apollo in Greek myths; its origin dates to Sumerian times. It is also linked with Crater and with the snake Hydra, on which it is often shown sitting.

Corvus lies in a bleak part of the sky and has no deep-sky objects of note.

CRATER—the Cup (kray-ter)
(see March through June monthly charts)

Crater is associated with Corvus both in mythology and in the sky. This small constellation sits to the right of Corvus. Crater's stars are not as bright as those of its neighbor, and its pattern is not as easy to recognize.

To astronomers, a crater is a bowl-shaped hole in the ground made when a meteorite hits a planet and explodes. The moon's surface is covered with craters. To ancient Greeks, a crater was a large bowl or cup with handles, like the kind that is filled with punch at a party (or with wine in Greek times). Both kinds of crater have a similar shape; Crater is the punch-bowl type.

The celestial Crater is directly south of the tail of Leo, the Lion. To see it as a bowl, look for a half-circle of stars just to the right of Corvus. The best time to see it is in the late spring from April through June.

In Greek mythology, Crater was a cup owned by Apollo and sometimes carried by Corvus.

CRUX—the Southern Cross (krucks)
(see Southern Sky chart)

The Southern Cross is one of the prettiest and best-known constellations. It is a shame it cannot be seen from the United States (except in Hawaii and southern Florida). It is far south of Virgo and it is the smallest constellation. The Cross would almost fit within the bowl of the Big Dipper.

Crux looks like a cross, and it is easy to understand how it got its name. Originally, however, it was part of Centaurus. It was first called the Cross by European navigators around 1500.

Crux points the way to the sky's south pole in the same way that the pointer stars in the bowl of the Big Dipper point to the sky's north pole. Trace a line from Gamma through Alpha and continue four times that distance in the same direction, and you will come to the "South Star"—a very faint star in Octans.

Crux is in a rich part of the Milky Way. It contains several beautiful star clusters and nebulae, including the famous Jewel Box and Coal Sack.

CYGNUS—the Swan (sig-nus)
(see July through November monthly charts)

Cygnus, a major constellation in the summer sky is high overhead in the early evening from July through September. Its brightest star is Deneb, one of the three stars of the Summer Triangle (see Lyra on page 89).

The constellation has two popular names. In ancient times it was called the Swan, but for the last few centuries it has also been called the Northern Cross. It looks like both. To see Cygnus as a swan flying southward, imagine that the faint star Beta is the swan's head. The neck and body extend northward through Gamma and end in Deneb (which means "tail" in ancient Arabic). One wing stretches to Delta and the other to Epsilon, and then to faint stars beyond, while the tail feathers are a half-ring of faint stars to either side of Deneb. To see Cygnus as a cross, imagine that Deneb is the top of the cross. The foot of the cross is the much fainter star Beta Cygni. The two arms extend from Gamma to Delta and Epsilon.

The Northern Cross is several times the size of Crux, the Southern Cross. At 8:00 P.M. at Christmas time, it stands upright on the northwestern horizon.

In Greek mythology, the Swan was originally a young boy, Phaeton, who was changed into a swan by the god Zeus.

Beta Cygni, also called Albireo (al-**beer**-e-oh), is a pretty double star. Viewed through a small telescope, the two stars appear blue and yellow, and the contrast is striking.

Cygnus lies in the Milky Way and contains within its boundaries several star clusters and nebulae visible through amateur telescopes. Three degrees east of Deneb is a luminous cloud called the North America Nebula because of its shape; it is visible through binoculars on a truly dark night. The Great Rift—a great cloud of relatively nearby dark dust that splits the Milky Way—begins near Deneb and extends southward.

A Brilliant Star

Deneb (**den**-eb) looks bright—and it actually is. If Deneb were put next to our sun, it would outshine the sun by over fifty thousand times. It is a true giant star. However, it is a long way away—1,600 light-years from the earth. Even at such an enormous distance, it still looks bright (it is magnitude 1.25). If it were as close as many other bright stars that we see, it would outshine all the stars of the sky. Deneb is the most luminous and the most distant bright star we can see. The light we see now from Deneb left it and began traveling to the earth around the year A.D. 400, toward the end of the Roman Empire.

Notice Deneb's blue-white color.

DELPHINUS—the Dolphin (del-**fi**-nus)
(see July through December monthly charts)

The dolphin is one of the smallest constellations that is easily identifiable. With a bit of imagination, it looks like a cute little dolphin leaping out of the water. It also looks like a small kite with a tail. It has no bright stars, but on a dark night over a dozen faint stars are visible.

The Dolphin is directly south of Cygnus and east of Aquila, and it is in the evening sky in the summer. The peculiar names of its two brightest stars—Sualocin and Rotanev—are "Nicolaus Venator" spelled backward. Nicholus was an astronomer at the Palermo Observatory and is the only person who has gotten away with naming stars after himself.

Dolphins were familiar creatures to the Greek and Phoenician sailors who placed this one in the sky.

DORADO—the Swordfish (doh-rah-do)
(see Southern Sky chart)

The swordfish is a string of faint stars near the sky's south pole, far south of Orion. It is not visible from the United States.

Dorado means "golden" in Spanish, and the constellation is sometimes called the Goldfish. This is not the kind of small, orange fish you might keep as a pet in a bowl, but rather a large, tasty fish related to the mahi-mahi served in seafood restaurants.

The Swordfish first appeared on Bayer's atlas in 1603, and, being modern, it has no mythology associated with it.

The Large Magellanic Cloud—a bright companion galaxy to our Milky Way—lies within Dorado.

DRACO—the Dragon (dray-ko)
(see all monthly charts)

The Dragon is a huge constellation of faint stars that winds between the Big and Little Dippers, curves around the Little Dipper, and then bends back to end near the bright star Vega. It does look like a dragon, and it is not hard to find once you know where to look (if the sky is dark).

We think of dragons as having heavy bodies, like those of huge horses or bulls, and being able to gallop quickly, but some dragons (like Draco) have a more "serpentine" or snakelike shape and move about on small legs. Three other serpents appear in the sky: Hydra, Hydrus, and Serpens.

The Dragon is circumpolar from the northern United States and Canada, but it is best seen in summer. It is high in the north at 9:00 P.M. in early August.

To find Draco, find the Big and Little Dippers. Draco's tail is a little more than one-third of the way from the North Star to the star at the end of the Big Dipper's bowl. The Dragon's body curves all the way around the bowl of the Little Dipper. It then bends sharply at a point about halfway between the North Star and the bright star Vega. The neck of the dragon extends southward toward a point a bit to the west of Vega, ending in Draco's head—a compact group of four stars about one-third of the way from Vega to the bowl of the Little Dipper.

Don't confuse the head of the Dragon with a similar small group of stars in Hercules.

In ancient mythology, dragons generally guarded treasures. This dragon guards the sky's north pole.

To the ancient Egyptians, these stars formed a hippopotamus.

A Former Pole Star

The faint star Thuban, which lies halfway between the middle of the handle of the Big Dipper and the bowl of the Little Dipper, was the North Star about five thousand years ago, when the Egyptian pyramids were built. The northern of two "air shafts" in the Great Pyramid was aligned toward Thuban. The pharaoh's ultimate destiny was the "imperishable" (circumpolar) stars, and the main imperishable star was Thuban. These stars symbolized immortality, because they do not rise or set. After death, the pharaoh ascended to them so that he, like them, would no longer die. Precession—a slow wobbling of the earth's axis—has carried the position of the sky's north pole from Thuban to Polaris during the last five millennia (see Ursa Minor).

EQUULEUS—the Little Horse or Colt (ee-kwo-lee-us)
(see August through December monthly charts)

Equuleus is a tiny and faint constellation that is nearly impossible to see. It has only a handful of faint stars, none brighter than magnitude 4, and there are no bright stars nearby to guide the way to it. You'll find it midway between Pegasus and Aquila in the early autumn sky.

Surprisingly, this insignificant constellation was recognized as long ago as the second century B.C. It is a companion to Pegasus, the much larger horse nearby.

ERIDANUS—the River (eh-rid-a-nus)
(see November through March monthly charts and Southern Sky chart)

The River is the second-longest constellation in the sky. Its long string of stars winds, like a river from near Orion far to the south. With the exception of its southernmost star, it is made up of only faint stars, and seeing it takes some practice. The southernmost part of it is below the horizon for viewers in the United States. It is in the evening sky in winter.

To find Eridanus, find Rigel, the bright blue star in Orion. The River begins with a faint star a short distance to the upper right of Rigel. The River extends as a looping stream of faint stars about one Orion's-length to the right and down a bit. It then curves back and down almost the same distance. It bends back to the left and extends far to the left, below the horizon, ending in the bright star Achernar (**ay**-ker-nar). Achernar is the ninth-brightest star in the sky, but it is not visible from the United States north of Miami or Hawaii. Achernar comes from the Arabic for "end of the river."

Eridanus is an ancient constellation that was associated with the Nile River in Egypt.

The star Epsilon Eridani is one of the closest solar-type stars (and the star around which Vulcan, the home planet of *Star Trek*'s Mr. Spock, supposedly orbits).

FORNAX—the Furnace (**for**-naks)
(see November through February monthly charts and Southern Sky chart)

This obscure constellation was invented by Lacaille to be a furnace for the use of the Sculptor, a nearby constellation he also invented. It is made up of a few faint stars far to the south of Cetus and lies largely within a bend in the River, Eridanus. It is in the far southern sky in late autumn and early winter.

GEMINI—the Twins (**gem**-eh-nye)
(see December through May monthly charts)

The winter sky is full of bright stars. Two that are equal in brightness and close together have been known as the "twin stars" for thousands of years. They are the heads of Gemini, twin brothers in Greek mythology. Gemini is one of the constellations of the zodiac, and the sun is within its boundaries from approximately June 20 to July 20.

Gemini is northeast of Orion. Look for it high overhead in winter and early spring. The Twins stand upright on the northwest horizon at 8:00 P.M. daylight time in the middle of May.

Gemini looks like two young men standing (or lying) side by side. It is two strings of stars stretching westward from the bright stars Castor (**kass**-tor) and Pollux (**poll**-ux). To remember which is which, note that Castor is nearest to Capella (the brightest star in Auriga) and Pollux is nearest to Procyon (the brightest star in the Small Dog).

In Greek mythology the twins were heroes who had enough adventures to fill a TV series; their best-known adventure was their travels with Jason to search for the golden fleece. Castor was an expert horseman, his twin Pollux an expert boxer; together they had lots of fun battling bad guys. Because they rose before the sun as winter storms ended and the sailing season resumed, they were popular with Greek sailors, who also looked to them for protection from pirates.

The star cluster M35 in Castor's foot is visible to the naked eye and is very pretty when viewed in binoculars or a small telescope. It is about 2,200 light-years distant in the Orion Arm of the Milky Way.

The Milky Way runs through Gemini's feet.

The Twin Stars

Castor and Pollux appear close together in the sky, but they are fifty-two and thirty-four light-years distant, respectively, and have no association with each other. Castor is a bluish white giant, and Pollux is an orange-yellow giant. Both are multiple-star systems: Castor is actually six stars, and Pollux is a binary star.

GRUS—the Crane (grus)
(see October and November monthly charts and Southern Sky chart)

The Crane is a southern constellation. It is not hard to spot just above the southern horizon in the middle of autumn, especially from the southern United States.

A crane is a water bird with a long neck, long legs, and a long bill. (It is also a construction machine with a "long neck" that lifts heavy objects.) Grus is not an ancient constellation; it first appeared on Bayer's star atlas in 1603.

To see Grus as a crane, find Pegasus and notice the length of one of the sides of the Great Square. Then find Fomalhaut, the bright star in the Southern Fish. Go directly south of Fomalhaut a distance slightly greater than the length of one of the sides of the Great Square of Pegasus. There you will see two medium-bright stars the same distance above the southern horizon; they are the Crane's body. The Crane's neck is a string of fainter stars that extend up and to the right of the star on the left (plus a few other stars nearby).

A modern constellation, the Crane has no associated mythology.

HERCULES—the strong man Hercules (her-cue-leez)
(see May through October monthly charts)

Hercules passes overhead in the summer. He has no very bright stars, but two bright stars (Vega and Arcturus) will guide you to him.

Today we call Hercules the Strong Man, but before Greek and Roman times he was known as the Kneeler—a man on bended knee. Who the kneeler was and what he was supposed to do was forgotten by the time of the ancient Greeks, but he may have been the Sumerian god of war. To us, Hercules is an early "Superman" whose strength was beyond that of normal men. In Greek mythology, he was given twelve labors, or challenges, to gain his freedom. The first was to slay a lion (Leo) that was unaffected by ordinary weapons. Hercules ended up strangling it with his bare hands, a feat also performed in the Old Testament by Samson. Another labor was to kill Hydra (another constellation), and in the process he killed the Crab (also a constellation, Cancer).

Hercules is standing (or kneeling) upside down. To see him, find a little box of four stars that lie one-third of the way from Vega to Arcturus. This box is called the Keystone, and it is Hercules' torso. His upper body is framed by two strings of faint stars that extend southward from the Keystone. His head is the star Alpha. His legs extend upward from the Keystone as two more strings of faint stars. His foot is on Draco's head, and one arm stretches from his upper body toward Vega.

You can also see Hercules as the letter H or as a butterfly.

Our sun is heading toward Hercules as it moves through the Milky Way.

A Bright Star Cluster

Amateur astronomers equipped with telescopes enjoy looking at the cluster of stars known by the romantic name M13 (its catalog number). This group of several hundred thousand stars looks like a sphere or globe, and it is the brightest globular cluster in the northern sky. Through small telescopes, it looks like a fuzzy round patch of light, but with a telescope at least 6 inches in diameter you can begin to see individual faint stars. It is about 25,000 light-years distant and magnitude 6. Look for M13 about one-third of the way from the star Eta to the star Zeta in the Keystone.

HOROLOGIUM—the Clock (hor-oh-low-jee-um)

(see January monthly chart and Southern Sky chart)

The clock is a string of stars lying far to the south in the winter sky. Only the top part of it is above the horizon as seen from the United States, but its stars are so faint that in reality you probably will not see it. It looks nothing like a clock, and there is no mythology associated with it.

This constellation is another mechanical invention of Lacaille. He gave it the terrible name Horologium Oscillatorium—the Pendulum Clock—now shortened to Horologium (which is almost as bad).

The northern part of the Clock is below a bend in the River, Eridanus. The bottom part is midway between the bright stars Canopus in Carina and Achernar in Eridanus.

HYDRA—the female Water Snake (hi-dra)
(see February through July monthly charts and Southern Sky chart)

We seldom see water snakes, but there are two in the sky: Hydra, the female, and Hydrus, the male. Hydra is an ancient constellation, but Hydrus first appeared in Bayer's 1603 chart.

Hydra is in the south in the spring. It is the largest constellation, zigzagging across one-quarter of the sky. Its stars are so faint and so far apart that it doesn't look much like a snake—or like anything else. On ancient star charts, Hydra's head is immediately below Cancer, and her body winds below Leo, Crater (which touches her back), and Corvus (who sits on her), and under Virgo. She is so long that her head is setting when her tail is rising.

Her brightest star, Alphard (**al**-fard), means "solitary one" in Arabic—a good name for such a lonely star. Alphard is below and to the west of Regulus in Leo.

In mythology, Hydra was the many-headed snake killed by Hercules as his second labor.

HYDRUS—the male Water Snake (hi-drus)
(see Southern Sky chart)

This constellation is a large, pretty triangle of stars near the sky's south pole. It is easily seen from South America, Africa, and Australia, but it is too far south to be seen from the United States.

Hydrus is a modern constellation that first appeared in Bayer's star atlas, and it has no mythology associated with it.

INDUS—the American Indian (in-dus)
(see Southern Sky chart)

Constellations are named after strange things, but the strangest may be Indus, the American Indian. America was a new, mostly unexplored land and American Indians a novelty to Europeans when Bayer included one in his famous star atlas in 1603. It was originally named by Keyser and Houtman.

Indus lies far to the south, below Capricornus in the autumn sky. We would be able to see its northernmost stars from the southern United States if those stars were brighter, but Indus has no bright stars. It is a small group of faint stars with no recognizable shape.

LACERTA—the Lizard (la-ser-ta)
(see August through January monthly charts)

Some parts of the sky are so empty you would think they are between constellations. Lacerta is such an empty part of the sky; although it passes high overhead in the autumn, its stars are very difficult to see. Hevelius, who invented it in 1687, said he put a lizard there because "nothing else would fit."

Lacerta is directly south of Cepheus and north of Pegasus.

The Lizard is in the Milky Way, and, although it has no bright stars, it has plenty of faint stars.

LEO—the Lion (lee-oh)
(see February through July monthly charts)

Leo is a major constellation that is best seen in the springtime. It is one of the few constellations that can be made to look like what it is named after. Leo is Latin for "lion."

Leo looks like a lion if you imagine a backward question mark marking his head and chest (Regulus is his heart) while a smaller right triangle of stars to the east marks his hindquarters and tail. We see him from the side, facing Cancer to the west and lying on his stomach. The backward question mark is an easily recognizable group of stars called the Sickle after the primitive harvesting tool with the same shape as the star pattern. Leo's head appears above the horizon first as he rises, and is also the first part of him to set.

Leo is one of the constellations of the zodiac, and the sun is in Leo from approximately August 10 to September 15.

Few of us see lions today except at the zoo, but in ancient Sumeria (now Iraq) five thousand years ago lions were familiar predators, coming down to the river valleys during the hot days of summer to hunt the sheep and goats—to the great annoyance of the shepherds. These stars have been seen as a lion since those prehistoric days. The famous Sphinx in Egypt may be Leo with the pharaoh's head. Today the reappearance of Leo in the evening sky announces the coming of spring, and the Lion is in the evening sky from March to July.

Gamma Leonis is a very pretty double star viewed through a small telescope.

The Royal Star

Regulus (**reg**-you-lus) is Latin for "little king"; it is one of the few stars with a Latin name. The star was named by Copernicus, the revolutionary astronomer who in 1543 proposed that the earth orbits the sun rather than the other way around, but Regulus has been associated with kingship for thousands of years (along with the other three royal stars that lie near the path of the sun: Antares in Scorpius, Aldebaran in Taurus, and Fomalhaut in Piscis Austrinus). Regulus is the twenty-first brightest star in the sky. It is a large white star one hundred times brighter than our sun, seventy-seven light-years distant, and magnitude 1.4.

LEO MINOR—the Small Lion (lee-oh my-ner)
(see February through July monthly charts)

The Small Lion lies north of Leo—the "big" lion—and south of Ursa Major. Leo Minor is a faint constellation that is best seen in the spring. It is a string of three dim stars midway between the bowl of the Big Dipper and the star Regulus in Leo. Leo Minor was devised by the Polish astronomer Hevelius to use up stars unclaimed by other constellations, and it first appeared on his star atlas of 1690.

LEPUS—the Hare or Rabbit (leap-us)
(see December through April monthly charts and Southern Sky chart)

Below Orion's feet is a rabbit hiding from the Hunter, perhaps hoping to go unnoticed while Orion hunts bigger game in the form of Taurus, the Bull. This ancient but modest constellation is often overlooked because of the grander constellations above it, but it is not hard to spot. It looks not like a rabbit but like a bent letter H lying on its side. It is in the sky at the same time as Orion—during the winter.

Gamma is a nice double star easily resolved in binoculars.

LIBRA—the Balance Scales (lee-bra)
(see May through September monthly charts)

Libra is a box of four medium-bright stars to the right of Scorpius. The box is standing on one end, so it resembles a diamond—perhaps a baseball diamond.

Libra is a set of balance scales. Contemporary bathroom scales are a flat device that you stand on, but in former times scales worked by balancing two pans hanging from a lever, like the "scales of justice" you see on court buildings. It doesn't take much imagination to see Libra as such old-fashioned scales. The Sumerians may originally have called these stars scales because the sun was here on the first day of autumn, when day and night are balanced in length.

Libra is the only nonanimal in the zodiac, which means "ring of animals." The sun is within its boundaries from approximately October 31 to November 22.

The stars of Libra were once seen as claws that belonged to Scorpius to the east. If you look at the Scorpion critically, he is missing his claws. Although it makes more sense for Libra's stars to form Scorpion's claws, in Roman times the claws were separated from Scorpius and given independence. As scales, they are associated with adjacent Virgo, who is often identified with Astraea, the goddess of justice.

Libra is at its best in the early summer, when it is in the southern sky.

Alpha is a pretty double star viewed through binoculars or small telescopes.

LUPUS—the Wolf (loo-pus)
(see June and July monthly charts and Southern Sky chart)

Lupus lies directly below Libra, and can be seen in the summer sky. Lupus has several bright stars but is hard to see because it is so low. It can't be seen from the northern United States, but from the southern states it is visible as two connected rings of stars. Look for it below Libra and to the lower right of Antares, the bright red star in Scorpius. The top part of Lupus is level with the lower part of Scorpius, so if you can't see the Scorpion's tail you won't see Lupus. The top part of Centaurus is to the right of the Wolf.

Lupus was originally an unspecified beast. On old illustrated star charts, the poor beast is usually shown being carried by Centaurus on his spear.

LYNX—the Lynx or Bobcat (links)
(see January through June monthly charts)

Lynx is so faint and uninteresting that the only reason to bother to find it is to be able to claim you have seen it. It covers a very large area of the sky north of Cancer and Gemini and between Ursa Major and Auriga in the late winter and spring sky.

Lynx was named in 1690 by Hevelius, who correctly stated that only a person with the eyes of a lynx could see it.

LYRA—the Harp (lie-ra)

(see May through November monthly charts)

The Harp is a compact, easy-to-recognize pattern of one very bright and five medium-bright stars. Vega dominates the group, which is small enough to fit within the bowl of the Big Dipper.

Lyra is nearly overhead at the end of summer and the beginning of fall.

It is not easy to see Lyra as a harp, but it is easy to see it as a parallelogram (or squashed box) with a hook on it. Begin with Vega. South of Vega is a parallelogram marked by four equally bright stars. Northeast of Vega is the hook—a fifth star, Epsilon (a "double-double star").

Lyra is a type of small handheld harp called a lyre that was popular in ancient Greece. In Greek mythology, it was the harp of Orpheus, whose adventure in the underworld is one of the more popular Greek myths.

Summer Triangle

Vega is the westernmost of three bright stars that form the Summer Triangle. Though not an official constellation (it is made up of stars from three constellations), the Summer Triangle is so easy to recognize that it is the first star pattern most people find in the summer sky. Once you locate the Summer Triangle, you can find your way around the rest of the sky.

As the name suggests, the Summer Triangle is at its best in summer, but it is visible much of the year. It is in the east late in the evening in June and in the west early in the evening at the end of December.

The other two stars of the Summer Triangle are Deneb in Cygnus and Altair in Aquila.

Vega

Vega (**vay**-ga or **vee**-ga) is a pretty star with a pretty name (Vega means "falling" in Arabic, and the Arabs thought of it as a bird falling from the sky). It is a nearby star only twenty-five light-years away, which is part of the reason it appears so bright. Intrinsically, it is fifty times brighter than our sun. Notice the contrast of Vega's bluish white color with the yellowish color of Arcturus to the west. Vega is magnitude 0 and is the fifth brightest star in the sky; it is the second brightest star in the northern sky (after Arcturus). It will become the North Star in about 12,500 years when the earth's axis precesses through almost half a cycle.

MENSA—Table Mountain (men-sa)
(see Southern Sky chart)

Mensa, Latin for "table," is named after a flat-topped hill called Table Mountain that lies near Cape Town, South Africa. It was named by Lacaille, who observed it near this spot in the 1750s. Mensa is near the sky's south pole and is too far to the south to be seen from the United States. This is no loss—it is a small constellation of only fifth-magnitude and fainter stars.

MICROSCOPIUM—the Microscope (my-kro-sco-pee-um)
(see September and October monthly charts and Southern Sky chart)

The Frenchman Lacaille loved to place machines in the sky when he was inventing new constellations in the 1750s. The Microscope is one of the few of his star patterns far enough north to be seen from the United States. It is a bleak group of dim stars that lie directly south of Capricornus. Like Capricornus, the Microscope is in the evening sky in early autumn.

MONOCEROS—the Unicorn (mo-no-ser-os)
(see January through May monthly charts)

The Unicorn is a huge constellation made up of only faint stars. Because it is next to some of the brightest constellations in the sky, it is often overlooked. It sits to the left of Orion and between the Large Dog and the Small Dog in the winter sky. It has no recognizable shape.

Monoceros first appeared on a globe produced by Plancius in 1613. A unicorn is an imaginary horselike animal with one straight horn coming out of its forehead.

The Milky Way runs through Monoceros, and its many interesting star clusters make rich viewing for observers with good binoculars or a telescope.

MUSCA—the Fly (muss-ka)
(see Southern Sky chart)

Musca is a small constellation that lies directly south of the Southern Cross—too far south to be seen from the United States. Musca originally appeared on Bayer's 1603 chart as Apis, the Bee, but it was renamed Musca, the Fly, by Lacaille in the 1750s.

NORMA—the Carpenter's Square (nor-ma)
(see July monthly chart and Southern Sky chart)

This very small group of stars lies so far south of the front part of Scorpius that it cannot be seen from the northern United States and is near the horizon from the southern states. It is a small ring of faint stars. The best time to see it is early on July evenings.

A carpenter's square is a tool that looks like a large letter L; it is used to make sure that angles are correct. The constellation, which looks nothing like any kind of square, was named by Lacaille in the 1750s.

OCTANS—the Octant (ak-tans)
(see Southern Sky chart)

This small constellation is directly above the earth's South Pole. It cannot be seen from the Northern Hemisphere, but (like Ursa Minor in the Northern Hemisphere) it never sets from the Southern Hemisphere. It has only very faint stars, one of which, 5.5-magnitude Sigma, could be considered the "South Star." However, Sigma is sixteen times fainter than the North Star and is barely visible.

An octant is an antique navigational device that was used to find the position of ships at sea. Lacaille invented this constellation in the 1750s.

OPHIUCHUS—the Serpent Bearer (oh-fee-you-kus)
(see June through October monthly charts)

This outline of a man occupies a large area of the summer sky north of Scorpius. Ophiuchus is holding a snake, or serpent (the constellation Serpens), in his bare hands. The serpent's head is to the right of Ophiuchus, his tail is to the left, and his body seems to cross in front. Since one constellation cannot be in front of another, Ophiuchus divides the snake into two parts—the head and the tail. No constellations are more intimately connected than the snake handler and his serpent.

Ophiuchus is high in the south early in the evening in July and August. It is not hard to imagine the outline of a giant man. He has no truly bright stars.

According to modern constellation boundaries, the sun passes through the southern edge of Ophiuchus, which makes it a constellation of the zodiac. Ophiuchus is not part of the traditional astrological zodiac of twelve equally spaced signs, but it is certainly the thirteenth constellation of the astronomical zodiac. A lot of people are born under Ophiuchus but don't know it—people born between November 30 and December 17.

Ophiuchus is a doctor, and snakes have long been associated with medicine (as in "snake oil"). The Greeks knew him by the name Aesculapius, a superphysician who tried the ultimate medical accomplishment: reviving the dead. This alarmed Pluto, god of the underworld, who worried that he would run out of "customers." Pluto protested to Zeus, the head god, who banished Aesculapius to the sky, still holding his serpent. When physicians today take the Hippocratic oath, they begin by swearing to Aesculapius (a.k.a. Ophiuchus) to do their duty.

The summer Milky Way runs through the eastern half of Ophiuchus, and it has many open and globular star clusters that are visible through a small telescope. The globular clusters M9, M10, M12, M14, M19, and M62 are bright enough to be seen in binoculars (M10 and M12 offer the best viewing).

The Pipe Nebula, a dark nebula similar to but smaller than the Great Rift in Cygnus, extends for about 7 degrees south-southeast of Theta. This nebula, about five thousand light-years from the earth, blocks light from the central hub of our galaxy. Observe the Pipe Nebula with the naked eye or with binoculars.

ORION—the Hunter (oh-rye-un)

(see December through April monthly charts)

Orion is the most magnificent constellation in the sky and many people's favorite. It is also one of the few constellations that looks like what it is named after. Orion looks like a man whose body is outlined by very bright stars.

The first part of Orion people see is his belt, a straight line of three bright, equally spaced stars. They are, from right to left, Mintaka (mean-**ta**-ka), Alnilam (**awl**-nee-lamb), and Alnitak (**awl**-nee-tock) (in Arabic, "girdle," "string of pearls," and "belt," respectively). In some countries, they are associated with the Three Wise Men. Spanning slightly less than 3 degrees in the sky, they are a convenient celestial yardstick.

Above Orion's belt are his shoulders—the stars Betelgeuse (**bay**-tel-juice) at left and Bellatrix (bell-**ah**-trix) at right. Orion's head is a tiny group of three stars where you would expect his head to be. A sword hangs from his belt. The sword is a string of many faint stars close together along with a bright nebula, or cloud of gas, that is the sword's jewel. Below are his knees or legs—the stars Saiph (sa-**if**) at left and Rigel (**rye**-gel) at right. Saiph is Arabic for "sword," although the star is in the wrong place to be part of Orion's sword, and Rigel is Arabic for "foot."

Orion is facing to the right (west). He is holding a shield—a long string of faint stars that stretch up toward the red star Aldebaran in Taurus, the Bull. The shield is shown as a lion skin on old star charts. In his other hand he holds a club—two strings of faint stars that extend up toward the feet of Gemini. The club is over his head as if he is about to strike. It is not easy to see the shield and club from within the glow of city lights, but they are a nice sight against a dark sky.

Orion is visible in the evening sky from December through March, although you can see him late at night as early as August. When Orion appears in the southeast in the evening, winter is about to begin.

Orion was a giant and a hunter who had many adventures. In one Greek myth, he boasted he could kill any animal alive. This offended the gods, who sent a scorpion to kill him. Orion and the scorpion (Scorpius) were then placed in the sky, but on opposite sides—Orion is in the winter sky, and Scorpius in the summer—and one rises while the other sets.

Orion is hunting Taurus, the Bull. A rabbit (Lepus), a more realistic target, is ignored below Orion's feet. To find the Bull, trace a line along Orion's belt and continue it to the right (west) about one Orion's length until you come to the bright red star Aldebaran, the Bull's eye. If you trace that line in the opposite direction (to the left, or east) an equal distance, you will come to Sirius, the brightest star in the sky. Sirius is the Dog Star in Canis Major, Orion's large hunting companion.

Many thousands of years ago (before Sumerian times), Orion might have been thought of as a Mother Goddess or Earth Goddess—quite a contrast to a Great Hunter! The Egyptians identified him with Osiris, the judge of the dead.

The Milky Way passes to the left of the main part of Orion. The Orion Arm of the Milky Way is the closest spiral arm to our solar system, and Earth lies on its inside edge. The whole area has a great number of bright stars and faint nebulae, and it is a fascinating part of the sky to look at with binoculars or a telescope.

Opposite Giants: Betelgeuse and Rigel

Orion contains two of the brightest stars in the sky. They are giants, but of the opposite kind: Betelgeuse is a red supergiant, and Rigel is a blue supergiant. The color contrast between them is striking. Although called a "red giant," Betelgeuse is actually orange in color.

Betelgeuse (which comes from "hand of the giant" in Arabic) is an enormous star. If we replaced our sun with it, the planets Mercury, Venus, Earth, and Mars would all orbit inside it. Betelgeuse is unstable, slowly changing its size and brightness, and it is the brightest variable star. It is ten thousand times brighter than our sun and about 520 light-years away (considerably closer than the other stars in Orion). The gruesome but funny movie and cartoon character whose name is pronounced "beetle-juice" was named after the star.

Rigel is the seventh brightest star in the sky and is magnitude 0. It is about fifty thousand times brighter than our sun and about the same size as Betelgeuse. It is 900 light-years away.

The Great Nebula

The jewel in Orion's sword is the brightest nebula in the sky. The word *nebula* is Latin for "cloud," and this nebula is an enormous cloud of hot hydrogen gas dozens of light-years across and 1,600 light-years from Earth. Stars are being born within it at the present time, and several brand new stars are lighting up the nebula and causing it to glow. The Trapezium, a group of four stars clustered tightly together, lies at the nebula's heart.

The Orion Nebula (M42) is barely visible without a telescope even in a dark sky. It is a very pretty sight viewed through even a small telescope, and considerable structure is visible through a good amateur telescope. It is one of the most popular targets for amateur astronomers.

PAVO—the Peacock (pah-vo)
(see Southern Sky chart)

The Peacock is a "new" constellation, appearing first on Bayer's atlas in 1603. It lies far south of Sagittarius and Capricornus—too far south to be visible from the United States. Peacocks were a novelty from India and Southeast Asia when Pavo was named.

PEGASUS—the Flying or Winged Horse (peg-a-sus)
(see August through January monthly charts)

Pegasus, a trio of bright stars with a sprinkling of much fainter stars nearby, is very easy to see in the autumn sky.

Most people see Pegasus as a large square of four stars called, simply, the Great Square of Pegasus. The Great Square, whose side lengths vary from 13 to 16 degrees, is not the same as Pegasus, however, because the Square's northeastern star is actually in the constellation Andromeda and therefore is not part of Pegasus. (This star is Alpha Andromedae.) Hence, the Great Square includes stars of two constellations. Formerly, it was possible for a star to be shared by two constellations, but when the official constellation boundaries were set in 1928, every star was assigned to only one constellation. (Remember, however, that the Great Square of Pegasus is not an official constellation.) Without binoculars, the Square may appear to be empty of stars.

To the ancient Sumerians and Egyptians, the Great Square was an irrigated field of grain. Pegasus is the front half of a winged horse who is upside down, flying to the west. According to Greek mythology, Pegasus was a winged horse created by Poseidon, the god of the oceans, from blood that had dripped from the head of Medusa into the sea. Pegasus was later flown by Perseus.

The Square points the way to other, fainter nearby constellations. Immediately to the south lies the westernmost fish of Pisces. Farther to the south is Aquarius. To the east is the easternmost fish of Pisces. Pisces and Aquarius are large but are made up of only faint stars, so the Square is very useful in locating them. Northeast of the Square (and connected to it) is Andromeda.

PERSEUS—the hero Perseus (pur-see-us)
(see October through April monthly charts)

Perseus lies midway between Cassiopeia and Taurus in the winter sky. At his highest position, he is overhead or even north of overhead for viewers in the United States.

Perseus is a man, but it is easiest to see him as a long, curving string of stars. The brightest star, Alpha, is in line with the three stars of Andromeda and looks like the "fourth star of Andromeda," to the east of the other three. The string begins south of the easternmost part of the W that forms Cassiopeia. It stretches southward in a long curve, and it stops short of the famous Pleiades star cluster. A short branch extends westward from the middle of the string to Algol, the one other bright star in Perseus.

The faintest part of the Milky Way passes through Perseus, and many dim stars and nice clusters of stars are within its boundaries.

It was Perseus who rescued Andromeda from Cetus and received the thanks of Cassiopeia and Cepheus. (See Andromeda for the full story.)

Perseus was worshiped during the days of the Roman Empire by the followers of Mithraism, now an extinct religion.

The sixth-magnitude open star cluster M34 is midway between Algol and Gamma Andromedae. It is about 1,400 light-years distant.

The Demon Star

Algol (**al**-gol) comes from the Arabic words for "the ghoul" or demon. Observers centuries ago were alarmed that this star grows noticeably fainter once every three days—something a good star was not supposed to do. It seemed to be slowly winking at observers.

Today we know that Algol (which is almost a hundred light-years from the earth) is actually two stars that eclipse each other once every orbit. When the brighter of the two stars is hidden by the fainter, Algol fades from magnitude 2.1 to 3.4 and becomes one-third as bright as normal for about ten hours. Compare it with Gamma Andromedae nearby, which remains at constant magnitude 2.1.

Algol's variability may have been known in ancient Greek times. It was rediscovered about 1667.

The Double Cluster

Halfway between the star Alpha in Perseus and the middle of the W of Cassiopeia is a pair of very distant 4.5 magnitude star clusters. Viewed with the naked eye, they look like two faint, fuzzy stars so close together that our moon would just fit between them. They are especially pretty viewed through binoculars or a small telescope, which shows hundreds of stars in each cluster. These are among the largest star clusters in our Milky Way. They are 7,000 to 8,000 light-years from the earth in the spiral arm of the Milky Way beyond the Orion Arm.

PHOENIX—the Phoenix (fee-nicks)

(see Southern Sky chart)

Phoenix was invented by Bayer in modern times to "use up" faint stars not included in other constellations. It is far south of Cetus and visible only from the southernmost United States.

The constellation is named after a mythical bird that is a symbol of rebirth. In Egyptian mythology, a phoenix is a bird that lives for 500 years and then sets itself on fire and dies, only to be reborn from its own ashes. A phoenix is also called a firebird.

PICTOR—the Painter's Easel (pick-tor)

(see Southern Sky chart)

Lacaille invented this small constellation while he was in South Africa in the 1750s. It is a string of faint stars that lie a short distance to the right of the very bright star Canopus. It is too far south to be seen from north of Hawaii or Miami. Lacaille imagined it as a painter's easel and palette.

PISCES—the Fishes (pie-sees)

(see September through February monthly charts)

Pisces is a large constellation of mostly faint stars visible in the autumn and winter sky. It is two fishes swimming in opposite directions, with their tails tied together.

Although the stars are faint, you can see two fishes here if you know exactly where to look and if the sky is dark. The western fish is a small circle of stars directly below the center of the Great Square of Pegasus. The eastern fish is an oval of fainter stars below the middle of Andromeda. The fishes are tied together by a string that we see as a long line of faint stars that first goes straight east from the western fish toward Cetus, then bends abruptly and—while staying west of Aries—reaches almost due north toward the eastern fish. It may take practice to see them, but once you spot them it is relatively easy to see them again.

We have ancient myths about the fishes and their adventures but little information about why these stars were originally named fishes or who these fishes were. In one Greek myth, they tied their tails together so they would not be separated, and we still see them this way today.

Pisces is a member of the zodiac, the band of constellations through which the sun passes in its yearly journey around the sky. The sun is within the boundaries of Pisces from approximately March 12 through April 18. Presently, the sun is just below the western fish on the first day of spring—the vernal equinox. To astrologers, this means that we are living in the "Age of Pisces."

PISCIS AUSTRINUS—the Southern Fish (pie-sees os-tra-nis)

(see September through December monthly charts and Southern Sky chart)

This constellation is unusual in that it has one very bright, very lonely star—Fomalhaut—along with some very dim stars. It is almost a one-star constellation.

The Southern Fish is to the lower left of Capricornus and can be seen in the fall. Look for it as the star Fomalhaut plus a line of very faint stars below this star and to the right.

Fomalhaut (**fo**-mel-hote; Arabic for "fish's mouth") is the eighteenth brightest star in the sky and is magnitude 1.19. It is about eleven times brighter than our sun and only twenty-five light-years away. It is useful for guiding us to nearby faint constellations such as Grus, Cetus, and Aquarius. Fomalhaut was one of the ancient royal stars—stars closely approached by the sun in its yearly trip around the sky.

PUPPIS—the ship's Stern (**pup**-is)
(see February through April monthly charts and Southern Sky chart)

The astronomer Lacaille divided Jason's huge ancient ship Argo, once the largest constellation, into three constellations: Vela, Carina, and Puppis. Puppis, the northernmost part, is the ship's stern, also called the "poop deck." It is visible in the winter.

Puppis fills a roughly L-shaped area of the sky that extends from directly to the left of Canis Major, the Large Dog, southward to a point under the Dog. This area has quite a few medium-bright stars, but it is difficult to see them as part of a ship.

Because the Milky Way runs through Puppis, many interesting objects can be seen within its boundaries by people equipped with a telescope. The brightest star clusters are M46 and M47, which are northeast of Sirius, and M93, which is southeast of Sirius.

....

The Brightest Star

The naked-eye star with the greatest intrinsic brightness may be Zeta Puppis, a second-magnitude star 30 degrees to the southeast of Sirius. Because it is over 2,000 light-years away, it does not look remarkable, but it may be sixty thousand times more luminous than our sun in the amount of visible light it radiates, and even brighter in the amount of ultraviolet light. It is a super-hot blue star.

....

PYXIS—the nautical Compass (**pick**-sis)
(see February through May monthly charts and Southern Sky chart)

When Lacaille created three constellations out of the ship Argo, he added Pyxis, the ship's magnetic compass. No ancient Greek sailing ship ever had a compass, but because of Lacaille's infatuation with mechanical inventions, the old ship now has a "modern" compass.

Pyxis has no bright stars, but because the Milky Way runs through it, many dim stars and some faint star clusters can be seen within it. It is a short string of faint stars to the left of Puppis, above the sail—approximately where a ship's compass should be on the stern deck. It is visible in the winter and early spring sky.

RETICULUM—the Reticle (re-tick-you-lum)
(see Southern Sky chart)

Reticulum is a small group of dim stars near the sky's south pole—much too far south to be seen from the United States.

Lacaille named it after the eyepiece with cross hairs (a reticle) that he used to measure star positions during his stay in South Africa, from 1750 to 1752—how unromantic! It is sometimes called the Net.

SAGITTA—the Arrow (sa-geet-a)
(see July through November monthly charts)

The word *sagitta* is Latin for "arrow," and this small group of stars certainly does look like an arrow. It is easy to imagine this constellation as an arrow fired by Sagittarius, in the south, toward the two birds Aquila, the Eagle, and Cygnus, the Swan. Even thought it is the third-smallest constellation and has no stars brighter than magnitude 4, it is surprisingly easy to see. Look for it one-quarter of the way from Altair in Aquila to Deneb in Cygnus in the evening sky in summer and early fall.

Sagitta lies in the Milky Way and is a pretty sight viewed in binoculars. With a length of 7 degrees, it barely fits within the field of view of wide-angle binoculars. M71 is a nice eighth-magnitude globular star cluster viewed through a telescope.

SAGITTARIUS—the Archer (sa-je-tare-ee-us)
(see July through October monthly charts and Southern Sky chart)

The Archer is a prominent and ancient constellation with many bright stars. You can see it low in the south in the evening in summer and early fall.

Most people see Sagittarius as a teapot. Four stars at the eastern end make up the handle, and three stars to the west outline the spout. The lid is a triangle of three stars above. When Sagittarius is in the southwest, the pot is tipped, pouring tea on the tail of Scorpius. A short line of faint stars above the handle is the teaspoon (and Corona Australis below is the lemon).

Sagittarius is a centaur of Sumerian origin later adopted by the Greeks. Many ancient imaginary creatures are made of two or more animals combined into one. One of the strangest was the centaur—a beast, half man and half horse. Centaurs were the ultimate hunter-warriors, combining the skill of men with the speed of horses. They were a pretty wild bunch, generally armed and dangerous, and were best avoided. This particular centaur is armed with a bow and arrow and is called the Archer. An unarmed, gentle centaur named Centaurus is farther to the south and is not visible from the United States.

The sun travels through the upper part of Sagittarius, which thus is a constellation of the zodiac, from approximately December 18 through January 18.

The western half of Sagittarius is filled with star clusters and nebulae that are pretty when viewed through a small telescope, and it is a wonderful place to explore on a summer evening. The eastern half of the constellation is comparatively boring.

Star Clusters

Sagittarius has far more than its fair share of bright star clusters. The best known is M22, a fifth-magnitude globular star cluster that can barely be seen without a telescope. It is one of the closest globular clusters to Earth, at a distance of about 10,000 light-years. It would be the most magnificent such cluster for North American observers if it were not so low in the sky. Other significant globular clusters in Sagittarius are M28, M54, M55 (quite a way to the east of the others), M69, and M70. Globular star clusters are concentrated toward Sagittarius because they orbit around the center of the Milky Way. All pass through this part of the sky at one time or another before dispersing to the outer parts of their orbits, which lie in all directions in the sky.

Lagoon, Trifid, and Omega

Two of the brightest and prettiest nebulae lie only 1½ degrees apart above the spout of the teapot.

The famous Lagoon Nebula, M8, is a fifth-magnitude glowing cloud of gas and dust over ½ degree in diameter. It is a spectacular object viewed through a telescope, nearly as impressive as the Great Nebula in Orion. The Lagoon Nebula is about 5,000 light-years distant and more than 100 light-years in diameter. It is associated with an open cluster in its eastern part.

The Trifid Nebula, M20, is a smaller but still striking eighth-magnitude nebula just north of M8. Its name comes from its three-part structure. It too is surrounded by stars.

A third bright nebula, M17, is called the Omega, Swan, or Horseshoe Nebula. It is smaller and more concentrated than M8. Though it is visible even in binoculars, a telescope shows a curved arc that resembles the neck of a swan, a horseshoe, or the Greek letter Ω (omega).

The Milky Way's Center

The center of the Milky Way lies far beyond the nearby stars of Sagittarius. It is located 5 degrees to the west of and slightly above the tip of the spout, above the tail of Scorpius. The center itself cannot be seen because intervening clouds of gas completely absorb light waves, but radio waves pass through the clouds, so the center can be pinpointed and studied by radio astronomers.

The Great Sagittarius Star Cloud is the visible part of the central hub of the Milky Way. It pokes above clouds of obscuring gas and dust, appearing as an irregular cloud of distant stars several degrees in extent immediately above the spout. It is easily apparent to the naked eye, and it looks even better in binoculars. It is about 30,000 light-years away and is as close to the center of the Milky Way as your eyes will see.

The Small Sagittarius Star Cloud is a small (1- by 2-degree) rectangular portion of the innermost arm of the Milky Way. Like the Great Sagittarius Star Cloud, it pokes above the obscuring material that blocks the light of most of the inner arm and the central hub. It is half as distant as the Great Cloud and is conspicuous on a dark night once you know where to look, about 10 degrees north of the center of the constellation. Use binoculars or a low-power, wide-angle telescope.

SCORPIUS—the Scorpion (skor-pee-us)
(see June through September monthly charts and Southern Sky chart)

The Scorpion is a major constellation in the summer sky. Because it is low on the southern horizon as seen from the United States, observers lose much of its splendor, but far south of the equator, where it passes overhead, it is a magnificent string of bright stars.

Scorpius truly looks like a scorpion, and people have been calling it the Scorpion since prehistoric times—for at least six thousand years. The bright red star Antares is his heart. His tail is a long string of bright stars that descends to the left of Antares and then curls back up to end in two stars close together that form his stinger. The front part of his body stretches a short distance to the right from Antares, ending in his claws—three stars in a north-south row.

Scorpius now has only three stars for stubby claws, but long ago the claws included the stars of Libra, to the right. Then the claws were huge, and Scorpius was a frightening creature.

In Greek mythology, Scorpius was the enemy of Orion, the Hunter. When Orion boasted that he could kill any living animal, the alarmed earth goddess sent a scorpion to kill *him*. The scorpion came to symbolize death and darkness; Orion, who was reborn, symbolized life and light. After Orion's death, both he and the scorpion were placed in the sky, but on opposite sides. One sets while the other rises, and so the battle between light and dark, between life and death, continues eternally.

Scorpius is a member of the zodiac, and the sun cuts across its northernmost part. According to the modern way in which the sky is divided, the sun is within its boundaries for only one week, from approximately November 23 through November 29. The sun then moves through Ophiuchus before continuing on to Sagittarius.

The Milky Way runs through the Scorpion, and, like Sagittarius, Scorpius is littered with star clusters visible in binoculars or a small telescope. Open clusters abound; two globular clusters of note are M4, a bright sixth-magnitude cluster only 1⅓ degrees west of Antares, and seventh-magnitude M80, 4½ degrees to the northwest of Antares.

The Rival of Mars

Hearts are red, and the Scorpion's heart is a red star. Antares (ann-**tair**-ees), Greek for "anti-Mars" (better translated as "rival of Mars" so named because the star rivals Mars in the redness of its color) is a giant almost ten thousand times brighter than our sun and 500 light-years distant. It is very similar to Betelgeuse in the Scorpion's enemy, Orion. Antares is one of the four ancient Persian royal stars—bright stars near the path of the sun.

Clusters in the Tail

Two especially large open star clusters, M6 and M7, are bright enough to be seen without binoculars and were known (although their nature was not) in ancient times. They lie above the Scorpion's stinger to the right of the top of the teapot of Sagittarius. M6 is 2,000 light-years distant, M7 less than 1,000. Use binoculars or a very low power, wide-angle telescope.

SCULPTOR—the Sculptor's Workshop (skulp-tor)
(see October through December monthly charts and Southern Sky chart)

This faint constellation lies south of Aquarius and Cetus in the autumn sky. Look for it as a shapeless group of dim stars of magnitude 4 and fainter to the left of the bright star Fomalhaut, in the Southern Fish. Sculptor was invented by Lacaille in the 1750s.

The sculptor's furnace, Fornax, is to the left of Sculptor. It is equally difficult to see.

SCUTUM—the Shield (skyoo-tum)
(see July through October monthly charts)

The Shield is a group of faint stars with no particular shape. It lies between Aquila, Sagittarius, and Ophiuchus in the summer sky.

The Shield was named by Hevelius in 1690 in honor of John Sobieski, the King of Poland, who had defeated the Turks in a major battle only seven years earlier. It was originally called Scutum Sobiescianum, but happily the name has since been shortened. It is the only surviving constellation whose origin is political in nature (all other constellations named to honor patrons or national heroes have thankfully been discarded).

Within Scutum is sixth-magnitude M11, one of the prettiest and most compact star clusters in the sky as seen through a small telescope. It contains hundreds of stars and is about 5,000 light-years from Earth.

Scutum is just south of the Great Rift that splits the Milky Way. Two large "star clouds" (dense portions of the Milky Way) that are bright enough to be seen with the unaided eye make the area a very enjoyable place to explore with binoculars and wide-angle telescopes.

SERPENS—the Serpent or snake (sir-pens)
(see June through October monthly charts)

Serpens is unique in that it is divided into two separate parts with a constellation between them. It is a giant snake held in the outstretched hands of Ophiuchus, the snake handler. Serpens does look like a snake. His head is a circle of faint stars near the constellation Corona Borealis, to the right of Ophiuchus. His body extends to the south and then bends eastward. It "crosses" Ophiuchus in a straight line and then "snakes" up and to the left, ending in a faint star in the direction of Altair in Aquila. The Snake's two parts are called Serpens Caput and Serpens Cauda from the Latin words for "head" and "tail" respectively.

You are supposed to imagine that the middle part of the snake crosses Ophiuchus's body. Because one constellation cannot be in front of another, poor Serpens is divided in two.

Snakes symbolize immortality because they shed their skin and are "reborn."

Serpens is visible in the southern sky at the same time as Ophiuchus—during early evenings in July and August.

The magnificent globular cluster M5 is second only to M13 (in Hercules) in the northern sky. It is magnitude 6 and can be seen with binoculars.

The double star Theta Serpentis is beautiful when viewed through a small telescope; it is two closely situated fifth-magnitude white stars.

SEXTANS—the Sextant (sex-tans)
(see February through June monthly charts)

This little constellation contains only faint stars of magnitude 4.5 or fainter, and it is barely visible. It is directly south of the west end of Leo and appears in the spring.

Hevelius named it in 1690 after the instrument he used to measure the positions of stars.

TAURUS—the Bull (tore-us)
(see November through April monthly charts)

Taurus is one of the major constellations of the winter sky. It has three bright stars and—equally important—two very bright star clusters. The Bull is above and to the right of Orion, the Hunter, west of Gemini, the Twins, and south of Auriga, the Charioteer. Orion is fighting the Bull and driving him backward, westward across the sky.

Taurus looks like the front end of a giant bull. The bright red star Aldebaran—the thirteenth brightest star in the sky—is one fiery eye. (His other eye is a much fainter star, so he appears to be squinting.) His face is a pretty V-shaped group of bright stars near Aldebaran. His horns extend up and to the left, ending in two bright stars directly above Orion. In his back is a pretty little cluster of stars called the Pleiades, or Seven Sisters.

Taurus is shown as just the front of a bull, with his hindquarters missing (a fate he shares with Pegasus, another half-animal constellation). He has been known as the Bull since prehistoric times, and he appears in art from ancient Sumeria. The Bull symbolized strength and fertility, and he was worshiped in ancient Egypt as the god Apis. He also appears in Greek mythology, where he is usually Zeus in disguise visiting his lady friends on the earth.

Taurus is a constellation of the zodiac, and the sun is within its boundaries from approximately May 14 through June 19.

The Bull's horns stick into the Milky Way, and many star clusters and nebulae are visible in the area for people equipped with a good telescope.

The Follower Star

Aldebaran (al-**deb**-are-on) means "follower" in Arabic; it follows the Pleiades across the sky. It is a giant star 150 times brighter than the sun and sixty-five light-years distant. Although it is called a "red giant," its color is actually orange. It is neither as big nor as distant as Antares or Betelgeuse, the two other bright red giants in the sky.

A line traced along Orion's belt and extended to the right (west) points to Aldebaran.

Aldebaran is one of the four royal stars of ancient Persia (bright stars near the path of the sun). The other three are Regulus, Antares, and Fomalhaut.

Hyades

The Bull's face is a cluster of stars called the Hyades (**hi**-a-deez). This cluster is so close to Earth that we can easily see the individual stars with our unaided eye. It looks even nicer through binoculars, but a telescope does not improve the view. Many of its stars are red and yellow, in contrast with the younger Pleiades star cluster, which has blue and white stars. The Hyades, at 150 light-years from Earth, is the second-closest star cluster (after the Ursa Major Moving Group; see Ursa Major).

Aldebaran happens to lie in front of the stars of the Hyades and is not part of it.

Pleiades

The Pleiades (**plee**-ah-deez) is a beautiful cluster of stars that rises an hour before the main part of Taurus. At one time, the Pleiades was considered a separate constellation, but now it is part of the Bull. Although called Seven Sisters in mythology (representing the seven daughters of Atlas), there are actually six bright stars and many faint ones. Why it should be called "Seven" Sisters when there are only six bright stars is the source of endless speculation; it is possible, but unlikely, that one has faded since they were named. You might see ten or so stars if your eyesight is exceptionally good, and binoculars will show several dozen. Its catalog number is M45.

The Pleiades is a young cluster (roughly sixty million years old) of bright blue stars 380 light-years from Earth and about 7 light-years across. It looks like a very little dipper.

TELESCOPIUM—the Telescope (tell-e-**sko**-pee-um)
(see August monthly chart and Southern Sky chart)

This rather blank area of the sky contains a small triangle of stars to the lower right of the tail of Scorpius. It is too far south to be seen from the United States except from the southern states, and then it is near the southern horizon in summer. It has only one star brighter than magnitude 4. It was invented by Lacaille to honor telescopes, and it has no mythology.

TRIANGULUM—the Triangle (tri-**ang**-you-lum)
(see October through March monthly charts)

The Triangle is below Andromeda and above Aries, and it is visible in the autumn. Although it is made up of rather faint stars, its simple triangular shape makes it easy to see.

Triangulum was invented by the ancient Greeks, who loved geometry.

The bright, nearby spiral galaxy M33 in the northern part of Triangulum can be seen with binoculars on a dark night. It is oriented face-on to the earth and has a low surface-brightness. Seen through a telescope, it is a formless haze of light larger than the moon.

TRIANGULUM AUSTRALE—the Southern Triangle (tri-**ang**-you-lum os-**tray**-lee)
(see Southern Sky chart)

The Southern Triangle is a group of three bright stars east of Alpha Centauri and near the sky's south pole. Although it is easily seen from the Southern Hemisphere, it cannot be seen from the United States.

The other triangle in the sky, Triangulum, is a Greek invention and is a mathematical triangle. The Southern Triangle is a device navigators used to plot their position on sea charts; it is used nowadays with a T-square and drafting board. The Southern Triangle was first described in 1503 by Amerigo Vespucci, the person for whom America is named, and it appeared on Bayer's atlas a hundred years later.

TUCANA—the Toucan (too-**can**-ah)
(see Southern Sky chart)

A toucan is a large, colorful bird with a big bill that lives in the American tropics. Toucan is a group of stars that "lives" near the sky's south pole. It was introduced in 1603 by

Bayer, who was fascinated by strange new objects from the New World. It is too far south to be seen from the United States.

URSA MAJOR—the Great Bear (ur-sa may-jer)
(see all monthly charts)

The Great Bear is the third-largest constellation of the northern sky. It contains the seven bright stars known as the Big Dipper, plus many fainter stars nearby. It can be seen best in the spring and early summer, but much of it is circumpolar and thus is always visible.

To see Ursa Major as a bear, first find the Big Dipper. The handle of the Big Dipper is the Great Bear's long tail, and the bowl is the hind part of his body. The Bear's neck and head are formed by a group of faint stars almost one Dipper's length to the west. His feet are fainter stars to the south and west. If you have a better-than-average imagination, you *might* see a bear.

If these stars don't look much like a bear, why is it called a bear? Perhaps people long ago noticed that these stars *act* like a bear. They rise in the spring, when bears come out of hibernation, and they set in the fall, when bears hibernate for the winter. During the winter, the celestial bear is low in the north and out of sight.

Perhaps the most curious aspect of the Great Bear is that it was called a bear by people in widely-separated places such as Europe, Siberia, and North America. Either these detached peoples independently thought up the idea that these stars should represent a bear, or the idea of the Great Bear was carried far and wide as people migrated more than ten thousand years ago. If this second reason is correct, as many people believe, the idea of calling these stars a bear dates back to the Ice Age and is one of the oldest human creations still in existence.

The two end stars in the bowl of the Dipper are called the Pointer Stars because they point to the North Star. Trace a line through them in the direction you would go if you were pouring, and continue one Dipper's length to reach the North Star. The Pointer Stars are separated by 5 degrees and are a convenient yardstick for what an arc of 5 degrees look like. (The length of the Big Dipper is 25 degrees.)

Find the arc made by the other two stars of the bowl and the three stars of the handle, and extend it southward to Arcturus to find that star and remind yourself of its name ("arc to Arcturus"). Then continue along the same huge arc and "speed on to Spica" in Virgo.

Mizar (**My**-zar), the second star from the end of the handle, is a pretty naked-eye double star for people with good eyesight. Mizar and its companion Alcor (Al-cor) are often called the horse and rider. Mizar is a close double star easily viewed through any telescope.

The Big Dipper

The seven brightest stars of the Great Bear make up the most familiar group of stars in the sky—the Big Dipper. Officially, the Big Dipper is not a constellation but is just part of Ursa Major. Before people had running water, they used dippers, or ladles, to scoop drinking water out of buckets.

These seven stars are called a dipper only in the United States and Canada. In England they are seen as a plough, in Germany as a wagon, and in France as a casserole pot. In ancient Sumeria, this group of stars was called a wagon; to the ancient Greeks, it was both a wagon and a bear; in ancient Egypt, it was the leg of a bull; and to the Chinese, it was their Emperor, being pulled around the sky's north pole in a wagon.

Strangely, no one knows how these stars came to be called a dipper. Perhaps the idea was brought to America from Africa by slaves who used to drink from dippers made from hollowed gourds. Before the Civil War, slaves called these stars the Drinking Gourd—which is pretty much what a dipper is.

Ursa Major Moving Group

The five middle stars of the Big Dipper plus several stars nearby are moving together on parallel paths through space and are related by birth. They form the Ursa Major Moving Group, the star cluster closest to the earth. It is so close—its center is about eighty light-years away—that its stars are spread over a huge area of the sky and for the most part seem completely unconnected to one another. Other possible members of the group are Sirius and stars in the constellations Auriga, Leo, and Ophiuchus. Only by knowing their distances and motions do we know that they form a group. Seen from a much greater distance, they would appear to be a few dozen stars in a very sparse open cluster.

URSA MINOR—the Small Bear (ur-sa my-ner)
(see all monthly charts)

The Small Bear does not look any more like a bear than does the Great Bear. What people see is the Little Dipper—a nice pattern of seven stars that does look like a scoop, or dipper. The brightest of its stars is Polaris (po-**lair**-is), the North Star; the only other bright stars are the two at the end of the bowl. The four stars in between are quite faint, and it takes a dark sky for the entire Little Dipper to be visible. The Little Dipper plus a few very faint stars nearby make up the Small Bear. The Bear's head and body are the bowl of the Little Dipper, and his tail is the handle.

Apparently, the Small Bear was invented between the eighth and sixth centuries B.C., by the ancient Greeks, who attributed its creation to the philosopher Thales.

The Small Bear is circumpolar. From the United States and Canada, it remains above the northern horizon and never sets. The Dipper's bowl is highest in early summer.

Polaris, the Pole Star

Polaris is a star that is famous because of *where* it is rather than *what* it is. It happens to lie above the Earth's North Pole and the earth's axis points to it. As the earth turns and the sky rotates overhead, the North Star stays in one place while the sky turns around it.

Polaris is almost exactly at the sky's north pole—the sky's pivot point. There is no corresponding bright star near the sky's south pole, so there is no bright "South Star." (Although there is a star near the South Celestial Pole, in Octans, it is so faint that it is almost invisible, and generally there is considered to be no "South Star.")

A common misconception is that the North Star is the brightest star in the sky. It is actually forty-eighth brightest at magnitude 2.

To find north, simply face the North Star. Its height above the horizon is equal to your latitude—something all scouts are supposed to know in case they get *really* lost.

The earth wobbles, or precesses, on its axis in a 25,800-year cycle, causing the axis to point to different parts of the sky in different millennia. When the Pyramids were built in Egypt, the axis pointed to Thuban in Draco. The axis is presently ¾ degree from the North Celestial Pole. The alignment will be closest in the year 2102, when Polaris will be just under ½ degree from the pole. In the distant future, Vega will be the pole star, although it will not be especially close to the pole. Observers on the earth will see no combination of a *bright* star so *close* to the North Celestial Pole as we do now (and will for the next few centuries).

VELA—the Sails (vee-la)

(see March and April monthly charts and Southern Sky chart)

This large constellation has many bright stars and would be wonderful viewing if it were not so far to the south that only its northern part is visible from the United States. It lies to the lower left of Canis Major and to the left of the bright star Canopus. The Milky Way runs through it.

Vela represents the sails of the huge ship Argo Navis, which Lacaille divided into three smaller constellations in the 1750s.

VIRGO—the Virgin or Young Maiden (ver-go)

(see April through August monthly charts)

Virgo is the second-largest constellation (after Hydra). It is visible in the evening sky in late spring and early summer.

Virgo, a young maiden who is associated with agriculture, represents both the spring planting and the autumn harvest. Virgo is especially associated with planting and with plowing the first furrow of spring, when a barren field is seeded and becomes fertile. On old star maps, she is sometimes shown as Astraea, Goddess of Justice; and she is sometimes seen on court buildings, holding a set of scales that looks suspiciously like Libra.

Virgo does not look much like a young girl; it does look like a letter Y that lies on its side most of the night. Spica is at the bottom of the Y.

Virgo is a constellation of the zodiac, and the sun is within its boundaries from approximately September 16 through October 30.

Spica

Spica (**spy**-ka) is the sixteenth brightest star in the sky. Because there are no bright stars nearby, it seems even brighter than it actually is. Spica is a blue-white star over 200 light-years from Earth.

Spica (which comes from the Latin word for "ear of wheat") has been associated with agriculture since prehistoric times.

VOLANS—the Flying Fish (vo-lans)
(see Southern Sky chart)

The Flying Fish is between Carina (the Keel) and the sky's south pole, too far south to be seen from the United States. It has no bright stars.

Volans was invented by Keyser and Houtman and appeared on Bayer's 1603 atlas. It swims beside the old ship Argo.

VULPECULA—the Fox (vul-peck-you-la)
(see June through November monthly charts)

The little Fox lies between Cygnus and Sagitta in the summer and autumn sky. It was invented by Hevelius in 1690 and is a shapeless association of dim stars of magnitude 4 and fainter. It was originally named Vulpecula and Anser, the Fox and the Goose, but only the fox remains today (apparently it ate the goose!). Lying within the Milky Way, it is a rich area to explore with a telescope, and several of its star clusters can be seen with binoculars. Its claim to fame is the Dumbbell Nebula that is situated within its borders.

....

The Dumbbell

The Dumbbell Nebulla, also known as M27, is a magnitude 6.5 cloud of gas shed by a dying star long ago; it is easily visible in binoculars and small telescopes. A showpiece of the summer sky, it gets its name from its bilobed shape, which resembles a weight lifter's dumbbell or barbell. To find the Dumbbell, first find Sagitta, the Arrow; the Dumbbell is 3⅓ degrees due north of the star at the tip of the Arrow. (The eighth-magnitude globular star cluster M71 is in the same binocular field of view.) The Dumbbell is about 2 light-years in diameter and 900 light-years distant.

....

Chapter Six

✦

TIPS ON OBSERVING THE SKY

Asking how to observe the sky might sound silly. Don't you just go outside at night and look up? However, there's a bit more to it than that. First, it is far better to observe from a dark place. You will see *many* more stars if the sky is dark. If you live in a city, you can't do much about the millions of city lights, but you can make sure the lights around your house are turned off. You can often observe the stars best while you are on vacation, especially in national parks and other remote areas where the night sky is amazingly dark. Also, it is better to observe the sky at a time of the month when the moon is not bright. Bright moonlight the week before and after the full moon turns even the darkest sky into perpetual twilight

Second, you should find an observation site away from trees and houses to see a larger portion of the sky. The most interesting part of the sky is the southern section, because it changes most as the sky turns overhead.

Third, it is important to be prepared for your nighttime viewing. If you're not comfortable, you won't enjoy sky gazing. Experienced sky watchers remember to dress warmly (hats are important in cold weather). Your body generates less heat to warm you when you're standing around stargazing than when you are moving around, as football fans know well. If you will be observing for a long period, as meteor watchers do, stretch out in a lounge chair or on a ground pad.

Fourth, you need to give your eyes time to adjust to the darkness. When you step outside from a brightly lit room, you cannot see much at first. Allow several minutes for your eyes to develop "night vision." Then you will be able to see faint stars and the Milky Way. Also avoid bright lights as you observe. Astronomers use a red flashlight to read notes and star charts. Red light does not affect night vision as much as white light; for reading, put a piece of red cellophane over the lens of a small flashlight.

✦ BINOCULARS ✦

Binoculars make stargazing much more enjoyable. They are portable and can easily be taken along on summer vacations to national parks and other dark places away from urban light. They are perfect aids for exploring the Milky Way and for viewing the larger and nearer star clusters.

The best binoculars for astronomy are labeled 7×50 or, preferably, 10×50. These binoculars magnify seven or ten times and have a lens diameter of 50 millimeters. Smaller binoculars, such as 7×35 or 6×24, have smaller lenses and do not gather enough light to show faint stars. Larger or higher-power binoculars, such as 11×80, are expensive and require the use of a tripod. If you wear glasses, be sure the binoculars you are thinking of purchasing will focus to infinity with your glasses off; you do not want to wear glasses while looking through lenses (whether binoculars or a telescope). Be sure the binoculars have center focus (both sides focus simultaneously); avoid focus-free binoculars. Shop at camera stores. Avoid the cheapest binoculars at discount houses, and expect to pay at least $100 for a good pair that will last a lifetime.

Chapter Seven

:✦:

OBSERVING SOLAR AND LUNAR ECLIPSES

As interesting as the sun and moon are in their regular motion across the sky, they are incomparably more fascinating when they align and one darkens. A rare sun-earth-moon alignment can create one of the most magnificent spectacles in nature.

Eclipses come in two flavors, solar and lunar. A solar eclipse occurs when the moon blocks and eclipses the light of the sun, causing the sun to darken. A lunar eclipse occurs when the moon moves into the shadow of the earth and darkens. Several eclipses take place each year, but solar eclipses seem much rarer because each solar eclipse can be seen only from the small part of the earth within the moon's shadow, while a lunar eclipse can be seen simultaneously by everyone on the half of the earth facing the moon. Both kinds of eclipse can be either partial or total; in all cases, a total eclipse is more interesting than a partial one.

Several sites on the World Wide Web provide detailed information on all eclipses—solar and lunar, major and minor—far into the future. Begin with either the Eclipse Home Page at http://planets.gsfc.nasa.gov/eclipse/eclipse.html or the U.S. Naval Observatory's Upcoming Eclipses site at http://riemann.usno.navy.mil/AA/data/docs/UpcomingEclipses.html.

Eclipse of the Sun

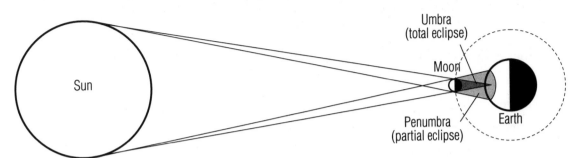

Figure 7.1 *A solar eclipse occurs when the moon moves in front of and blocks the sun.*

Eclipse of the Moon

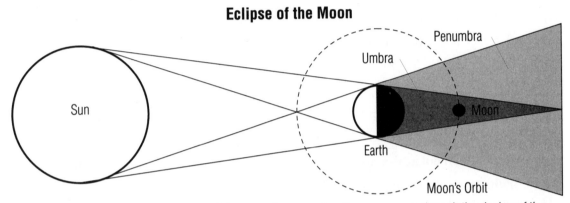

Figure 7.2 *A lunar eclipse is an eclipse of the moon; it occurs when the moon moves through the shadow of the earth and darkens.*

LUNAR ECLIPSES

At least twice and sometimes three times a year, the full moon moves into the shadow of the earth and darkens for up to a few hours. Everyone on the side of the earth facing the moon sees the eclipse simultaneously, but depending on your location you see it during the evening, late at night, or early in the morning. (You cannot see a daytime lunar eclipse because only the full moon is eclipsed; since the full moon lies opposite the sun, it is always below the horizon when the sun is above it.)

Let's start by exploring what happens when the moon moves into the shadow of the earth. A shadow is surprisingly complex. Every shadow has two parts: the dark central *umbra* and the surrounding, lighter *penumbra*. Look at it first from a position on the moon. If you are standing on the moon within the umbra, the sun is completely blocked by the earth and the eclipse is total at your location. If you are standing within the penumbra, the sun is only partially blocked, and the eclipse is partial at your location. As seen from the earth, the part of the moon in the penumbra is slightly darkened because some sunlight is still striking it, while the part in the umbra is very dark. Each eclipse is different, and not all are equally interesting. (Some are not interesting at all.)

Lunar eclipses are one of three types, depending on whether the moon moves into the penumbra only, partly into the umbra, or fully into the umbra. In a *penumbral* eclipse, the moon moves within the penumbra of the earth's shadow but does not enter the umbra. The moon darkens very little; because penumbral eclipses are hard to see, they often are not even announced in newspapers. During a *partial* eclipse, part (but not all) of the moon moves into the umbra, and that part of the moon darkens dramatically. The moon does not disappear during partial eclipses, but they are definitely worth watching. A *total* eclipse happens only if the moon moves fully within the umbra, and then the entire moon goes dark and sometimes even disappears. Total lunar eclipses are grand sky spectacles and are not to be missed.

A lunar eclipse goes through a sequence of stages, whose times are printed in newspapers and science magazines. Although the descriptions may seem confusing in print, it is useful to know what the stages refer to. In a penumbral eclipse, the moon moves into the penumbra and then out again, and generally no one even notices. A partial eclipse has five stages, including a maximum: moon moves into penumbra; moon moves into umbra; maximum eclipse; moon leaves umbra; moon leaves penumbra. A total eclipse has two more stages, for a total of seven: moon moves into penumbra; moon begins to move into umbra; moon moves completely within umbra (totality begins); maximum eclipse; moon begins to leave umbra (totality ends); moon completely leaves umbra; moon leaves penumbra. The eclipse is total during the time the moon is completely within the umbra, and that is the best time to watch it.

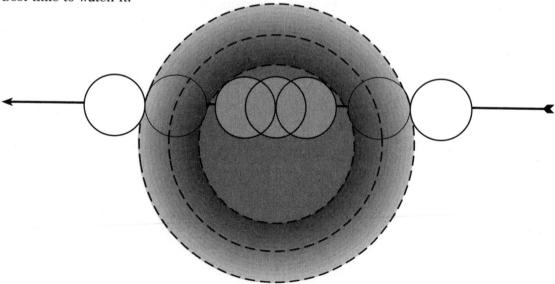

Not surprisingly, the most interesting eclipses are total. Only then does the moon darken enough to take on a ghostly appearance—or even disappear—and only then does it take on strange, eerie colors. During a lunar eclipse, the moon often becomes orange or deep red. Since the moon is lit only by sunlight, which is white, where do these strange colors come from? They come from sunlight refracted around the edge of the earth and onto the moon. White sunlight enters the earth's atmosphere, where most of the light is refracted and scattered away. Blue light scatters well, which is why the sky is blue. Red light passes through our atmosphere relatively unaffected (it is refracted least), which is why sunrises and sunsets are red. Unrefracted reddened sunlight passes through the atmosphere at the edge of the earth—where the earth's sunrises and sunsets are seen—and continues on to the moon, giving it its reddish color. The light that reaches the moon is tinted by all the earth's sunrises and sunsets.

During some total lunar eclipses, the moon takes on a pale orange color but remains relatively bright. At the other extreme, the moon can become so deeply red that it disappears entirely and cannot be seen even in binoculars. Sunsets display the same variation—some are colorless, while some are breathtaking. Ironically, the color and darkness of a lunar eclipse and of a sunset depend on similar atmospheric conditions. If the weather is clear and dry in the part of the atmosphere at the edge of the earth where sunlight is refracted, the moon will redden little and the eclipse will be bright. A large amount of dust in the atmosphere reddens sunlight; the lunar eclipse will be redder and darker. Major volcanic eruptions throw massive amounts of dust into the high atmosphere. For years after the 1991 eruption of Mount Pinatubo in the Philippines, eclipses were incredibly dark. Eclipses are as variable as the weather, and their appearance is not fully predictable. This uncertainty adds interest because we can forecast what to expect, but then we have to watch to see if we were right.

TOTAL LUNAR ECLIPSES VISIBLE FROM NORTH AMERICA

Date	Date
2000 Jan. 21	2014 Apr. 15
2001 Jan. 9	2014 Oct. 8
2003 May 16	2015 Apr. 4
2003 Nov. 9	2015 Sep. 28
2004 Oct. 28	2018 Jan. 31
2007 Mar. 3	2019 Jan. 21
2007 Aug. 28	2021 May 26
2008 Feb. 21	2022 May 16
2010 Dec. 21	2022 Nov. 8
2011 Dec. 10	2025 Mar. 14

Table 7.1 *This table lists total lunar eclipses through the year 2025 that will be visible from at least part of North America. Some will occur in the evening, others in the morning. In addition, a few partial eclipses (not listed here) will be visible from North America during these years.*

In contrast to a solar eclipse, no filters or special precautions are needed to observe a lunar eclipse. After all, the eclipsed moon is simply a huge gray rock in the shade! Watch through binoculars or a telescope to better see the colors.

A lunar eclipse offers several things to watch for as it slowly unfolds. Let's walk through a total eclipse. If the moon is above the horizon before the eclipse begins, note the brightness of the full moon. When completely full, the moon is several times brighter than it is even the day before and after, when it *looks* full. Take a moment to notice how very bright the completely full moon is. At the time the moon enters the penumbral part of the earth's shadow (which you can find out from the newspaper or announcements from a local planetarium or science museum), see if you can tell that the moon has begun to darken. The effect is very subtle, and the edge of the penumbra cannot be detected. Is one side of the moon darker than another? If so, by how much? By the time the moon begins to enter the umbra, it is clear which side of the moon is deepest in shadow. The earth's umbra does have a fairly sharp edge, and you will notice when the moon crosses its boundary. It now looks as if the moon has had a bite taken out of it. Is there color to the umbra? (Probably not, because bright, unreddened sunlight is falling on the rest of the moon.) When do you first notice hints of color? Is it orange or red?

As the moon moves progressively deeper into the umbra, the "bite" grows in size, and the curvature of the edge of the umbra becomes apparent. Does the darkening moon make it easier to see faint stars? Monitor the sky around the moon to watch stars appear as the moon's light wanes and the sky darkens. You can read a book by the light of the full moon. When does the sky become too dark to read by moonlight? By watching the moon move deeper into the umbra, can you predict how dark it will be during totality and what its color will be then? When only a sliver of moon is left outside the umbra, the moon has a very odd shape in the sky, and whatever color it will have at totality should be apparent. When does the moon stop casting a shadow?

You can time the moment of the onset of totality to within a minute or two just by watching. How dark is the moon during totality? What is its color, and is the color uniform across the moon's face? Which (if any) major features on the moon can you still recognize? How dark has the sky become? Can you see faint stars, and even the Milky Way? If the moon does not move directly through the center of the umbra, one side will be brighter than the other. Can you anticipate, by subtle changes in the shading, when totality will end? How do the colors fade as brightness returns? When can you again begin to discern the moon's major surface features? When do faint stars fade to invisibility as the sky brightens? The last stages of a lunar eclipse are an anticlimax that mirrors the early stages; by now most observers are thinking about going to bed.

If the eclipse takes place while the moon is rising or setting, there is the added interest of a moonrise or moonset and the greater reddening caused by light reflected off the eclipsed moon passing through our atmosphere a second time. Excellent photo opportunities present themselves when the eclipsed moon is near the horizon.

Attempt to watch the whole eclipse, even if at intervals, in order to appreciate the many changes that occur. An eclipse is a process that unfolds, not a momentary event.

SOLAR ECLIPSES

No celestial spectacle—not even a world-class sunset—is as sensational as a total solar eclipse. In past times, battles stopped and brave men trembled when the sun went dark during the day, and even today in many areas of the world a total eclipse is cause for general panic and great alarm. Some people travel great distances at great expense to see one, and for some it becomes that year's annual vacation. People may be affected at a deep emotional level, and even animals change their behavior. No one carries on business as usual during a total solar eclipse.

Paradoxically, although there are more solar eclipses than lunar eclipses in an average year—four or five solar versus two or three lunar—solar eclipses are seen by far fewer people due to the relative sizes of the shadows of the earth and the moon. The earth is so large that the umbra of its shadow completely engulfs the moon during a lunar eclipse, and when it does everyone on the side of the earth facing the moon can watch the eclipse at the same time. The much smaller umbra of the moon, which barely reaches the earth,

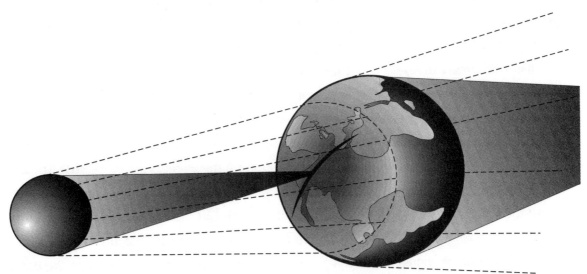

Figure 7.4 *A solar eclipse is seen as partial from much of the earth, but only people within a narrow path see it as total.*

has a width of no more than 167 miles (and often much less). During a solar eclipse, the shadow of the moon traces out a long, thin path—called the "path of totality"—that moves across the earth's surface. Only the relatively few people within that narrow line see the eclipse as total, while far more see it as a less interesting partial eclipse. Because the shadow is moving quickly, totality lasts for no more than a few minutes—yet people will pay $1,000 per minute to stand in the shadow of the moon.

In one of the great coincidences of nature, the moon is 400 times smaller than the sun but 400 times closer to the earth; hence the sun and the moon have the same *apparent size* in the sky (½-degree diameter). This coincidence allows the moon to cover the sun, but just barely. If the moon were a little smaller or a little more distant, it would not cover the sun and there would be no total solar eclipses. If it were much closer or much larger, it would block not only the disk of the sun but also its wispy corona, which gives a total eclipse so much of its beauty.

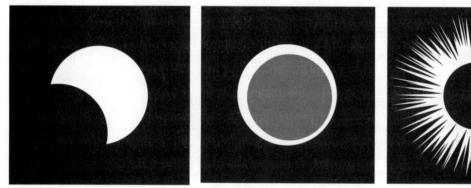

Figure 7.5 *Partial, Annular, and Total Solar Eclipses*

Just as there are different types of lunar eclipses and several stages in each, there are different types of solar eclipses: partial, total, and annular. The moon's shadow, like that of the earth, has an outer penumbra and an inner umbra. When you stand (on the earth) in the moon's umbra, the moon completely blocks the sun and you are in darkness; the solar eclipse is total. When you stand in the penumbra, the moon is aligned so that it only partial blocks the sun, leaving a crescent of the sun's disk to shine around the edge of the moon; the eclipse is partial. All total eclipses are partial in their initial and final stages.

Partial and total solar eclipses have their lunar counterparts, but the third type of solar eclipse is unique. Although the moon lies at the right average distance from the earth to completely (but barely) cover the sun, the moon's orbit is not round. Its maximum and

> ### ✦ ECLIPSES ✦
>
> *Total eclipses are the rage today, but in the distant future they will no longer occur. The moon is slowly receding from the earth at the rate of 1½ inches per year— roughly the rate at which your fingernails grow—and its angular size is diminishing proportionately. Today, the moon barely covers the sun, but our distant descendants will not see total solar eclipses; they will enjoy annular eclipses only. The last total solar eclipse will be visible in the year A.D. 600,000,000.*

minimum distances are 252,700 miles and 221,500 miles, respectively. If an eclipse takes place when the moon is at a more distant point in its orbit, the moon does not appear large enough from the earth to completely cover the sun. Instead, the moon is superimposed on the face of the sun, blocking most of the sun's disk but leaving a ring of sunlight to shine around the edge of the moon. Such an eclipse is called *annular*, after the Latin word for "ring." It is rather unusual to see the sun as a thin ring in the sky, and annular eclipses are interesting in their own right. But the sky does not grow as dark as it does during a total eclipse, and the auxiliary phenomena are absent.

Most solar eclipses you will see are partial. To see a total eclipse, you must be within the narrow path of totality. For about two thousand miles on either side of this path, observers see what looks like a bite being taken out of the sun. The closer you are to the center, the bigger the bite. People on several continents see the eclipse as partial. Partial eclipses, however, are much less interesting, and require the use of sun filters or special techniques for safe observation.

When the sun is partially blocked by the moon, the part that remains visible is as bright as always. Even when 90 percent of the sun is eclipsed, the remaining 10 percent is too intense for human eyes, but to see simply the shape of the sun while it is partially eclipsed requires only very simple equipment.

The old standby is a pinhole viewing box. This device is especially popular with schools, perhaps because it involves simple hands-on construction. Begin with a shoe box or similar small box, and discard the lid. In one end, cut away a small section of cardboard roughly a square inch in size, and tape a piece of tinfoil over the hole (it is impossible to make a proper pinhole in coarse cardboard). Punch a pinhole in the foil. There is no correct size—a large pinhole gives a bright but fuzzy image, while a smaller pinhole casts a fainter, sharper shadow. Tape a piece of white paper (a 3-by-5 file card works well) on the inside of the opposite end of the box. Hold the box, now an "eclipse viewer," so that sunlight falls through the pinhole and onto the card and the box shades the card. This is a perfect project for third-graders.

Using a mirror is even simpler and more effective. Reflect the sun's image onto the north-facing wall of a building to see an image of the sun. Smaller mirrors give fainter images and must be positioned closer to the building (several tens of feet); mirrors a foot square reflect a brilliant image and can be a hundred feet or more away. Attach the mirror to something solid, and fasten a large sheet of smooth white cardboard to the wall for a first-class image that can be viewed by a crowd or even photographed with standard cameras.

These special techniques are necessary only when the sun is partially eclipsed (including annular eclipses). For the few moments of totality, when the sun's surface is completely blocked by the moon, the part of the sun that remains visible—its outer corona—is not too bright to be viewed directly. (We see the corona only during an eclipse because normally it is overwhelmed by bright sunlight.) Set aside filters,

TOTAL SOLAR ECLIPSES	
Date	**Location**
1998 Feb. 26	northern South America, Caribbean
1999 Aug. 11	Europe, Iran, India
2001 Jun. 21	South Africa
2002 Dec. 4	South Africa, southern Indian Ocean
2006 Mar. 29	Africa, Mediterranean, Turkey, Ukraine, Siberia
2009 Jul. 22	China, western Pacific Ocean
2012 Nov. 13	northern Australia, South Pacific
2016 Mar. 9	Indonesia, western Pacific
2017 Aug. 21	United States from Oregon to South Carolina
2019 Jul. 2	Chile, Argentina
2020 Dec. 14	Chile, Argentina (again)
2024 Apr. 8	Mexico, United States from Texas to New England, Newfoundland

Table 7.2 *This table lists major total solar eclipses through the year 2025. It omits partial eclipses and total eclipses visible only from inaccessible areas of the earth. Eclipses that take place over warmer oceans are visited by specially chartered cruise ships on popular "eclipse expeditions."*

projection boxes, and mirrors during totality and observe the sun in all its glory. The sun will appear surprisingly small, so use binoculars or a low-power telescope. Tripod-mounted binoculars are ideal for viewing a total eclipse. Because they encompass a wide angle of the sky, they show the entire corona, which spans several degrees. The corona is too large to fit within the field of view of a telescope. Be sure to turn the binoculars or telescope away when totality ends; this happens gradually enough to give you adequate warning.

A partial solar eclipse is not a complicated affair. Prepare and test your filters or projection box in advance, especially if you will be sharing the eclipse with others. At the moment the eclipse begins, you will notice a notch taken out of the sun's edge. That notch slowly grows larger until maximum eclipse and then recedes. If you are using a telescope, you might notice sunspots being eclipsed and then revealed again, adding a bit of novelty to an otherwise slow event. With high magnification, you will notice that the edge of the moon is not smooth. The profile of craters and mountains will be silhouetted against the sun, and you will see the true measure of the moon's roughness.

If more than half the sun is covered, the sun takes on a curious crescent shape—a shape we don't usually associate with the sun. Pinholes will cast crescent-shaped shadows. Look for bright little shimmering crescents under trees where the overlapping leaves create natural pinholes.

If the eclipse is nearly total (as it is in all annular eclipses), notice how much the sky darkens. Does it become a deeper shade of blue? Look around at shadows, which seem somehow different.

An eclipse that takes place at sunrise or sunset has all the added effects of a normal sunrise or sunset thrown in. A sunrise or sunset partial or annular eclipse can be quite spectacular and is second only to a total eclipse.

A total eclipse offers all the features of a partial eclipse plus the glorious brief moments of totality. As totality approaches and the sky darkens, there is a sense of an impending storm. The sky grows darker, the temperature begins to drop, and a slight breeze may begin to stir and possibly even develop into a pronounced wind. People seldom observe a total eclipse alone, and the general excitement and anticipation in the air can reach incredible levels.

About ten minutes before totality, eerie bands of light may ripple over the landscape, passing mysteriously over people, trees, and houses as if borne by the wind itself. They travel slowly enough for a person to keep up with them by running. These "shadow bands" are an atmospheric phenomenon that has never been satisfactorily explained.

The moon's shadow approaches from the west, and the sky in that direction darkens as if to herald a silent storm. The darkening accelerates during the last minutes before totality, and very soon the ultrathin crescent of sunlight breaks up into a series of brilliant beads. These beads are produced by sunlight passing through valleys and other depressions along the moon's edge. Finally, one bead is left, creating the beautiful "diamond ring" effect. The diamond shrinks to nothingness before you have time to catch your breath. Totality has arrived, and the corona with its quiet majesty shines down upon you.

The sky, though dark, is not a midnight sky with its myriad of stars but instead more like deep twilight, with only a few stars and the brighter planets visible. The horizon remains bright in the distance, and the brightness swiftly shifts from east to west as the center of the shadow passes over from west to east.

The light of the sun's corona is usually described as white with a bluish tinge, and it can display a rich, delicate structure. If you look close to the edge of the moon through binoculars, you may catch sight of reddish prominences hovering above the sun.

All too quickly, a brilliant jewel of light appears at the outer edge of the moon's rim, announcing the end of totality. The phenomena previously seen are now repeated in reverse order, until once again the sun is shining brightly, and the eclipse is just a fresh memory.

Don't forget to take photographs. Even if you are not equipped with the specialized equipment necessary to capture the delicate shadings of the corona, the shots of people watching make a great souvenir. If you have a video camera, let it run continuously throughout the entire eclipse to capture the sound, if nothing else.

All who experience a total eclipse of the sun come away with a great sense of privilege at having been present at such a dramatic, awe-inspiring event. There is a feeling of having come face to face with the forces of the cosmos.

Chapter Eight

✦

WHERE TO GO FROM HERE

This book is only a starting point. What should you do if you want to learn more about the sky? Begin at your local **planetarium**. If there is no planetarium in your town, there will probably be one in a nearby city. A planetarium simulates the night sky in an indoor theater and presents multimedia shows that describe discoveries in astronomy. An astronomy museum and bookstore may be attached. Planetariums exist to help people learn about the stars, and the staff will be happy to answer your questions.

The best way to learn about something is to hang out with people who are knowledgeable and enthusiastic about the subject. Check out a local **astronomy club**. Astronomy clubs often conduct "star parties" at which members gather to look at the sky through a variety of telescopes. Your local planetarium or science museum will know about any astronomy clubs in your area, and a comprehensive list is posted at *Sky & Telescope* magazine's Web site at http://www.skypub.com.

Two excellent **astronomy magazines** are *Astronomy* (1027 N. Seventh St., Milwaukee, WI 53233) and *Sky & Telescope* (P.O. Box 9111, Belmont, MA 02178-9111). *Astronomy* claims to be the more colorful of the two and is aimed at armchair astronomers. *Sky & Telescope* has a long reputation for excellence in interpreting astronomy. Both carry advertisements for astronomy items, including telescopes, and both publish annual guides to planetariums, astronomy clubs, and equipment vendors.

Travelers need maps and guidebooks, especially when they are in unfamiliar territory, and skygazers are no exception. The charts in this book are intended to orient the sky as it appears at different times of the year. To explore the constellations thoroughly, you'll want a **star atlas** and **observing guides**. Many atlases are available, from simple sets of charts that show only the stars you'll see with your unaided eye to multiple-volume atlases that are works of cartographic art and show all the faint objects visible in a large amateur telescope. The most complete star atlases are available on CD-ROM and run on desktop computers. Observing guides describe in great detail the thousands of star clusters, nebulae, and galaxies that have been charted. Like a guide to the hotels and sights of a city in a foreign land, these guides tell you what to expect when you arrive at your telescopic destination. Check the advertisements in astronomy magazines for descriptions of the many atlases and guides in print.

If you have a personal computer, you can explore the sky with the hundreds of **astronomy computer programs** available for DOS, Windows, and Mac OS operating systems. Programs show the positions of the stars and planets at any given time, show the constellations in great detail, and simulate eclipses and the motions of the planets. Astronomy software will let you look into the future and plan observing sessions (when does Mars rise tomorrow? next April?), maintain personalized observing logs, and generate tables of planet or comet positions and sunset or moonrise times. Armchair astronomers will find picture collections on CD-ROM to browse as well as games with astronomical themes and educational software intended for school use. More good astronomy software exists than a person could possibly look at; the problem is to identify the better programs. Check monthly reviews in *Astronomy* and *Sky & Telescope* for recommendations. Lists of available software are posted on the World Wide Web at the Astronomy Software Revue site at http://www.skypub.com/software/mosley.html and Planetarium Software at http://www.seds.org/billa/astrosoftware.html.

Finally, a universe of astronomy information is available for free on the Internet's **World Wide Web**—even on cloudy nights when you cannot see the stars. You'll find unlimited news, pictures, information, and software. Good places to start are Sky Online at http://www.skypub.com and *Astronomy* magazine at http://www.kalmbach.com/astro/astronomy.html. Links to these places and more are found at the Griffith Observatory's web site at http://www.GriffithObs.org. Your local planetarium or science museum undoubtedly has a Web site that would be a place to begin your further exploration of the wonders of the sky.

Index

What readers are saying about

Needlemouse

★★★★★

'I was charmed by this tale of unrequited love, redemption and hedgehogs. A feel-good book' – Heather, Netgalley

★★★★★

'An eccentrically heartwarming tale of stepping out of your comfort zone. I was rooting for Sylvia to get the happy ending she so deserves' – Lottie, Netgalley

★★★★★

'A lovely story with delightful characters. I loved this novel and would highly recommend, especially if you are a fan of Ruth Hogan and Gail Honeyman' – Mary, Netgalley

★★★★★

'This is an absolutely superb novel about someone who is dissatisfied with her life but feels it's difficult to change. I would highly recommend to anyone who likes a quirky novel to entertain them' – Sue, Netgalley

★★★★★

'A delightful and heartwarming novel that I thoroughly enjoyed. It had a charming story written with compassion and empathy, interesting and likeable characters, and a poignant ending' – Joan, Netgalley

★★★★★

'Oh how I adored this book which is reminiscent of *Eleanor Oliphant is Completely Fine*' – Justine, Netgalley

★★★★★

'I like a book that makes me feel uplifted, that soothes the soul, and this book certainly did that. Sylvia is definitely one of my favourite fictional characters' – Joanne, Netgalley

Jane O'Connor is a former primary school teacher turned academic and writer. She was born and brought up in Surrey and lived in London until she moved to the West Midlands in her mid-thirties. Jane's PhD was about child stars and she is now a Reader at Birmingham City University where she researches children's experiences of celebrity, media and everyday life. Jane lives in Sutton Coldfield with her husband and two young sons in a house full of pirates, dinosaurs, superheroes and lots of books. She really likes all animals, especially hedgehogs.

Needlemouse is her debut novel.

JANE O'CONNOR

NEEDLE MOUSE

EBURY
PRESS

First published by Ebury Press in 2019

1 3 5 7 9 10 8 6 4 2

Ebury Press, an imprint of Ebury Publishing
20 Vauxhall Bridge Road,
London SW1V 2SA

Ebury Press is part of the Penguin Random House group of companies
whose addresses can be found at global.penguinrandomhouse.com

Copyright © Jane O'Connor, 2019

Jane O'Connor has asserted her right to be identified as the author of this
work in accordance with the Copyright, Designs and Patents Act 1988

www.penguin.co.uk

A CIP catalogue record for this book is available from the British Library

ISBN 9781529103281

Typeset in 11.75/15.5 pt Adobe Caslon Pro
by Integra Software Services Pvt. Ltd, Pondicherry

Printed and bound in Great Britain by Clays Ltd, Elcograf S.p.A.

Penguin Random House is committed to a sustainable future
for our business, our readers and our planet. This book is
made from Forest Stewardship Council® certified paper.

For Graham, with love.
And for hedgehogs everywhere ...

Autumn

The European hedgehog (*Erinaceus europaeus*) is so called due to its fondness for foraging in hedges and other undergrowth, and the pig-like grunts it makes as it does so. Hedgehogs are nocturnal animals and only come out at night. If you see a hedgehog during the day it usually means it is sick or injured.

Hedgehogs are covered in up to seven thousand spines which are a defence mechanism. When it feels threatened, the hedgehog can draw itself into a ball to protect its vulnerable underbody from predators such as badgers and foxes. Unfortunately, hedgehogs also ball up in response to traffic, which is why so many of them end up being killed on busy roads.

It is vital that during the autumn hedgehogs build up enough fat reserves to see them through the winter. They can roam up to two miles every night looking for food such as beetles, slugs and earthworms. Hedgehogs have also been considered a delicacy themselves over the years. For example, baked hedgehog used to be a traditional Romany dish made by rolling hedgehogs in clay and placing them in the embers of a bonfire. After cooking the prickles would come away when the clay was broken open.

Jonas Entwistle, *The Hedgehog Year*

Wednesday 2 September

I look forward to this day all year. Not because I enjoy getting older (heaven's no), but because Prof takes me out somewhere special for lunch on my birthday, just the two of us. He likes to surprise me with the venue and I love it when he takes the lead. Last year he took me to a very upmarket French restaurant where he decided, rather impetuously I thought, to order the snails. Prof's face as he made his way through them! I did laugh.

We are exactly the same age, Prof and I. Well, I say exactly: I am actually forty-one days older than him as his birthday isn't until October, but I don't suppose that matters. I just think of us as the same age, fifty-two, and that's nice. I suppose it would be even better if he was a little bit older than me, but being the same age gives us one more thing in common and that's the way I like to think about it.

I got into work about ten to nine. I always get there before Prof so I can make sure everything is perfect for him when he arrives – computer on, blinds up, post laid out on his desk. He came bursting through the door at quarter past, holding up his black leather briefcase as if it were a trophy. It made me giggle as he knew it would – I think that's why he does silly things like that. He needs a strong cup of tea (two teabags) as soon as he gets to his desk, to 'get the cogs working' as he puts it, and I couldn't help tutting with frustration as Margaret fussed around making her coffee, blocking my way to the kettle.

'Won't be a minute, Sylvia,' she said as she poured milk slowly into her mug and then reached for the sweetener. 'Patience is a virtue, remember.'

I glared at her as she sailed past with her drink and had to overcome the urge to put my foot out to trip her up.

Tea duly made and delivered, Prof and I then had our golden time together. This is my favourite part of the day, when we spend ten, or maybe even fifteen, minutes going through his diary, discussing the meetings he has to attend and the people who are coming to see him. Often Prof has earmarked time for writing in his daily schedule and this is when my shielding of him becomes invaluable. I see myself very much as his defender, fending off the hordes of students and faculty staff who are desperate for a piece of him. They would suck Prof dry if they had the chance. He doesn't know the half of it, what I do for him, how I keep them at bay so he can just get on, but he is safe in the knowledge that my loyalty to him is complete.

'Lunch today then, Sylvia?' Prof said, swivelling round in his chair to face me when we had finished going through the day's business.

I nodded and managed to say 'yes, please,' as I tried not to look overly eager at the prospect of Prof's full attention for an hour and a half and us looking to all the world like a proper couple.

'Righto, we'll leave around noon.' He turned back to his computer, immediately absorbed in the on-screen text as I slipped back to my desk and tried to concentrate on typing up the minutes from yesterday's finance meeting. I sat in anticipation from 11.30 onwards, not knowing exactly when Prof would be ready to go, covertly touching up my face every few minutes behind my computer screen. Finally, at twenty past twelve, he caught my eye through the glass partition and held up five fingers. I nodded in agreement and gave myself a final spritz of perfume while he finished up with his emails.

'OK, let's get going,' he said, clapping his hands together and beaming at me as I dropped my make-up on the floor in a fluster. 'I'll meet you in the lobby when you're ready,' he said with a backwards wave as he grabbed his jacket off the coat rack and went out the door.

I knelt down to retrieve my lipstick which had rolled right under my desk and ignored Margaret's nasty little snigger as I bumped my head on the way back up. I took a couple of deep breaths to compose myself before heading out into the corridor, relieved that Prof had not been witness to the ungainly scene.

He stood in the entrance hall downstairs, talking into his mobile, and I watched fondly as he repeatedly stepped back from the electronic doors that he kept opening by mistake. He always paces up and down when he speaks on the phone; I notice little things like that about him, it's part of what makes us so close. He saw me and indicated the doors and we walked through them together into bright sunshine. Prof finished his call and put on his aviator sunglasses which, along with his tailored blue suit and open-necked shirt, made him look completely dashing. He has changed so little in the fifteen years I have worked for him, a more generous sprinkling of grey in his hair perhaps, a slight darkening under the eyes, a thickening around the middle, I suppose, but there's no denying he is still a fine figure of a man. I couldn't help but gaze at him as he hailed us a cab. 'Antonio's in Drayton Street,' he instructed the driver and I climbed in beside him.

A moment's awkward silence ensued as we both adjusted to the dim coolness of the car's interior and then, just as I was about to comment on the weather, Prof's phone started ringing again. Throwing an apologetic look in my direction he answered it and spent the rest of the journey thrashing out the finer details of a research project with one of his academic colleagues. Disappointed that my precious time with him was already being shared, I distracted myself by watching the shabby roads around our university slowly transform into a more salubrious area of London until we came to a stop outside an unremarkable-looking Italian restaurant in a side street off the Fulham Road.

I got out and the taxi hovered while Prof finished his call, paid and got a receipt. His attention back on me, he did a silly mock bow on the pavement. 'Shall we go in?' he said.

I smiled as he held the door for me and we entered the busy trattoria. The décor in the room was uninspired to say the least. Red and white gingham cloths covered the many tables, bunches of fake herbs hung from the ceiling, and an amateurish fresco of the Coliseum covered the right-hand wall. There was an open kitchen at the far end where several teenage chefs were urgently making pizzas and shoving them into ovens using huge wooden spatulas. I felt a slight dip in spirits as I had hoped for somewhere a little more elegant for our special lunch.

'Madame?' I allowed a waiter to help me off with my jacket and took the seat opposite Prof at the window table that he had reserved, trying to ignore another minor wave of disappointment that he hadn't rushed over to pull it out for me. Prof seemed somewhat distracted and ordered a bottle of house red with no consultation whatsoever. He examined the menu for what seemed like a long time, turning it over once or twice to make sure he hadn't missed anything, then he sighed, put it down between us and started fiddling with the cutlery, arranging and rearranging it around his wicker plate mat. I had glanced at my menu and automatically identified the least calorific dish – the food, for me, being the least interesting part of this lunchtime by a mile. We ordered when the wine arrived and Prof poured himself a large glass. Then, as somewhat of an afterthought, he poured some for me. He took a long drink, put down the glass and stared intently at the mural.

'It's all over, Sylvia,' he said finally, his eyes flicking back to meet mine.

Panic rose as I thought for a moment that he meant the department was closing or that my job was being made redundant. 'What do you mean?' I whispered, my fingers clutching the edge of the table.

'Me and Martha. She wants a divorce.'

The words hung between us as I tried to get a handle on what he was telling me. My initial reaction was to laugh with relief and joy, but I could tell by his hangdog expression that this wasn't happy news for him. I altered the tone of my surprised response halfway through from celebration to commiseration and hoped it hit the right note.

'She's been sleeping with Julian,' he said taking another big swig of wine. I looked at him blankly.

'That guy who's been designing our extension. The architect. Julian Delaroche,' he said his name as if I should have known. 'He with the Jag and the hipster beard,' he said, tutting and shaking his head. 'She's in love this time, apparently. She wants me out.'

A frenzied combination of emotions and thoughts swirled round my head as I took a sip of my wine, buying myself time before I responded. I needed to get this right. Was he looking for advice from a friend, a new love ... or just a shoulder to cry on?

'You know I'm always here for you, Carl,' I said, careful not to stray from our professional relationship, but hoping he picked up the alternative meaning.

'Yes, I know, Sylvia.' He patted the side of my arm. 'I don't know what I'd do without you. You're my rock.' He held my gaze for a second as I flushed pink with pride.

'What's going to happen?' I said, aslant of the questions I really wanted to ask.

'I'm moving into the house in Dulwich.' I remembered as he spoke that they had bought a place a few years back as a rental property. 'I've given the tenants a month's notice. What else can I do? The boys will stay with me every other weekend.'

'And Julian?'

'Julian is moving in.' Prof shrugged his shoulders and opened his palms in a helpless gesture that made me want to jump into his lap, but I sufficed with a head tilt and was just reaching for his hand when the food arrived.

There was a flurry of plates and Parmesan and pepper mills and then all was quiet again as we contemplated our meal. I wondered if Prof would be able to eat, he seemed so upset, and I considered asking if he would prefer to go for a walk along the river but the sight of his lasagne seemed to revive him and he ate with gusto. I pushed my penne around, adept at making it look like I was eating when I wasn't; but truly, today I couldn't have eaten a thing anyway. He and Martha had split up so many times, but they always ended up getting back together. More than anything I wanted to dare to hope that it was different this time – he had said the 'D' word, after all, which had never been mentioned before. Surely this would mean that we could be together at last? It would have to be after a discreet period of time, of course, so as to avoid any scandal or malicious gossip. I understand the importance of reputation for a man of Prof's standing.

I waited for him to say more about it, but it seemed that the subject was closed and my heart sank when he began telling me about the exciting new research project he was planning with Dr Bastow. I nodded along, asking relevant questions, but I could have screamed. I was desperate to know all the details of his fall out with Martha, but I knew better than to try to steer the conversation back to where I wanted it when he had already moved it on.

It occurred to me, as we were having coffee, that he hadn't asked me one question during the whole meal or even said 'Happy Birthday' and I felt a surge of annoyance that I immediately squashed down, reminding myself that he was in the midst of an intensely difficult time. Having repositioned myself emotionally towards his well-being, rather than mine, I was able to watch him drink his coffee with renewed affection.

'Why did you choose this place?' I asked him with a smile.

He looked round as if noticing his surroundings for the first time. 'Don't you like it?' A question at last.

'It's lovely. Thank you.'

'I don't know, really. There's a conference coming up in Rome and that was in my head and everyone likes Italian food. Imagine if we were in Rome right now, wouldn't that be wonderful?' He put his cup down and raised an eyebrow. 'You do like Italian food, don't you?' Another question – and, thrillingly, a possible hint about accompanying him to an international conference at last.

'Yes, I most certainly do. I love it.' I smiled again, surreptitiously moving my napkin from my lap over my untouched plate of pasta.

'Good, that's good,' he said distractedly as he motioned to the waiter for the bill.

11

'Sylvia, I need to get across town to meet up with a potential new PhD student, Lola somebody or another. She's a bright spark, by all accounts, and the Dean wants her on board in the department. I'll be in the office again later this afternoon.' I could tell he was back in work mode now as he fished the university credit card out of his wallet. 'Are you all right to jump in a cab back to campus?'

'Yes. Yes, that's fine.'

I was a little taken aback at the abrupt end to our lunch, given the intimacy with which we had spoken, but I tried hard not to let it show as we walked out onto the pavement. He hailed a taxi almost immediately, which I assumed was for me, but he leapt in without a backwards glance. I was left standing alone, squinting against the afternoon sun, wondering just how brilliant a student must be to have a professor trek across London to meet them.

I took in Prof's last cup of tea as usual about ten to five and found him rooting through one of his overflowing desk drawers. He stopped when I came in and ran his hands through his hair, making it stick up in the most endearing manner, before picking up his mug. 'Sorry about earlier,' he said, taking a biscuit from the plate I had brought in for him.

'It's fine. I got the tube back here no problem.' I had completely forgiven him and had spent the afternoon going over the delicious divorce news in my mind, trying to work out how long it would be before he was free to be with me.

'Oh yes, me rushing off to meet Lola.' He paused and frowned and then a curious look crossed his face which I couldn't fathom. 'No, I actually meant sorry about offloading on you about Martha. It's just that I think it's only fair you know what's going on, as we work together and so on.' He opened another drawer as I considered the hideous possibility that he had told me about the divorce for purely professional reasons. It had to be more than that, and then there was the hint of a trip to Rome. I opened my mouth to reassure him, but he was already immersed in the contents of the new drawer.

'Too much stuff, Sylvia, that's the trouble,' he said, dragging out a pile of yellowing papers and dumping them in the bin.

'Can I help? What are you looking for?' I asked, snapping out of my reverie and fighting the urge to tidy the mess up for him.

'Just that article about … oh, here it is.' He held up an ancient magazine in triumph.

'Good,' I smiled, happy he had found what he wanted.

He continued sorting through the drawer and pulled out a blue velvet-covered lined notebook that I recalled him receiving as a secret Santa present several Christmases ago at the staff party. The very same party, in fact, where he had kissed me passionately under the mistletoe in the corridor, away from prying eyes, before running his hands down my back and murmuring in my ear that I smelt wonderful. By the time I had regained my composure he had disappeared back into the festive fray and we have never spoken of it since. We both know, though, that the connection was there and that it is only a matter of time before we will begin our love affair in earnest.

'Do you want this? It's rather nice' he said, turning it over in his hands and then holding it out to me, 'and I'm not going to use it.'

I was torn between my desire not to hurt Prof's feelings and my deep disappointment that this appeared to be as close to a birthday present that I was going to get from him this year. In the end I nodded, unable to refuse any offering, however small, that came from him.

'Here you go, then, you can write down all your secrets in it. Happy birthday!' He laughed and passed it into my open hands. I felt the brush of his suit cuff on my wrist, sending tingles all along my arm. 'Thank you,' I mouthed, although, to my humiliation, no sound would come out. 'You might as well have this as well to go with it,' he said as an afterthought, passing me a shabby plastic box with a picture of a ballpoint pen on the lid. I bit my lip and took it from him with another meek 'thank you' and slunk back to my desk to lick my wounds.

I put the journal and the pen box on my desk and kept glancing at them as I finished up for the day. I couldn't understand how Prof could be so cruel as to think that a second-hand journal and a cheap pen would suffice as my gift, especially given the countless hours I spend searching the shops for perfect presents for him, and I experienced the familiar confusion that he so often provokes in me. I could barely bring myself to be civil as he walked past me and out of the office with a cheery 'Bye, Sylvia, see you tomorrow.' He even had the audacity to wink at me as he pulled on his coat.

I sat for a little while longer assimilating the events of the day, trying to decide whether I should feel hopeful or utterly dejected. Eventually I picked up the box and opened it, intending at least to get some use out of the pen. I gasped when I saw what was inside. An exquisite gold bracelet with charms of diamond-studded stars lay on a bed of white and pink rose petals. I picked it up with shaking hands and tears sprung to my eyes. I grabbed the blue velvet notebook and opened it at the first page.

'Sylvia, you are my absolute star.' Prof had written in his flourishing style, 'Wishing you a very happy birthday. Carl x'.

I held it to my chest as pure elation flowed through me. My Prof, my darling Prof.

So here it is, my personal journal gifted to me by Prof. Starting today I am going to write down everything that

15

happens between us and everything about myself that I never get the chance to tell him. I like to think that when we are in our dotage we can sit and read it, laugh a little, perhaps, at the capricious nature of love, and remember our journey and how we finally ended up having a life together.

Saturday 5 September

I met Millie for coffee in town this morning to talk about arrangements for Mother's eightieth birthday dinner, Kamal's aunties' upcoming visit from India, and a few other inconsequential things. Crystal came too, a bit later – she was shopping for an outfit for her start-of-year prom. This is now the thing for sixteen-year-olds – very American – and Kamal had given her a small fortune to buy the perfect dress. I felt the familiar discomfort when Crystal arrived and shifted as subtly as I could in my seat to extend the space between us by a few inches. Millie may have picked up on it, though, as she shot me a puzzled look.

'Let's see the dress then,' Millie trilled, pulling at the carrier bag her daughter had shoved under the table as she slouched down into her seat. I knew it wouldn't go well. Crystal is a much more conservative dresser than her mother and cringes with embarrassment at some of Millie's more outlandish outfits, such as the lime-green dungarees and work boots she had on today.

'It doesn't matter, Mum, you won't like it.' But Crystal's protests were no match for my sister's determination. I had to suppress a smirk as Millie held up a three-quarter length brown nylon shift with long sleeves and a round neck. She looked confused and then hopeful.

'That's a bit plain, darling, are you going to jazz it up a bit?'

'No,' Crystal replied sulkily.

'Oh, well I'm sure it's all the rage; I must be out of touch with teenage fashion.' Millie looked at me for support and I raised my eyebrows noncommittally and took a sip of my black coffee.

'Did you spend all the money Daddy gave you on it?'

Crystal shook her head and rummaged in her bag handing Millie back four of the five twenty-pound notes Kamal had given her.

'Keep it, darling, buy some fabulous shoes or something to go with it,' Millie urged.

Crystal sighed and put the money back in her purse. We sat in uncomfortable silence for a minute until Crystal's phone beeped and she snatched it off the table as if someone had thrown her a lifeline. 'It's Lewis; he wants me to meet him at the library.'

'OK, but please be back by seven for dinner, darling. Daddy is doing a roast.' Crystal wrinkled her nose in distaste at the thought and Millie, with an anxious expression on her face, watched her leave. Then she shifted gear, back on to more comfortable child-boasting ground as she stirred another sugar into her Frappuccino. 'Exciting news, darling. Crystal's had one of her drawings chosen for an exhibition of talented teenage artists.' I feigned interest as she told me about it at length, wondering who on earth would want to look at one of Crystal's gloomy compositions.

It was only when we were leaving ourselves that we realised Crystal had left her carrier bag under the table. 'I do worry about her,' said Millie pulling out the top of the dress and rubbing the cheap nylon fabric between her fingers. 'And this Lewis boy she spends all her time with? I'm sorry, but he is such a nerd. Can you use that word any more or does it have some awful connotation? And he's so dull, darling, you can't get two words out of him.'

I held back from saying he sounds perfect for Crystal. Millie still seems to be under the impression that her daughter will one day transform into an exuberant, flamboyant socialite, a younger version of herself, ready to set the world alight with her sparkling wit and verve.

'And what sixteen-year-olds meet at a library in this day and age? I thought all the libraries had closed, anyway. What are they going to do there? Everything they could want to read is online, isn't it?'

'Maybe they just want to be somewhere quiet?' I suggested mildly.

'And she's got a lovely figure under all those baggy shirts she wears. At her age I wanted to be part of the action, meeting different people, having fun, being impulsive ...'

'I know, Millie, I remember it well.'

19

'You can't get these years back again. Being young and beautiful doesn't last forever.'

I nodded sagely in agreement, trying to look like I cared about Crystal's wasted youth as I held the door open for her. She finally noticed my bracelet and her fingers reached out to touch it as it sparkled in the light.

'That's so pretty. Where did you get it?'

'I treated myself, for my birthday.' I have never let on to Millie how special Prof is to me. I couldn't bear her pragmatic opinions or, worse, constant teasing.

'Well, good for you, darling. You deserve nice things,' Millie said absently as she looked for where she had parked the car.

Kamal was holding the fort in the deli for the afternoon and looked hassled and dishevelled when we got back. He was serving a tall Nigerian woman in traditional dress and headgear whose three children were running riot round the shop as he tried to get her complicated requirements right. 'No, not those – I want to try the peppery ones. My husband likes the chicken you do – no, not that much, he can't have everything he wants,' the woman laughed and Kamal scowled as he caught sight of me behind Millie.

'Hi, baby, how's it going?' Millie is eternally cheerful, as a counterfoil to Kamal's terminal grumpiness, but she knows just how to handle him. He ignored her as he finished serving the customer and when she and her children had gone he took off his apron and threw it on the counter.

'You said you'd be back by three.' He held up three fingers for emphasis.

'I know, darling, sorry. We got chatting and Crystal took ages choosing her dress.'

He glared at me accusingly, as if it was my fault, as Millie turned towards the counter to check out the cash register.

'You have done so well, though,' she said as she lifted out a wad of tens. 'My lovely husband.' She took his face in her left hand and gently stroked his cheek. All the tension seeped from him in the wake of her loving admiration.

'My God, woman, you take the piss. You really do.' He flicked a tea towel at her bottom and she jumped out the way. Then he grabbed her in a hug and they kissed like teenagers. As usual, I felt like I was invisible and backed out the door. I was eager to get home anyway to proofread Prof's latest journal article on inequalities in the secondary school system in England and Wales.

Friday 11 September

It was Mother's eightieth birthday dinner at Millie and Kamal's this evening and we all had to pretend to be happy about it.

I had come in the side way and came across Kamal and Millie in the garden. They didn't see me at first. They were sitting on the swinging bench together, Millie with her legs to the side under her paisley shawl, curled against Kamal who sat face on with his arm protectively around her. They were talking softly to each other, looking ahead across the garden towards the beech trees at the far end which were gently swaying in the warm evening breeze. The kitchen door was open and the radio was on, a delicious spicy smell drifting out along with Jazz FM. For a moment I just watched them, feeling their togetherness and intimacy as if I was somehow wedged between them, part of their muted words and entwined lives. Then came the stab of being apart from that, alone, as usual and a wave of melancholy swept over me. I had to shake myself out of it, of course. There is no place for maudlin at a supper party.

I packed the painful feelings away and composed a cheerful expression on my face as I strode towards them, saying, 'Gosh, you two look cosy! Room for a little one?'

Kamal's face was a picture. He still is never quite sure with English humour, not knowing whether we are joking or not. After all these years, I suppose some things are unlearnable. Plus, I think he is always silently terrified that I am going to blow his cover and reveal our horrible little secret to Millie, but truly, that is something that I would never ever do.

Millie, as always, was pleased to see me and jumped up, taking me by the hand into the kitchen to show me what they'd made, desperate as usual for Mother's approval. A feast of coconut fish curry, raita, rice, fresh light naans, a dish with okra and cauliflower pakoras. Millie and Crystal had also rather impressively made a cake in the shape of a West Highland Terrier with chocolate buttons for eyes and a slice of strawberry for a tongue in honour of Mother's snappy little dog, Hamish.

Mother arrived soon after and seemed quietly pleased with the effort. Dressed in cream linen, as usual she looked immaculate, belying a trip to the beauty salon earlier for hair, nails and eyebrow grooming. I marvelled at how she sat dead straight in her garden chair, as if she had a broom up her back, with her ankles neatly crossed and a benign expression arranged on her face. She nibbled at the food and said the right things about the cake, but she always manages to give the impression of being slightly disappointed in all of us – or perhaps with life in general. I have never been able to work it out.

Millie and I have talked about it at length and I have to say that it seems to bother her a lot more than it does me. But that's Millie all over, she's a people-pleaser. She just wants everybody to be happy and I think, in a way, Mother has always let her take responsibility for that so she doesn't have to.

It was warm enough to eat outside (I had two small spoonfuls of rice and one of fish curry) and it was beautiful, really, until the bats started fluttering across the garden and Crystal got scared.

'Silly girl! We used to have bats inside our house in Kochi,' Kamal teased her. 'Uncle Prakash used to catch them and put them up my shirt – so tickly!' He laughed his rolling hearty laugh and Millie looked lovingly at him. She likes him to share stories from his childhood in India with Crystal, for him to try and make it real for her.

Millie worries that Crystal is not 'in touch' enough with her heritage and is always trying to encourage the girl to email her relatives in Kerala and wear a sari and learn Indian dancing. As far as I can see, the more she pushes, the more Crystal stubbornly digs her heels in. Even tonight she refused to eat the curry and had an avocado salad instead that Millie made her quietly in the kitchen when everyone was talking. I also saw her feed Hamish her pakoras under the table and that was naughty, because Kamal makes them especially for her because they're supposed to be her favourite.

Utterly spoilt in my view. Who cares if she feels Indian or not? She lives in South London, for goodness' sake; being mixed race is hardly something unusual or worth making a fuss about.

It's not Crystal's fault that I don't like her. I have tried, over the years, not to let the past affect my relationship with her (the last thing I want is Millie picking up on it) but I know she knows there is a problem there. I can't quite hide my lack of genuine enthusiasm about Crystal's many and varied achievements over the years. Her first steps, first words, writing her name, passing her ballet exams – the list goes on and on – and with each occasion the news has been delivered to me like a special present that I am invited to share in the joy of opening. And no matter how hard I have tried, and still try, to look pleased and say the right things, there is a note of discord in my voice and in my reactions that chills and often kills the moment. To Millie's credit, she still includes me in everything the damn child ever does or plans to do, or wants to do. We have detailed discussions about what I can get her for birthdays and Christmas and Crystal writes gushing thank-you cards for Auntie Sylvia that are, I suspect, dictated by Millie. It is an orchestrated relationship, I suppose, not a real one. It may sound cruel, but I wouldn't care if I never saw Crystal again and I suspect she feels the same way about me. But we both hang in there for Millie's sake.

Anyway, Mother seemed to like her presents. Millie had made her a complicated hand-embroidered cushion cover that had all sorts of meanings related to her life that she did explain to me at some point but which I have now totally forgotten. I gave her a silver-framed picture of her and Father at their pearl anniversary, which was only about three months before he died and it's the last nice picture we have of him before the cancer made him lose all that weight and his face went waxy. She always loved Father more than she did us, so there was no point giving her a picture of her with me and Millie. Crystal gave her some floral soap and a set of bath salts that I thought was a bit weak and thoughtless but I said nothing.

The doorbell rang around ten and Crystal rushed to answer it. She slunk back into the garden with Lewis standing behind her like a shadow, his long brown hair hanging lankly over the shoulders of his leather biker jacket.

'Is it OK if we go up to my room to listen to music?' Crystal asked, staring at her feet in embarrassment. Mother sniffed loudly in disgust as Millie agreed. I think Millie wanted to make a point to Mother that, unlike her, she is a liberal, accepting parent, because I know she can't stand Lewis under normal circumstances. Kamal went up after about twenty minutes anyway and ushered Lewis out. I heard Crystal slam her bedroom door and took that as my cue to leave. I was halfway out the door when I remembered I had left my wrap on one of the garden chairs and Millie offered to go out the back and fetch it. I was standing in the hall when Kamal came out the lounge.

'I thought you'd gone,' he said.

I looked myself up and down pointedly. 'Nope. Still here, Kamal.'

'You could make it a bit less obvious, you know,' he said.

'I don't know what you mean,' I replied, although I did suspect I hadn't covered up my negative feelings towards Crystal quite as well as usual during the evening, given the fact that I really didn't want to be there.

Kamal pointed to the montage of photos of his daughter that covered the hall wall. There was Crystal opening her birthday presents aged six, beaming a big, gappy smile; there she was again, on the back of a pony, aged ten, scared but thrilled with Kamal holding the reins; one of her messily eating an ice cream as a toddler, and the one of Millie cradling her as a newborn that still made me tremble with emotion. 'She's just a kid, Sylvia. Nothing is her fault.'

He waited for me to respond, which I didn't. Instead I pulled myself up tall and gave him an unpleasant, scornful look. I really do struggle to recall what I ever thought was attractive about him. He sighed impatiently and we scowled at each other through narrowed eyes until Millie bustled back in through the kitchen. 'Here we go, darling. Can't have you catching a chill, can we? Safe journey home.' She kissed me on both cheeks as Kamal disappeared upstairs.

'Isn't it wonderful how we all get on so well as a family?' she mused as she helped me on with my wrap.

'Yes, Millie, it's totally wonderful,' I replied, mystified as ever by my sister's unshakeable childlike commitment to seeing life as a thoroughly warm and fun experience for everyone. 'Thank you for a super evening,' I said as I stepped out into the balmy evening air and headed towards the bus stop.

Saturday 12 September

I went to the hedgehog sanctuary as usual this morning. I volunteer there on Tuesdays after work as well as at the weekends. It gives me an excuse not to help out in Millie and Kamal's deli, and it is at least something to talk about when colleagues ask the de rigueur questions about what I did last night or at the weekend. The other advantage is that volunteering there makes people think I'm a nicer person than I actually am, which can come in useful. For example, last December Charlotte from accounts was criticising me behind my back for not buying any of the ghastly Christmas cards she was selling to support a wildlife hospital she'd visited on holiday. Two or three colleagues apparently jumped to my defence in the staffroom saying how I give up lots of my time working at a hedgehog rescue centre and couldn't reasonably be expected to contribute to any other animal charity.

This was reported to me by Margaret, as I try to avoid the staffroom at all costs. If I do ever venture down there, it's out of sheer boredom or to check my pigeonhole. It's surprising how interested people are in hedgehogs – an interest that generally demonstrates itself to be both intense, yet extremely short-lived, which suits me fine. I have stock answers to the most common hedgehog questions (Do they all have fleas? Why do they always get run over? Where do they go when they hibernate?) and that tends to permanently satisfy their Erinaceus curiosity. Millie was the same when I first started there, but I don't think I have ever discussed hedgehogs with her since. She knows vaguely that that's what I do when I'm not at work and approves of my community spirit – and that's as far as it goes. I've never mentioned it to Prof, although I don't know why. I like to exude an aura of sensual mystery, I suppose, and don't want him to conjure an image in his head of me in my wellies cleaning out hedgehog pens in a back street in Sydenham.

Old Jonas who runs it is a sad sack of a man, keeping his wife Paula's memory alive by carrying on with her beloved sanctuary. A cardigan in human form is the best way to describe him, with his jumble of woollies and pockets full of handkerchiefs and toffees. He wears bicycle clips around his trousers for reasons I have yet to fathom and, on chilly days, he pulls a brown woolly hat right down over his ears. He has curly grey hair and a matching beard, ancient thick-rimmed specs held together with masking tape, and the rotund figure of a man who enjoys too much cake. He smells of earth and animals and tea and is about as harmless a person as you could ever hope to meet.

His house, a crumbling post-war semi covered in greying pebble dash, has been frozen in time since Paula died. It's clean and homely inside, but everything's faded and nothing is ever replaced. The television and phone are huge and old-fashioned, the carpets are worn, the kitchen appliances all show signs of DIY repairs, and Jonas must be the only person in London to still have a VHS recorder and a cassette player. The bottom half of the back door is covered in dog scratches and peeling paint. It opens straight on to a little patio with a bench along the outside wall of the house where Jonas likes to sit and have his breakfast, come rain or shine. His garden is a muddle of sheds, plant pots and hutches, with a patch of lawn in the middle and overflowing flower beds and vegetable plots round the outside. Coming here is like being transported back to the 1940s, with the tin watering cans and runner beans tied up with string, the push-along mower and patched-up fences, and Jonas himself, of course, usually bent double over a spade as if he's digging for victory.

Jonas and Paula brought up their three daughters here, Harriet, Katie and Carrie, and surrounded by all those women for so many years, Jonas always had a male dog as a pet, 'to even things out a bit', as he explains it. He has kept up this tradition, even though it is just him on his own now, and his current companion, Igor, is a Jack Russell–spaniel crossbreed that he got from Battersea dog's home when his beloved collie

Jake died last summer. Igor is an odd-looking animal, covered in an explosion of brown and white splodges with the sharp mouth of a Jack and the stockiness of a spaniel. But his fierce appearance belies a soppy pup who adores Jonas and follows him everywhere he goes either physically, or if he is too comfy lying in his basket or in the sunshine, with his soulful brown eyes.

The garage where the hedgehogs are kept is on the far left of the garden, away from the house, and is quite cosy with all the cages along one side and an electric fire, sink and wooden table and chairs on the other. Any spare wall space is covered with posters and pictures of hedgehogs that Jonas has acquired over the years and various hedgehog ornaments and knick-knacks are lined up along the window ledge. The hogs come to us with all sorts of injuries and illnesses and Jonas does his best to nurse them back to health. There are heat pads in the cages for those who are really young or poorly and some hutches on the patio for the ones who are nearly ready to be released back into the wild, so they can get used to the weather and the smells of outside again.

An ancient crab-apple tree sits between the garage and the toolshed, its low-hanging branches laden with bird feeders surrounded by the constant flutter of blue tits and chaffinches. The actual bird table has been colonised by next door's cats who seem to be on a rota system, taking it in turns to curl up on the wooden perch, blinking in the sun or sheltering from the rain, tormenting Igor by being just out of his reach. Jack and Jill, an unwanted rabbit and guinea pig pair who were left in a box on Jonas's doorstep one frosty morning two or three years ago, enjoy a custom-made hutch and run that take up a good third of the lawn. Jill's high-pitched squeaks fascinate Igor and he spends hours with his nose pressed against the wire netting, watching her chew manically on dandelion leaves, her ginger fur sticking up from her head in tufts. Jack, in contrast, is a calm, sleek creature who looks like he's been carved out of mahogany by a master craftsman. He sits, statuesque in the corner of the run, plotting his escape, so Jonas says, but I think he's quite happy just taking it all in, really.

It's not cheap, keeping it going and feeding all the animals, and what with the vet's bills for the hedgehogs and having the garage constantly heated, it adds up to quite a sum each month. Jonas pours far too much of his own money into the place, although he thinks I don't know that. We have a collection box on the counter in the newsagent's on the corner, and the local Women's Institute do a cake sale for us once a year but, apart from the occasional gift left in the wills of Paula's friends as they shuffle off, that is the extent of the sanctuary's financial resources.

Jonas wrote a lovely, quirky little booklet called *The Hedgehog Year* a while back, containing lots of useful and interesting information about hedgehogs. I typed it up for him from his handwritten jottings and made some copies at work. We put them out for our occasional visitors to purchase for a suggested donation of fifty pence in a bid to boost funds. They haven't been a roaring success, to be honest, and most remain in a yellowing pile on the garage table. I have reassured Jonas several times that poor returns are no reflection of quality – I know this from the disappointing sales of Prof's last book, which is actually quite brilliant. But Jonas doesn't seem bothered one way or another about whether anyone buys his leaflets and says he just wanted to put it all down on paper.

There used to be quite a crowd of us volunteers, but the others have either died (the old ones) or lost interest (the young ones) so it's mainly just Jonas and me these days. Jonas is hoping one of his three daughters or their children will take over at some point, and I humour him with that, although I think it's unlikely. Having said that, his second youngest granddaughter, Sophie, seemed to love the hogs when she visited this morning.

'Why is that one curled up in a ball?' she asked Jonas, pointing at a young sow who had been found weak and hungry in someone's garden shed.

'Because she's frightened, lass,' explained Jonas, in his rolling Yorkshire accent that has never faded despite decades spent living in London. 'She feels protected like that, surrounded by her spikes. No one can get to her soft vulnerable parts. Nothing can hurt her when she's balled up like that.'

'Why don't they stay like that all the time then, if it's nice and safe for them?' asked Sophie, with the logic of a five-year-old, looking round at the variety of injured hedgehogs with concern.

'Because they have to move about, lass. They have to find food and mates and make a nest for themselves and their babies.'

'They have to live, don't they, Grandad?' she said, nodding her head wisely.

'Aye lass. They have to live,' Jonas replied, smiling proudly at Sophie and patting her blonde head as if she had just uncovered some profound mystery. I rolled my eyes at Igor as I swept the floor.

Her next question was more pragmatic. 'How can you tell which hedgehogs are boys and which are girls?' she asked innocently.

Jonas delighted in demonstrating to her what we call the 'casserole technique' of gender identification, whereby the hog is placed on a Pyrex dish and held up, enabling its important parts to be examined, prickle free, from underneath. Sophie naturally thought that was hilarious and carried on giggling as Jonas shambled off to make the tea. Before he got back, Sophie's mother, Katie, flung open the garage door and smiled at her daughter indulgently.

'There you are,' she said, taking Sophie's hand. 'I've been looking all over the house for you. We only popped in to collect Grandad's washing. We'll be late for Isabel's party if we don't get a move on. Hello and goodbye, Sylvia!'

Jonas was quite subdued when he got back with the tea and found Sophie was gone.

'She was late for a party. She wanted to stay,' I assured him as we sat with our tea looking at the three Bakewell tarts he had put out on the plate.

I attempted to shift the mood by starting a conversation about current educational issues, which I thought would interest him as he is, after all, a retired English teacher.

'Did you realise, Jonas, that fifty-five per cent of white working-class boys finish compulsory education without basic skills in reading, writing and arithmetic?'

'Is that so?' he replied reaching for a tart.

'Yes. My professor has been leading a research project examining the reasons for this. It's really quite fascinating what he has found out,' I said proudly. (I call Prof 'my professor' when I talk to Jonas, out of respect, really, and also because I don't want Jonas to know how I feel about him.)

'I dare say,' said Jonas, chewing absently.

'There are inherent problems in the way these children are taught, according to my professor. Teachers simply don't connect with these boys on their level and so they feel alienated and then they can't learn. Did you realise that when you were teaching?' I knew I was being provocative, but his indifference to Prof's research was making my hackles rise. I have lost count of the number of times I have generously tried to share Prof's findings, theories and insights with Jonas only to be met with mild interest at best, or stony unresponsiveness at worst. It seems to me that people like Prof go through blood, sweat and tears to try and make this world a better place, whilst people like Jonas sit idly with pastry crumbs on their beards, not caring one way or another.

After a long silence, during which I wondered if he was going to answer me at all, Jonas sighed and said, 'Sometimes kids just don't want to learn what they're being taught, Sylvia. That's their choice at the end of the day.' Then he got up to check the thermometer and I stared furiously at his back. He really is the most exasperating thickie.

Thank the Lord I get to spend my working week with someone as erudite, cultured and intelligent as Prof. He enriches me beyond words and I can't wait to get back to him after the weekend. Mondays are far and away the best day of the week for me. Last Monday, though, Prof was at a conference in Cardiff so I had to tolerate an extra day of separation. I always offer to accompany him to these events, saying, 'Would it be helpful if I came with you to Brussels/Manchester/Chicago?' or wherever he is off to (the international ones are the worst as he can be away for days at a time). But he always says something like, 'It would be great to have you there, Sylvia, but the budget won't cover it' or 'We need you here holding the fort' or 'Perhaps next time we can organise that' and I say, 'Fine.' It is hard for me to keep asking, but the pain of him being away is worse than the short amount of time I feel embarrassed for suggesting it, so I have worked out that it's better to ask just in case he agrees one day. And I make it such a professional thing by saying, 'Will you be needing administrative support whilst you are away?' or 'Will you need help organising your symposium?' so it's not like he is rejecting me in any personal way. He never says he has missed me when he gets back, but I know that he has. I do wish he would say it though, just once.

Anyway, poor Prof had only just got back from Cardiff on the Tuesday after a pig of a journey, when Yvonne Gilbert came bursting into the office in tears wanting to see him. I told her that she would have to email and make an appointment like everyone else and emphasised that Professor Lomax is an extremely busy man. She begged and pleaded and made such a fuss that Prof came out of his sanctum and asked what was going on. Seeing her chance she started on about not being ready for her PhD viva voce examination the next day, and did he think her project was perfectly useless and could he help her go through some practice questions and please and please and please? He gave in, of course. He's too nice, that's his problem, and to add insult to injury he even gave me a slightly disapproving look. Not because I had let the girl come and bother him, but because I hadn't let her go straight in. How did that happen? How did I become the baddie in that situation? I seethed with anger all the while she was in there, my mood made even worse by Margaret's patronising advice regarding the importance of empathising with students' emotional needs. 'It's not only the practical issues they need help with, Sylvia. We have to recognise the stress that many of our young people experience when they are at university. It was all on that course that I went on about student well-being.'

'Oh, do shut up, Margaret, you don't know anything about it,' I snapped, craning my neck to see into Prof's office.

I couldn't do any work and sat fuming at my desk as Yvonne got his full attention and I was left out in the cold. When she was still in with Prof after ten minutes and it became clear that she wasn't to be dismissed quickly, I pulled up her electronic file to see what I could find out. Pleasingly, I discovered that she had a few hundred pounds in unpaid tuition fees outstanding on her account. A brief call to the student finance department soon put that right, and as I was putting the phone down she came out of Prof's office and gave me a horribly smug smile. I smiled back with genuine pleasure and wished her luck with her viva tomorrow, which wouldn't go ahead now anyway if she didn't pay her fees in full. That would be a nice panic for her later in the day. I envisaged the desperate phone calls to the bank, perhaps to her parents, the sleepless night agonising over whether the funds had gone through.

'Hope it all goes well,' I added brightly and she gave me a puzzled little backward glance. Margaret opened her mouth to speak but the glacial look I gave her stopped her in her tracks and she turned back to her work, tutting loudly.

This is what I do. I assist Prof by always being on his side and supporting him in any way I can. If other people have to be pricked and prodded out of his way, then so be it. Prof's well-being is my ultimate concern, not theirs. He needs time to focus on his writing and his research. That's what's important. That's where he makes the difference and that's where his genius lies. Not in helping doe-eyed girls with their dissertations or sorting out arguments about office size among middle-aged academics who should have better things to worry about. He appreciates me, I know he does, and I have a very important place in his life. It works both ways, though, and Prof ensures that I am made to feel special and that everyone else knows that I am his indispensable right-hand woman.

There's all the little things that show that he cares, not just the annual birthday lunch. For example, he always brings me a treat back from any meeting that he attends – a pack of biscuits, perhaps, or a mini muffin (he doesn't know I don't eat them and I wouldn't dream of hurting his feelings). I remember one day when I was sniffing and sneezing at my desk he came back from a senior management meeting with a ginger and lemon teabag in a paper envelope. He put it on my desk as he walked past saying, 'Here you go, Sylvia, this might help your cold.' I was so touched by his thoughtfulness. I just stared at the teabag and before I could say thank you, he was gone into his office. I know it's silly and sentimental, but I still have that teabag. I have never opened it. I keep it in my bedside table drawer and sometimes, if I have had a particularly difficult day, I find it calming to take it out and breathe in its aroma before I go to sleep.

Every second Wednesday he treats me to what he calls a 'working lunch' in the staff canteen. We do talk about work mainly, but sometimes the conversation moves onto more personal territory and he tells me about what his boys have been up to or updates me on his father's illness or his house extension. I always listen intently to whatever he wishes to share with me and try to provide supportive comments. Over the years I have heard a lot about his soon-to-be ex-wife, carefully hiding my glee beneath a concerned face when he has confided in me about her appalling behaviour.

Prof also likes to tell me about his research and finds it incredibly helpful to use me as a sounding board as he thinks through his ideas. I am thrilled that he values my opinion, although I never have anything critical to say as he is way beyond me intellectually. I tell him how interesting I find his work and that's why he has given me the honour of proofreading all his papers and book manuscripts before they go to the publishers.

'You are so good with the details, Sylvia,' he always says, as he passes me another one of his stuffed plastic folders. 'What would I do without you to look after me?' I hurry home, looking forward to spending the evening immersing myself in Prof's work, delighting in finding missing commas and correcting spelling mistakes, playing my small part in his superb contributions to the field of Educational Sociology. I don't mind the extra hours I put in for free doing this for him. In fact, I enjoy it, and it makes the time I am away from him easier to bear.

Monday 21 September

I was getting ready to go home this afternoon when Prof's soon to be ex-wife Martha came storming into the office to pick up some documents that Prof keeps in his desk, relating to the boys' passports. I must admit I am always fascinated to have a good look at her and to carefully note their interaction, so I sank back down into my chair and rebooted my computer. She was wearing a sort of black cape, which swamped her skinny frame, and thigh-high black suede boots that had a pantomime feel about them. She has a black bob with a short fringe and she was wearing the bright red lipstick which I gather is something of a personal motif. No other make-up, mind, just the lipstick, making her look both glamorous and oddly unfinished. I saw Prof look up from his computer and see her come in and he jolted in his chair as if he'd been caught stealing. He stood up, sat down again, took off his glasses, then put them on again and pretended to be engrossed in his work as she threw open his office door. She had her back to me at this point and, annoyingly, she closed the door behind her, so I couldn't hear what was said, but Prof was obviously thrown by her turning up like that, unannounced. She didn't stay long. Prof fumbled in his desk and passed her the papers she wanted. She snatched them off him and came out into the main office where I was able to give her a withering look that said all it needed to say about what I thought about her and the way she had treated Prof.

It clearly irked her and she stopped in her tracks on her way out, turning to face me full on. 'Do you have something you want to say, Sylvia?' she snapped.

I simply continued staring at her with a stern expression on my face, adding in a slight head shake to reinforce my disapproval.

'I don't know what fairy story he's told you,' she said loudly so Prof could hear her, 'but please don't waste your time feeling sorry for him.' She did a nasty, scoffing laugh as she said the last bit and with a final poisonous glare at Prof through the glass partition she strode out the door.

Prof actually bit his lip, bless him, like a small child. I just wanted to run in and throw my arms around him. What he must have gone through, being married to that dreadful woman, and then for her to behave as if he was the villain of the piece. I had to stay seated for several minutes until I had stopped shaking with anger and then went in to Prof to see if I could soothe him in any way, at the very least with a cup of tea. He was rather curt and dismissive of me, which was hurtful, and he didn't even look up from his screen, but I forgive him as he was clearly distressed by Martha's visit.

I thought for a long time about what I could do to get back at her, both for belittling me and for upsetting Prof. Finally, I settled on leaving some unfavourable, anonymous online reviews of the art gallery she manages, making sure I mentioned her by name. It wasn't enough to settle me, but a better idea will come when I feel calmer. It always does.

Thursday 1 October

I was gazing out of the window this morning, watching a new batch of enthusiastic students being given a campus tour by a bored-looking Dr Bastow, when my mobile burst into noisy life on my desk. I sprang to answer it, hoping that Prof hadn't heard it ring. It's one of his pet hates, phones going off in the office or in lectures or meetings; even a muffled vibration is enough to darken his mood when he is in the middle of speaking or reading or listening to something important. As a mark of respect to him I always have my phone either turned off or on silent at work even though it means I sometimes miss calls from the bank or Mother or, less commonly, Jonas. Today, as I picked it up, I realised that I had used it this morning to call Mother and that she had said she would call me back so I had left it on and then forgotten about it.

'You were supposed to call back hours ago,' I snapped, furtively checking through the glass divide that Prof hadn't been disturbed.

'What? Was I? What do you mean?' It was Millie, not Mother, and she was as confused as I was

'Millie. I thought it was Mother. It doesn't matter. Is everything all right?'

'Yes, fine. Listen, darling, sorry to ring you at work, I know you don't like it, but I had to talk to you about something exciting.' Millie sounded fit to burst, so, with some trepidation, I encouraged her to continue.

'Una Shipman came into the shop today – do you remember her? They used to live next door to us in Purbeck Road and she had that gorgeous son who we both fancied. He rode a motorbike and was in a band. You used to say that you were going to marry him one day.'

I had no idea where Millie was going with this, but was beginning to feel most uncomfortable. I checked again that Prof couldn't see or hear me on the phone, but he was engrossed in editing an article – glasses on, shirtsleeves pushed up, slight frown. I loved watching him while he worked.

'What about him? We were all teenagers, Millie, that was a long time ago.'

'Well, apparently he has recently divorced his second wife and is single again. He's living back at Una's at the moment while they sort out selling the house and everything and Una says he is really down in the dumps and could do with some cheering up.'

'And?' I was getting impatient at this irrelevant stream of information, but was not prepared for what came next.

'And I told her that you were also still single and looking for love and that you two should go out for dinner and see what happens. Darling, are you there? Did you hear me?'

'I am not going for dinner with Neil Shipman, Millie. What on earth were you thinking? What do you take me for?' I saw Margaret's head pop up in interest at this and moved further into the corner away from her flapping ears, annoyed with myself for giving her an insight into my personal life.

My harsh tone took Millie aback and put her on the defensive. 'What's the problem, darling? This could be wonderful for you. You used to really like him. Don't you remember that diary you used to keep of all his comings and goings and everything he wore and everything he ever said to you? You were mad about him. And now here is a chance to make it real. You are both of … of a certain age, both single – you could be perfect for each other. You have to be brave, take a risk, see what happens.'

'I'm not prepared to discuss it with you any longer, Millie. How dare you decide what I need and what I should do? I'm perfectly fine as I am and I don't need to go chasing after some has-been rocker who lives with his mother!' I was whispering furiously down the phone by this point, with one eye still on Prof.

'For heaven's sake, darling. You waste so much time and energy trying to ensure that nobody pities you. Why don't you just admit how lonely you are?'

I hung up and tossed the phone back onto my desk as if it had offended me itself. Hot tears sprung to my eyes and, horror of horrors, Prof chose that exact moment to throw open his office door and come striding out, academic paper in one hand, empty coffee cup in the other.

'This is really very good, you know. Really very good,' he said absently as he poured himself another coffee from the jug. I grabbed the watering can from my desk and turned to water the windowsill plants to hide my upset, knocking over a small potted fern in my haste.

'Careful, Sylvia,' Prof called as he re-entered his sanctum and closed the door.

'Everything all right, Sylvia?' Margaret asked with exaggerated concern when he had gone. 'It's just that you sounded a little bit upset on the phone. Boyfriend trouble, is it? It must be awful still being single at your age. I don't know how you bear it, really I don't. Still, at least you've got your hedgehogs.' She picked up her mug and sailed past me to the kitchen, her spiteful missile neatly despatched, as I picked up the fallen plant and burned with shame.

I was put out for the rest of the day. I'm not sure what I was most upset about: Prof seeing me in such a dither, letting Margaret get to me, the fact that Millie obviously perceives me as such a sad case or the fact that she had discussed me with Una Shipman and made ridiculous plans behind my back. Whichever it was, I couldn't face eating anything when I got home and sat sipping peppermint tea with a copy of the paper that had so impressed Prof on the table in front of me. I was trying to concentrate on it, to understand what he had admired about it, but was finding it difficult to follow the complex, and rather dull, argument about the relationship between pedagogy and religion. When the phone in the kitchen rang I knew it would be Millie and ignored it. Then my mobile rang, which I also ignored. Ten minutes later the landline rang again and I answered it crossly, my concentration completely shot for the evening.

'Am I forgiven?' Millie was using her sweetest voice with a hint of humour. It was hard to stay angry.

'I suppose so.'

'Will you please just meet him for dinner? It's all arranged. Next Wednesday at seven thirty at Stones in Covent Garden. Kamal can pick you up afterwards if you don't want to get the bus home.'

I sighed, sensing defeat. 'I don't understand why this is so important to you.'

'It just is. I love you. I want you to be happy, darling. Please go.'

'You are emotionally manipulative, do you know that?'

'I know. It's one of my best features. I'll tell Una to tell Neil to expect you at seven thirty. I'll book the table for you both. Do you want me to come over after work on Wednesday and help you get ready?'

'No, I'll manage, thank you, Millie.' I was momentarily amused by imagining how I would look if I let Millie have free rein with my clothes and make-up. 'How will I recognise him?'

'Apparently, he hasn't changed all that much according to Una. Good luck, can't wait to hear how it goes.'

Millie hung up as I contemplated having dinner with a tattooed man in his mid-fifties, clad in leather, with a goatee and long hair.

Tuesday 6 October

I arrived at Jonas's around six o'clock and found him in the garden, carefully deadheading the roses that grow up the back wall next to the raspberry canes.

'It's a shame when they're done for the year,' he said, pulling off a pinkish-brown bloom and throwing it into the wicker basket by his feet, flanked by a sleeping Igor. 'Paula's favourite flower, they were. By a mile.' He gave a little chuckle and I felt obliged to show interest.

'Really?' I asked dutifully.

'Oh aye. That's how we met, you see, because of the roses. And my grandmother dying, of course.'

I waited for him to elucidate further but he just nodded and carried on plucking the flowers.

'Dad, you don't explain things properly.'

I looked round at the female voice and saw it was Katie, holding two cups of tea and smiling broadly. Her long brown hair was pinned up and she was still wearing her white optician's overall under her coat, indicating she had come straight from work. She is the best-looking of the sisters in my opinion, in a wholesome sort of way, even though she's in her early forties now. Her younger sister, Carrie, is tall and very hippyish in her style, often looking a bit of a mess as she eschews make-up and hairdressers, whilst Harriet, the oldest, is the opposite – a somewhat intimidating, highly successful corporate lawyer with expensive perfume and designer clothes. All three of them have Jonas's light-blue eyes, though, despite their different looks; they are all very fond of each other and they adore their father.

I took one of the cups with thanks and Katie continued, 'Mum worked in a flower shop in Bridlington, Sylvia, where they both grew up. Dad's mum sent him to get some roses for his grandmother's funeral and they didn't have any in that day.'

'No roses, in a florist,' Jonas repeated, shaking his head.

'Anyway, Mum was so embarrassed that she told Dad to wait in the shop and she ran all the way back home and picked a big bunch of roses from her family's own back garden and brought them back and gave them to Dad.'

'All the way back to Argyle Street she ran, uphill it was. And she left me in charge of the till, told me to serve any customers that came in. I could've been a robber. I used to say to her, "Paula, you are too trusting of folk." But that's the way she were.'

Katie put her hand on Jonas's shoulder and handed him his tea. 'She was, Dad.'

'I knew I had to marry her then,' said Jonas taking a thirsty gulp and wiping his beard with a hankie. 'I couldn't let a lass like that get away.'

I remember Millie declaring much the same about Kamal when she got back with him from India, and how Mother had raised her eyes and commented to me later that she predicted it would all be over by Christmas. She was wrong, of course. Despite what I think about Kamal, he and Millie are clearly made for each other. When you know, you know – and that's how I feel about Prof.

'Time to go in, it'll be dark soon,' Katie said, doing up her coat as I stood gazing at the faded roses, wondering why I am even bothering to meet Neil tomorrow.

Wednesday 7 October

I've had a hideous evening.

I knew it would be a mistake to meet Neil and how right I was. It wasn't worth going all the way home and then into town again so I went straight to Covent Garden after work and had a wander round, watching the street performers before going to Stones, arriving there a fashionable seven minutes after the agreed time. As the waitress led me through the beige and brown restaurant, lit with low-hung chandeliers, I realised I was holding my breath with anticipation despite my annoyance about the whole affair. I needn't have bothered with my orchestrated lateness because he wasn't there anyway, and irritation mixed with embarrassment started to rise up in my chest. I ordered a glass of tap water (if he didn't come at all, at least then I wouldn't have to wait for the bill) and stared unseeingly at the menu for several minutes, silently berating myself for agreeing to this charade in the first place.

'Sylvia?' The pleasant male voice matched the warm smile of the attractive man who had appeared in front of me. I laid down my menu and nodded, wishing I had made the effort to go home and get changed after all.

'How nice to see you again. I'm Neil.' He held out his hand and I shook it – a cool, firm handshake that matched his steady gaze.

'Yes, I know. I'm Sylvia,' I said unnecessarily.

'Yes, I know,' he said and smiled again. 'May I sit down?'

'Please do,' I said somewhat overeagerly and we both gave little nervous laughs.

'One tap water,' declared the waitress pointedly as she placed a glass in front of me, overdone with ice and a wedge of lime.

'Not drinking?' asked Neil after he'd ordered a beer.

'Well, I wasn't sure if —'

'If I'd turn up?' He raised his eyebrows and the creases around his eyes temporarily disappeared. He had a beautiful face for a man of his age. A face that spoke of a life filled with laughter and warmth and adventure, of summers on the beach and winters skiing down mountains. His greying hair was cropped close to his head and his eyes were hazel with hints of green around the pupils. He was fit, too: long and lean and muscular with a relaxed way about him that suggested a man at ease with himself and his place in the world. He was dressed in baggy chinos, cowboy-style boots and a blue T-shirt with a grey linen jacket. Smart casual to a tee, with a little bit of edge, and perfect for both his age and the occasion. I was acutely aware of my lack of effort with my own appearance and although I was wearing a pleasant enough skirt and blouse, my brown cardigan brought the ensemble down. I shrugged it off as Neil hung his jacket on the back of his chair. I felt a tinge of regret that I hadn't reapplied my make-up since this morning and that my hair was hanging limply on my shoulders, crying out for a brush. Mousey was how I looked and mousey was how I felt.

Neil shifted in his seat and politely turned his attention to me. 'So, long time no see. What have you been up to all these years?'

To his credit, he tried to look interested as I falteringly accounted for the last thirty-five years of my life, which sounded as dull and uneventful to me as they must have done to him. I tried to keep my tone light, as if I was delighted with how everything had turned out. I recounted the series of administrative positions I had held in colleges and universities, the outright purchase of my flat in South London using my uncle's inheritance money, my various trips abroad. I didn't mention Prof. In response to his inevitable question about husbands and children, I breezily dismissed both as not being at all what I wanted.

Neil looked at me in silence when I had finished, and I realised he was waiting for me to continue, to get onto the good stuff, the meaty stuff of my life, the achievements, the loves, the passions, the disasters, the defining moments. I briefly considered telling him about the hedgehog sanctuary, but decided against it.

'That's it, really.' I took a sip of my water and he cleared his throat and fiddled with his watch. 'How about you?'

It was a relief to get the focus off me and, like most men, he enjoyed the opportunity to talk about himself. He told me about his career as a music journalist, which had taken him all over the world, and about his love of going to gigs and festivals and discovering new bands. He told me about his first wife, Mia, who had died when their daughter Holly was only a baby and how he had brought her up on his own until he met his second wife, a Japanese singer of some renown apparently, called Emiko. They had a whirlwind romance and got married quite quickly, but apparently she soon discovered that she couldn't stand living in England and had recently moved back to Tokyo, taking their young son with her. He was in the process of selling the family home whilst trying to work out how to manage being a father to two children of vastly different ages in different continents. He recounted all this without self-pity, but in a pragmatic, mature manner.

'She was too young for me, I suppose,' he said thoughtfully, taking a long draught of his beer. 'Or perhaps I was too old for her.'

It was the story of a life well-lived – he had taken risks, he had followed his passions, he had been hurt, he had experienced terrible loss – but he had had much joy and love and he clearly adored his children.

The comparison to my meek and sheltered life hung unspoken between us as the waitress delivered our food. He had ordered only a main course, steak and chips, and I had gone for a salad, as usual, which I pushed around my plate. He ate quickly and we talked a little about the road we both grew up in and some of the neighbours that we had had.

It was glaringly apparent that I was of no interest to him, either physically, mentally or emotionally, which was fine by me as my heart belongs to Prof. Even so, I have to admit it was nice listening to Neil talk and reminiscing about the old days when we were all so young. I saw him glance at his watch and towards the door and felt a surge of unprecedented panic. I don't know what possessed me, but I found myself suggesting cocktails. He hesitated for a moment and then politely agreed, signalling to the waitress to take our order. I drank my mojito rather too quickly as he sipped his Old-Fashioned and we talked about the time he and his brother had broken a pane in Father's greenhouse with their cricket ball and how they had had to weed his vegetable patch all summer to make up for it.

The rum and the shared stories combined to create an artificial feeling of closeness with Neil for a moment, and I found myself blurting out, 'Do you know I used to keep a diary about you?'

He looked at me with a quizzical expression. 'What do you mean?'

'Well, I used to write down every day what you were wearing and where you went and what time you came back and if you spoke to me, or anyone else in the family, what you said and what I, or they said ...'

He frowned. 'You spied on me?'

'No, of course not. It was just, I suppose I liked you, was interested in you, you were the most exciting person in our street. I wanted to know what you were like, what you were doing. I didn't do it for long, just a few weeks – no, it was just a few days, actually, now I think about it ...'

'It sounds like you spied on me, Sylvia,' he said.

I could sense the warm atmosphere dissolving around us and quickly changed the subject, asking him about his mother and his current domestic set up. He answered my questions in a perfunctory way and then excused himself to go to the bathroom. I took the opportunity of a few minutes respite to plan how I could backtrack to the regretful sharing of the diary and downplay it, cancel it out, and try to end the evening on a more positive note. I decided to tell him it was a joke and worked out how I would explain that I have an offbeat sense of humour. It would be fine, he would understand and we could move forward, just as friends, obviously (my romantic desires lie elsewhere), but it would be nice to meet up with such an attractive man every now and then for dinner and a chat. Perhaps even have a companion to be a plus one at weddings and the like – he was lovely company, after all. Buoyed up, I finished the last of my mojito, ordered another cocktail for us both, and awaited his return with confident anticipation.

After five minutes, the dreadful possibility crept into my mind that he wasn't coming back. After fifteen minutes, it was a certainty. I looked around the restaurant at all the other couples and groups of friends laughing and eating, oblivious to my predicament, and shrank into myself, to the small, proud place where no one can hurt me. I stood up on shaky legs and then sat down again. How did one deal with this situation? I couldn't just go; the bill had to be paid. I indicated to the waitress and asked for it.

'Don't worry, your friend paid on his way out,' she said, beaming as if I should be delighted at this news. 'But you will need to pay for those last two drinks.'

I handed over the money and stumbled past her towards the door. I looked up and down the road but he was nowhere to be seen.

I rang Millie as soon as I got home and told her what had happened. I covered my upset by saying how angry I was and how rude Neil had been to leave like that. I also ranted at her for making me go to meet him in the first place. Millie listened without interrupting and then commented enigmatically, 'You can tell a lot about yourself by the way someone leaves you, darling.'

'What on earth is that supposed to mean?' I really was angry by now. 'Don't you dare give me any of your self-help nonsense!'

'Don't be cross, sweetie, he was obviously just not interested and didn't want to hurt your feelings by telling you.'

'*I* wasn't interested,' I shouted. 'For your information, I have a man in my life.'

It's not often Millie is speechless, but that took her off guard for a moment.

'Really? Who?'

'It doesn't matter, it's not important. It's none of your business.'

'I'm sorry you're upset, darling. I really did think you'd like to catch up with each other and I didn't know you were already seeing someone. How could I know that if you didn't tell me? I don't spy on *you*, you know.' This last comment was said teasingly, with affection.

'I told him, Millie, how embarrassing is that? I told him I watched him and kept a diary about him and that's why he left. I don't know what I was thinking telling him that, what must he think of me?'

'But he already knew that, darling.' Millie sounded confused. 'I told his mum about it in the shop and I also told him at the time. Sorry, honey, I thought you knew that he knew. It's not really a big deal, is it? You were only fifteen or so and everyone thought it was a hoot.

I'm sure he's not that easily rattled. Now, tell me about this man you're seeing.'

I watched a moth fly in the open window and knock against the ceiling lampshade again and again in the self-destructive dance all of its kind seem compelled to perform, and suddenly felt incredibly weary.

'I'm not seeing anyone, Millie. I'm going to bed now. Goodnight.' I hung up the phone and went into my bedroom.

I have taken Prof's teabag out of the bedside table drawer and laid it beside me on the pillow so I can smell it while I go to sleep.

Thursday 15 October

Is there a difference between willing and wanting? I'm
not sure any more. Apparently, in German, there is a
word which can mean either and there is no way to
know in translation which meaning is right. I know this
because I heard Prof discussing it with his new PhD
student, the brilliant Lola, when I took them in their
coffee. A grown woman called Lola! How ridiculous.
She is not the usual post-grad type, actually. Older, a bit
more world-weary-looking but obviously she was quite
a looker in her youth. She has long blonde hair which
is too young for her (dry-looking at the ends) and she
was wearing a denim jacket and a load of silver and
turquoise jewellery.

Anyway, Prof was very pleased to see her when
she arrived this afternoon. He came out of his inner
sanctum and shook her hand, said he was happy to see
her again and that he was looking forward to working
with her. Their meeting went on well over the allotted
hour. They sat deep in conversation – well, she did most
of the talking in her soft Irish accent – and I could see
Prof was interested because he sat at his desk the whole
time; when he is bored he wanders round the office like

a restless dog waiting for his walkies. I usually take that as a sign to go in and rescue him via a fictitious urgent phone call from the Dean or a forgotten Skype meeting with an overseas colleague. I kept my eye on his body language throughout in case he needed me in such a way, but he seemed fine so I left them to it, although after an hour and twenty minutes I did open the door and remind him that he had Simon Belington booked in for a tutorial at half past.

'Is he here yet?' Prof asked without looking up from the papers Lola had given him to look at.

'No, not yet,' I stammered, feeling a bit taken aback, 'but he is due soon.'

Prof just nodded and gave me what I felt was a rather dismissive smile so I backed out of the room with that annoying, uncontrollable blush reddening my cheeks. I didn't like that at all; I feel it gave the wrong impression to Lola and I don't want her thinking that she is more important than the other students or to underestimate my role in scheduling and protecting Prof's time. I also hate it when Prof makes me feel as if I am a fusspot or a nag when all I ever try to do is look after him and help his days go smoothly. Lola came out a couple of minutes later with that inspired, excited look that Prof's students tend to leave with when their work is going well and they can't wait to get back to their computer and continue writing their masterpiece, buoyed up with his approval.

'Just a minute, please,' I called after her as she fumbled with the office door handle, juggling files and her bag.

'Yes?' She turned with an impatient smile.

'You need to fill in a tutorial record sheet.' I like all Prof's records to be up to date as you never know when the Dean will do an audit.

'I'll email it to you; I have to pick my son up from school now,' she called over her shoulder as she rushed out.

I narrowed my eyes at her departing back. Not only did she keep Prof nearly half an hour longer than scheduled, but she didn't fill in the paperwork either. I wonder what her husband or partner thinks of her doing this doctorate? I'm sure he's not well pleased, given the commitment involved, especially if they have children. I doubt she'll stay the course. I've seen these mature students before and they rarely complete. They take on too much, wanting to do it all before they get too old, having a last-chance grasp at an academic career, trying to live up to the image of themselves they had when they were younger, before work and marriage and families and mortgages came along to steal all their time, energy and money. There's no doubt students like Lola *want* to do a PhD but are they willing to make the sacrifices necessary for such a prolonged and intensive piece of research? By the look of her, I'm guessing not. She's had her bit of attention from Prof but he will now want some pretty impressive writing from her by the end of the week, based on their discussion, and the proof, as they say, is always in the pudding.

Simon turned up five minutes later, looking like a whipped puppy as usual. I can't imagine why skinny boys think that skinny jeans make them look anything other than weedy and ridiculous. His fringe was all in his face, his acne was worse than ever, and I swear he was wearing eyeliner. I ushered him in to the inner sanctum and Prof and I shared a lovely little amused look over Simon's head that said *What a state!* and that settled me and made me feel connected to Prof again.

I asked him later about Lola, on the pretence that I needed to provide some information about her to the student record office. His face lit up as he recounted how she was an absolute rising star in the world of Educational Sociology and that her Master's degree dissertation had been published in a high-ranking journal and was causing quite a stir in academic circles. He was honoured that she had chosen him to supervise her thesis and enthused about her 'astounding level of intellect' and 'incredible insights'. I couldn't think of anything to say, so I just nodded blandly and got back to my work. I don't want him to think I am even slightly impressed. I am both willing and wanting her to never come back.

Saturday 17 October

I went to see a film with Millie this evening, the new George Clooney one. How tedious that man is with his vanity projects and perfect profile, but Millie has loved him ever since *ER* and Kamal refuses to go the cinema (says he can't stand sitting still for so long, but I think he just finds it pointless). I wanted to go to the multiplex, but Millie insisted on the Ritzy – she is truly obsessed with Brixton, says she likes the buzz. This evening Mills was wearing leather trousers, an orange bandana and hoop earrings that gave her a distinct piratey look which I assume wasn't deliberate, but you never really know with my sister. She had a huge piece of carrot cake and a hot chocolate in the cinema café before we went in. I try not to comment but I worry about her weight, I really do. I had a peppermint tea served to me by a girl covered in rose and thorn tattoos with piercings on every visible orifice and with the sort of cut-glass accent that is usually associated with royalty. You would think, having been employed in universities for most of my working life, I would be numb to the countless ways that young people insist on shoving their 'individuality' in everyone's face, but I have to admit even I was rather surprised at this juxtaposition. I was about to comment on this to Millie when I noticed she was staring after the girl as she stomped back behind the bar in her Doctor Martens.

'You know who that is, don't you?' I could see Millie was animated in the way she gets when she recognises anyone even remotely famous.

'I haven't the faintest idea.' I sipped my tea dismissively, ready to be unimpressed at Millie's triumphant naming of some has-been reality TV star.

'That's Bethany, Shona and Ian's daughter.'

I stared long and hard at the waitress as she stood frowning behind the counter, trying to comprehend how that could possibly be the case.

'No, Millie. It can't be, she's only what? Nine or ten maybe at the most …' I was faltering, panicking really. That familiar surge of dread came over me, the one that rears up from somewhere deep inside when I'm faced with irrefutable proof that so much time has passed, that friends' children have grown up, that everyone's life has moved on and ahead into new pastures. All except me. All except my life.

But even as I was trying to dismiss her, forcing my attention away from this grown-up girl with the tattoos and the attitude, Millie was up from her chair and rushing over to her. I couldn't hear what she said, but she cast her usual Millie spell on the girl and they were hugging and chatting like best friends within moments.

Millie indicated over to me as I knew she would and I managed to arrange my face into a semblance of a smile, a contented smile I like to think, and lifted my hand in a slightly embarrassed wave. Bethany acknowledged me with a small nod before turning her attention back to Millie who had her phone out by now and was tapping in precious new numbers. She was flushed with excitement when she finally made her way back to the table and gabbled on as if she had just met one of her heroes.

'I can't believe she's all grown-up. She's twenty-two now, graduated from Brighton University with a degree in graphic design last summer. Shona and Ian have moved back to Wimbledon – how fab is that? Beth's given me Shona's number so I'm going to call her tomorrow and hopefully arrange a meet-up. Wouldn't it be amazing to catch up with Shona again after all these years? We used to have such a laugh, didn't we?' Millie looked at me at this point and I smiled thinly, nodding my head. 'You did like Shona, didn't you?' Millie was clearly irritated at my lack of enthusiasm.

'Yes, of course,' I replied curtly, hoping she would drop the subject.

The truth is, that whether I liked Shona or not, and I suppose I did back then, I do not, under any circumstances, want to see her now. Millie doesn't – can't – understand, how hard it is to have catch-ups with people when you have absolutely nothing new to report and nobody else you can talk about. She can't know how such interactions leave you exposed, with nowhere to hide, and when you think it can't get any more painful, then comes the pitying stare. *No partner, no children, how sad*, you can see them thinking. Then they feel embarrassed for you and they try to say something that will make you feel better, like: 'Oh well, you've still got your freedom. Do you do a lot of travelling?' (no, not really) or 'Haven't met the right one yet, hey?' which sounds ever more ridiculous the further I get into my fifties. Then, almost imperceptibly, their mind shifts to thinking, *No partner, no children, how weird* ... and they look at you like you are an unanswered question. You are residing at the destination they spent their whole adult lives ensuring they didn't arrive at. Every divorce, every pregnancy, every relationship they took a chance on, every bad decision they ever made, at least took them on a different path than the one that led here – to being an undefined woman in a world fixated with definitions. If only Prof would hurry up and be ready for our relationship to properly begin, then this awful feeling of living in limbo would be but a distant memory.

But I couldn't say any of this to Millie, of course. I picked up my bag and said we'd miss the beginning of the film if we didn't get a move on and she made a slightly barbed comment, which I ignored, about being surprised I was so keen to see George Clooney; it's not like her to be sarcastic.

The film was better than I had expected and I tried to enjoy it, but my mind kept flitting back to Lola. Every time a woman came on screen I saw something to remind me of Lola's hair, or eyes or voice. I got an unpleasant, uncomfortable feeling when I recalled the way she'd sat talking to Prof, so animated and passionate about her research and I hadn't liked the way he'd looked at her. I kept going over it in my head, trying to work out whether his enthusiasm was purely to do with her thesis or whether it was about her as a person.

No! I know I am being silly. I must stop this. She is not his type physically at all, far too buxom and earthy. But she does have an attractive face with those wide, high cheekbones and those ice-blue eyes. She reminds me of a Scandinavian milkmaid, if there is such a thing, and a saucy one at that. Certainly not an academic in any shape or form. She is also probably married or in a relationship, and she definitely has at least one child. I think long blonde hair simply triggers an unconscious response in men and they are attracted to the woman without any real reason. These days, with extensions and colourists and so on, anyone can have hair like that. My goodness, how often have I seen the most slender, beautifully dressed women with manes of perfect long blonde hair walking ahead of me in the richer parts of London, turning heads from passing men, only to catch a glance of their face and realise with a shock that they are in their sixties or even seventies. It's the hair that does it. Imagine Lola bald or with a crewcut: Prof wouldn't give her the time of day.

All this ruminating over hair meant that I lost the thread of the film halfway through and then had the uncomfortable reality check of realising I was sitting in a large dark room full of strangers, watching a made-up story. The suspension of disbelief should not be taken for granted.

'Are you all right?' Millie asked, cocking her head to one side as we stood waiting for our buses afterwards 'You're very quiet.'

'Yes, why wouldn't I be?'

'Oh, don't be so spikey, Sylvia, I'm only asking because I care about you. You seem a bit distracted tonight, that's all. Do you want to come back to ours and Kamal can drop you home later?'

Absolutely not! I don't want Kamal within a hundred yards of me. He makes my skin crawl, was what I wanted to say. But I sufficed with a small smile and reassured her I'd be fine, but thanks anyway, just tired.

'I'm sorry about the Neil thing, darling. I did think you might like each other.' She put her hand on my arm and I shrugged it off and stared at the pavement.

Millie's bus came first and as she stepped on she turned around and shoved a book into my bag. 'I wanted to give you this, it might help,' she blustered as she tried to give me a hug.

The bus had pulled away by the time I had retrieved it. It was a flimsy paperback with a dumpy middle-aged woman on the front holding a flower, entitled *You and the Menopause: Surviving the Change.* Typical of my sister to assume she knows me better than I know myself. I hastily shoved it back in my bag before anyone else at the bus stop saw it. That change happened relatively smoothly several years ago and I certainly didn't need a book to help me survive it. The only change I am interested in at the moment is getting Lola out of Prof's life and out of mine. Permanently.

Tuesday 20 October

I have been searching through Lola's personnel and academic files trying to get a handle on who exactly she is and what she's about. Basic information: she is a thirty-three-year-old single mother of an eight-year-old boy. She has very good undergraduate and Master's degrees in Sociology from a prestigious university back in her native Ireland. She is currently working part-time as a lecturer at a local sixth form college and is enrolled on the PhD here with Prof as her supervisor. Because of her 'amazing' MA dissertation she has got a bursary from the university to do the PhD and this pays her fees and some travel and living expenses too, but obviously not enough for her to give up her job. Her next of kin is her mother, so no partner on the scene. She doesn't have any disabilities or special needs, but she is allergic to nuts and keeps an epi-pen with her at all times. We are also required to keep one in the office for health and safety reasons. She dropped it in yesterday, looking flustered and embarrassed. She had her little boy with her as it was some sort of teaching training day at his school – he is called Ned and is rather cute with glasses and messy brown hair. He stood at the corner of my desk, munching his way through a bag of jelly babies, watching me eat my quinoa salad with concern.

'Is that all you have for lunch?' he asked me. Then he offered me one of his sweets, which I politely declined.

I noticed Lola reach into her bag and stuff a chocolate biscuit into her mouth as she was leaving, saying to Ned that she was starving. She really could do with losing a bit of weight. She is not fat as such, but she is definitely curvy, with big wobbly boobs that seem constantly on the verge of falling out of her top. It annoys me when women just eat whatever they want and don't try to stay slim and elegant. I have spent most of my adult life controlling and limiting what I eat to ensure that I don't go over a size eight. Eating too much has been a constant source of anxiety to me, not to the extent of having an eating disorder, but enough to be aware of everything I eat and how many calories it contains and never allowing myself to go over 1300 calories a day. Ever. Additionally, two days a week I only eat 500 calories and once a month I do a weekend juice fast.

Jonas finds my eating habits perplexing. For him food, the sweeter the better, is to be enjoyed as often as possible. In all the years I have volunteered at that sanctuary never once have I eaten a biscuit, cake, scone or toffee but that doesn't stop him from offering me at least one of those items every time I go there and then looking surprised when I decline. Paula was just as rotund and used to show her love by baking for him,

I gather, so it doesn't take much to work out why he comfort eats.

But I know Prof loves skinny women, so I don't mind sacrificing food for being slender. It's part of how I show that I love him, demonstrates my commitment to him. If I ever feel hungry or start to crave sweet things or crisps I think of him and enjoy the denial. I suppose that's what is meant by 'love is suffering', and I am happy to suffer for him. Martha is a stick insect. Prof adored her edgy look; he had photos of her all over his office until this most final split, and for a while I thought about trying to emulate it. I even got my hair cut into a bob, but I looked like an ageing schoolgirl, so I wore it in a bun until it had grown shoulder-length again. Clothes-wise, I can't carry off high fashion and killer heels. I have my own subtle but expensive way of dressing, with silk blouses and cashmere cardigans and knee-length skirts or well-cut suits in muted blues and greys, which I feel is much more becoming to my role and personality. I always wear matching underwear as well, even though Prof doesn't see it. At the weekends, I'm more relaxed about how I dress; I've even been known to spend the weekend in my pyjamas after I get back from the sanctuary, reading old articles and books by Prof. But for work, for Prof, I love to make the effort.

Like today, for example. It was the monthly departmental finance meeting so I dressed carefully in my pale-pink silk blouse and plum suit, with a string of pearls round my neck for an elegant touch. I always feel a responsibility to turn out nicely for these events as my appearance and demeanour reflect on Prof. I am, after all, his personal assistant, and if I look shabby, colleagues may assume we aren't running a tight ship over in Darwin building, and that would never do. I love to see Prof suited and booted for these formal gatherings. He usually wears his charcoal grey Italian single-breasted suit with a sharp white shirt (he gets them professionally laundered) and a cerise or silver and black striped tie. Today, however, he was dressed in a double-breasted navy suit that I hadn't seen before, a light-blue shirt and a dark-red tie. He looked divine and I had the absolute pleasure of sitting next to him. It was a 9 a.m. meeting and he still smelled of his morning shower gel, a lemony, minty scent that I will try and remember and track down to buy for myself. His hair was slicked back with wax, giving it a slightly damp look, and his cheeks were flushed pink from his morning shave. I breathed him in as I organised my notebook and pen, ready to take the minutes.

'Coffee, is there coffee?' Prof craned his neck irritably to look round the room and creased his brow in displeasure as he realised the vital drink was missing. I jumped up, rushed out the door and down the corridor to the kitchen. The catering girl was leaning against the counter in the narrow galley texting on her phone, her mouth chewing steadily on gum, a tray of cups beside her on the side. She looked up lazily as I strode in and then back to her phone.

'Where is the tea and coffee for the meeting room? Is it ready? There should be pastries too.' It was my fault, really, as it's my responsibility to ensure everything in the room is ready before the faculty arrives. I didn't know how I had overlooked this. I had been so focused on making sure I had copied the agenda and the relevant paperwork for everyone that I had forgotten to check the catering had been delivered.

'Yeah, it's all on the side, I was just going to bring it.' She still couldn't draw her eyes away from the screen and I could feel my anger rising.

'They have already started. It needs to be there by ten to. This is completely unacceptable.' My voice trembled with fury.

'All right, love, wind your neck in, I'm just coming.' She sniffed loudly, not even slightly perturbed by my tone. 'I just need to send this text.'

I snatched the phone off her and it was as if I had flicked an invisible switch, changing her mood from bored insolence to pure rage. 'What the hell do you think you're doing, you stupid old cow?' She grabbed for the phone and I held it out of her reach, forcing her to take a step towards me. She was so close now I could see the pale roots of her dyed black hair, the sloppily covered spots on her reddening face, and smell her greasy body odour.

'Get the catering delivered to the meeting room immediately.' My voice shook as I tried to assert my authority, realising with a fearful start that I may have picked a fight with someone with vastly different personal boundaries of behaviour than myself. She lunged towards me and I gave a little yelp as I stepped back, bumping into a large, solid person behind me.

'What on earth is going on in here?' It was Prof, filling the doorway of the little kitchen, a look of exasperation on his face. 'Sylvia?'

I hastily gave the girl back her phone and she stood glowering at me.

'She's a nutcase, that woman. She stole my phone!' She held the item right up to Prof's face as if he needed clarification of what she was referring to.

'Sylvia?' he said again in confusion.

'She was texting, we needed the coffee, she is totally incompetent at her job, lazy and rude ...' She lunged for me again and Prof put his arm between us.

'Look, I don't know what is going on here but I need to get back to the meeting. I will speak to you about this later, Sylvia. And ... what's your name?' He noticed her identity badge. 'Janine, I will be speaking to your manager. Sue, isn't it?' Janine nodded meekly, used to a man in authority taking control, looking for all the world like the naughty schoolgirl she undoubtedly used to be.

'Now, can we have this damn coffee and get on?' He picked up the tray himself and stormed off down the corridor. I shot the now deflated Janine a poisonous look, grabbed the platter of mini Danish pastries and trotted after him, mentally constructing my defence as I went.

Prof, consummate professional that he is, showed no indication that the fracas in the kitchen had perturbed him at all and chaired the meeting with his usual combination of efficiency, diplomacy and humour. I kept my head down and took the minutes diligently, not daring to look in his direction. The last item on the agenda concerned funding for PhD students to go to international conferences. The recurrence and subsequent rejection of this issue that came up at every finance meeting was something of a long-standing joke and I waited with pen poised to note the latest reason for vetoing this possibility before we moved on to any other business and the close of the meeting. Mine was not the only head to shoot up in surprise when Prof announced that we would be welcoming a student representative to put forward the case for such funding and then there would follow a vote on whether to take it forward.

'Could you go and fetch Miss Maguire, please, Sylvia. She should be waiting outside.' I got up like an automaton and walked across the room. I could see her blonde hair through the glass in the door and, as I opened it, the whiff of her musky perfume caused a wave of nausea that I had to swallow down.

'Come in, Lola,' I said and she flounced past me without saying thank you.

I closed the door and went to go back to my seat then realised that Lola had already sat herself down in it. I glanced urgently at Prof. Surely he wouldn't allow that? He must have seen that I was still there. But he said nothing and instead launched into a fawning introduction of Lola as an 'outstanding doctoral student' and a complicated explanation of why her research needed to be presented at the upcoming conference in Rome. I stood awkwardly by the door, waiting for his proposal to be rejected by the faculty members, but some were already nodding earnestly, Dr Bastow and Dr Kofi staring at Lola's cleavage in the inappropriately low-cut top she had chosen to wear this morning.

'Can we hear from Ms Maguire, please?' I could have cheered for Professor Scott with her grey bun and half-moon specs who was clearly not ready to acquiesce solely on the basis of Lola's physical appearance.

Prof waved his hand theatrically in Lola's direction and Lola widened her eyes and cleared her throat before addressing the room, hesitantly at first and then, with frequent glances at Prof for reassurance, with more confidence.

'The conference in Rome is about social class and education. It is a large conference with people, erm, I mean, delegates from all over the world.' She paused and then added unnecessarily, 'It's an international conference.'

'Yes, most are,' Professor Scott said, not unkindly. 'Could you please explain to us why it is important that you attend.' She picked up her pen expectantly, smiled, and looked at Lola over the rim of her glasses.

'It's, erm, I mean, my research is in that area.'

'Go on.'

'I am exploring how the use of language in the home impacts on the educational attainment of children in the English school system and comparing this to a similar cohort in Germany.'

'And do you speak German, Ms Maguire?'

'Yes, I do.' Lola was gaining momentum now. 'My mother is German, so I speak it fluently and I think it is important to compare the educational experiences of children in different countries.' Professor Scott raised her eyes in anticipation of further elucidation. 'In relation to restricted codes – that is, the limited vocabulary and literacy levels some children start school with and how this may affect their final exam results when they leave school.'

She had pressed the right button with Imogen Scott by mentioning young children and she beamed at Lola.

'Yes, literacy in the early years is vitally important. What an interesting project. I can see why this will be of relevance to the conference. Professor Lomax,' she said, turning to Prof, 'I assume you will also be attending?

We don't want one of our new academics all at sea; an accompanying mentor would be most helpful.'

'Most certainly, Imogen. I will hold her hand all the way.'

Everyone laughed, Lola loudest of all, and I looked on with dismay as the table agreed unanimously that if her paper was accepted then Lola should be funded to attend the Rome conference with Prof, and started to gather their papers together ready for the end of the meeting.

'But ... but ...'

'Yes, Sylvia?' Imogen turned towards me.

'We have never done this before ... I mean, there is no form for this funding.' I tailed off, realising how pathetic I sounded.

'Well, let's not allow the lack of a form to stand in the way of sharing significant research with the international academic community, eh Sylvia?' Dr Bastow said, as he stood and reached for his coat, his eyes glued to Lola's cleavage.

There were a few quiet guffaws at that and I felt my cheeks redden as I gathered up the paperwork. The temptation to note on the minutes that Lola's request for funding had been rejected was strong, but I knew it was a fait accompli. This wasn't a decision that could get forgotten in a pile of papers or lose its way en route to the finance office. Prof was expecting Lola to accompany him to Rome and accompany him she would. To add to the sting, it would be my job to book her place at the conference and organise her travel and hotel arrangements.

'Lola, once we know that your paper has definitely been accepted by the conference committee, Sylvia will sort everything out for you.' Myself, Prof and Lola were the last people in the room and they were glowing with their success. 'Just tell her when you want to travel and so on. Well done. You presented your case articulately and you deserve this opportunity.' He patted her on the shoulder and they held what seemed to be an inappropriately long and happy look.

As Lola gathered her things and left, I was caught between wanting to linger and spend a few moments alone with Prof and being anxious that he would reprimand me about the earlier squabble with the tea girl.

'I'm sorry about earlier, in the kitchen,' I muttered, hoping to diffuse any residual anger he might still have about the incident.

'What?' He looked at me blankly.

'The tea girl in the kitchen, the phone … the coffee. It got a bit out of hand, but really, she was rude and incompetent.'

'Oh yes, yes,' Prof waved his hand dismissively. 'Let's not have anything like that again.' I opened my mouth to explain my position further but he had already walked out the door.

I sat in the empty meeting room, the polished mahogany table covered with the usual detritus of a meeting and covered my eyes with my palms feeling a headache coming on. In one foul swoop Lola had been elevated from lowly student status to being on an equal footing with the academics in the department and now I was expected to serve her as I served them. I lifted my palms and looked with disdain at her empty coffee cup, the rim smeared with red lipstick and the half-eaten pastry in the saucer. Every fibre in my being wanted to walk out the room and leave the mess behind, but I knew I couldn't and calling the tea girl to come and clear it away was definitely not an option. I collected the crockery and rubbish onto one of the trays and carried it back down towards the kitchen.

Lola was standing a few metres along, blocking my way, talking animatedly to an entranced Dr Kofi about how thrilled she was to be studying under Prof. I stood behind her for several moments waiting for her to finish and move or at least for her to sense my presence, but she didn't or pretended not to. 'Excuse me,' I had to say in the end and she still didn't acknowledge me, just moved slightly towards Dr Kofi so I could squeeze through the gap with my laden tray. I felt like a skivvy and burned with indignation as I made my way to the kitchen and almost threw the tray onto the counter. The cups rattled, but none fell off and I turned on my heel and walked straight out, leaving the washing-up to somebody else. I saw her waiting for the lift at the end of the corridor so turned right instead and took the stairs back up to the third floor. She was already waiting by my desk as I arrived, flushed and annoyed, a few minutes later.

I sat down and turned on my computer, ignoring her as she had ignored me.

'Sylvia,' she said in a sing-song voice, a trace of humour in her tone. She waited until I finally looked up at her.

She was smiling broadly, still thrilled by her success in the meeting room. 'I need to talk to you about registering for the Rome conference.'

I stared at her without speaking and then turned back to my computer.

'I can't do it now. I'm too busy. You'll have to email me the completed form.' I carried on typing and refused to look up until I heard the door close and was sure she had gone.

'You really are—' Margaret began in an admonishing tone, but was cut short by her phone ringing, saving me the trouble of telling her to mind her own business.

Friday 23 October

I endured an excruciating evening out tonight with Shona and a couple of others from the old 'gang' organised by Millie. Dear lord, I love my sister but I do wish that, just for once, she could let an opportunity for socialising pass her by. Her urge to be involved in as many people's lives as possible leaves me stone cold, I'm afraid, and it was precisely as awful as I had anticipated.

I arrived ten minutes late and was still the first one there, completely typical of my history of meeting up with this group. The bar was one of a chain that, for some reason, seem to be designed to emulate Victorian workhouses, with scrubbed wooden tables, plain white walls and bucket-like chrome lights. I still can't get used to the smell of bars and pubs these days, all pine disinfectant at the beginning of the evening and horrible body odours and emissions at the end. I preferred it when everything smelt of cigarettes – at least it felt properly adult.

I was just getting over the shock of my vodka and tonic being served to me in a jam jar (a jam jar! I must remember to tell Prof; that's just the sort of pretension that would amuse him) when Millie and Kamal walked in hand in hand. Millie was beaming at me, Kamal, half a step behind her, was giving me a death stare as usual. The cheek of him, always acting as if I am the enemy when it was both of us who betrayed Millie.

'Are they here yet?' Millie asked eagerly as she shrugged off a fascinating hat and poncho combination in garish yellow.

'Not yet,' I replied. 'Are you joining us as well, Kamal?' I knew he wasn't; he hadn't even sat down, let alone taken off his coat.

'No, no,' he muttered, giving no reason or apology. Typically bloody rude.

'You know he hates loud music, Sylvia. See you later, darling.' Millie pulled Kamal down for a kiss, during which he somehow managed to give me another angry glare, which I did my best to ignore.

'Have fun,' he said touching her face. 'Call me when you are ready to come home.'

He hurried out, bumping briefly into Shona who was on her way in. Always one for a big entrance, Shona stood in the doorway squealing with excitement, waving manically at Millie who rushed over to give her an enormous hug as if she'd just been let out of prison. It was pathetic, actually – two grown women behaving like schoolgirls. I sipped my drink nonchalantly, hoping nobody was watching. I had unwittingly chosen the worst seat at the table, directly opposite a huge mirror. I have never understood why they do that in bars – who on earth wants to see the harsh reality of what they look like after a couple of drinks?

I was shocked at how old I looked in that environment. In my regular life, at work, at home, I am used to the mirrors and the lighting and it's hard to see any definite changes on a day-to-day basis. But it had been so long since I'd sat in a bar with make-up on and the cracks really have started to show. There is a tiredness around my eyes that no amount of sleep ever seems to remedy, and my forehead is, if not lined, then certainly more bony than it used to be as the layer of youthful, plumping fat has disappeared – one of the few drawbacks of dieting, unfortunately. Thanks to my regular use of 'honey-brown' dye there is no grey in my hair, but it's not shiny, any more, and my neck is simply old, no disguising it. I am still thin, though, whippet-thin as Father used to say, although I do sometimes worry it may make me look rather androgynous, especially next to curvy women like Lola.

I used to go out with this group a lot when we were in our twenties and early thirties. They were Millie's friends, really, Emma and Shona from school and Tig, Shazia and Annabel from art college. We had the usual fun, I suppose, although I was always somewhat on the outside of the clique. All of us were single and navigating the ups and downs of dating. It seemed like a game, really, the possibility of being left alone and old was a distant and unreal destination that none of us actually believed we'd ever reach. Our regular Friday night round-ups of the week's dating triumphs and disasters were particularly entertaining. I wasn't as ribald and open as some of the girls, especially Emma and Tig – my goodness, their sex lives were enough to make anyone blush – but I usually had something to throw in the ring for the group to have a giggle over: being asked on a date by my dentist, for example, or getting a bunch of red roses sent to me from the man who came round to fix my boiler. There were so many available men back then. There was usually someone on the scene who you liked or who liked you, or very occasionally both, and when one was pulled offstage – returning to a childhood sweetheart or backpacking round the world – another one or two would appear in their place.

When it comes to actual relationships, though, my experience is quite limited. I went out with Stewart at university. Boring, dependable, reliable, mechanical engineer Stewart. I met him in Fresher's week and we didn't break up until two years after graduation when he suddenly announced he didn't love me any more, and disappeared to China to teach English. I wasn't overly heartbroken. He was more of a security blanket than a great passion, to be honest, and there was always the nagging feeling that I was missing out, especially when I saw the fun Millie was having being single with her friends. She was still at art college then, a much funkier place than the solid, middle-class university I had chosen. She was always dyeing her hair wacky colours and having different bits of herself pierced and wearing crazy clothes.

Our mother couldn't have looked more disapproving. She has always treated Millie's eccentricities like a mystery that she can see no point in solving and continues to be bemused by her to this day. I was more of a recognisable quantity. Mother could see in me the essential suburban regularity and provincial reserve that have always guided her manner and behaviour. Stewart fitted well into this, until he couldn't stand it any longer and wanted some adventure.

I wanted adventure too. I wanted to be more like Millie, I suppose, in the way she looked and how she was always so relaxed with men, but I didn't have the courage to risk rejection or social embarrassment. Being in her shadow was a nice compromise for me. I could enjoy her eventful love life vicariously, and could experiment a little with make-up and clothes without having to fully become that person or claim that lifestyle. Millie didn't seem to mind, although a couple of her friends made snide comments to me occasionally which I ignored. She is such an inclusive person, if you want to be around her then she will make you welcome, that's her way, that's what makes her so adorable and so loved by everyone. That's how we passed our twenties and early thirties really, although by the time we hit our thirties the group had pared down to the four of us who were still single – me, Millie, Emma and Tig, the Friday night crowd.

It didn't really seem to matter what I did as a job back then as I naively assumed that eventually I would find 'the one', get married and that that would define me and be my life. I remember the flood of relief when I thought I had met him at last. Eugene was such a flirt and all the women loved him. He was the office manager at the college I worked at before I got my present job, and he was an absolute sweetheart. Or so I thought until the day I found some horribly explicit images on his hard drive and dropped him like a burning coal. That was around the time Millie went to India and brought Kamal back with her like the ultimate holiday souvenir.

It all changed very quickly after that and the girlie camaraderie and Friday nights out started to dwindle. Somehow, subtly, over the course of that year when I turned thirty-five, my world changed, and suddenly it wasn't about having everything to look forward to any more, having it all ahead of me. It was about a disturbing new feeling of being left behind and past my prime. A new younger generation of women seemed to be taking centre stage in the bars and clubs, rising up from the ranks of their career-driven mid-twenties, ready to bag themselves a serious relationship before they hit the big three-o.

They seemed shinier, with glossier hair, whiter teeth and more fashionable clothes. The music I listened to and loved and associated with going out became retro rather than current.

That year things changed for everyone. Millie had Kamal, Tig went on tour with her repertory company, Emma got a nursing job in Australia, Annabel got engaged to a car salesman called Lance and moved to Eastbourne, and Shazia married her on-off boyfriend, immediately fell pregnant, and joined Shona in the ranks of the smug yummy mummies. It was as if, in those short few months, my life closed up behind my back and refused to reopen. It felt as if everyone had held hands and crossed a secret line that nobody had told me about. I was alone, really alone, for the first time in my adult life. I was happy for Millie that she had Kamal, but when things turned so unpleasant between him and me it made it difficult to spend as much time with her, especially if he was there.

I tried to meet someone of my own, rather half-heartedly attending speed-dating events and salsa classes, but I was horribly self-conscious and it was all too deliberate somehow. This wasn't how it was supposed to be. I wanted the romance, the perfect man to pursue me – and for me to feel special and desired, not desperate and trying too hard. I remember that the sting of feeling like a failure in love hit me particularly hard at the christening of Shona and Ian's youngest son.

'Don't leave it too late, Sylvia,' Shona's mum warned me in an important voice as she cradled her latest grandchild. 'I know what you career girls are like, but there's nothing like having a newborn in your arms to make you realise what matters in life.' She cooed at the baby as I stared at her, wondering how anyone could be so unintentionally spiteful. She looked up and nodded at me as if she had shared some profound, rare wisdom and I went off to find the bar as I experienced for the first time, but definitely not the last, the disconcerting sensation of being an outsider in my own life. At home that evening I set up an internet dating profile, determined to get back into the kind of life that made sense to me and everyone else.

How on earth can you describe yourself in words without sounding as though you are trying to sell yourself? It was humiliating, the whole process. I didn't feel excited about it, I felt sick to my stomach that my life had come to this. I posted my profile on the site, nonetheless, and responses from men started to trickle in. I met a few of them for coffee or lunch but never felt any special connection and, more often than not, felt utterly repulsed by their self-satisfied boasting or, worse, nervous attempts at conversation or clumsy sexual overtures. There was one man, Geoff, who seemed all right and we went out a couple of times, but then he just stopped calling and texting and I saw him back up on the dating site looking for someone new. That was another kick in the teeth and left me wondering: What did I do wrong? Why did he lose interest? I considered emailing him and asking, and in a way I wish I had, but my pride wouldn't let me, not for someone as bland as him. I wasn't going to give him the ego boost of thinking that I cared if he wanted me or not.

I managed to convince myself that Geoff had saved me the trouble of extricating myself from our burgeoning relationship, but it still stung and my self-esteem was battered and bruised. Sometimes I wonder if that rejection was part of the reason why I lost all judgement and made my huge mistake with Kamal several weeks later, although I'm not sure I will ever fully understand why I did it. After that unforgivable incident, and what happened afterwards, I decided I would never waste time on any other man who wasn't worthy of me. I would wait until I found my absolute perfect match and then I would do everything in my power to make him mine, whilst protecting my pride and the depth of my emotional neediness. Next time I would be in complete control and would not put myself in a position to be rejected or hurt. And then, the semester after I started my new job at the university, as if by magic, Prof appeared.

The first time I saw him he was being shown around by the departing professor, Linda Kapoor, a tiny, harried woman who seemed perpetually surprised and rather overwhelmed by the success of her academic career and who, one suspected, had long been counting down the years and days until her retirement. Prof could not have been more of a contrast, both in his strong, imposing physicality and in his laid-back, confident manner. I had my back to the office, watering the plants on the windowsill, when I heard them come in, Professor Kapoor wittering on about door codes and broken lifts and tea-making facilities. I smelt him before I saw him. His aftershave surrounded me in a wave of masculine, musky scent that made my knees go weak.

'And this is Sylvia Penton who will be your personal assistant.'

I paused for a second, composing myself, before I turned around.

'Very pleased to meet you, Sylvia.' Prof was already holding out his hand by the time I faced him and he shook mine firmly, looking me straight in the eye as if we already knew and liked each other. My impression was of a bear of a man, heavyset, the sort of man who fills a room, with a voice to match. He had a weather-beaten tanned face (he had just returned from skiing, I later discovered), light brown eyes and jet-black hair with the odd touch of grey, swept back from his forehead in a style that Millie would have described as oily, but which to me seemed sweetly old-fashioned. He was what my father would have described as a man's man. And to make him even more perfect, he was wearing a beautifully cut slate-grey suit with a crisp white shirt and a navy striped tie, making him that rarest of breeds: the well-dressed academic.

I could feel the blush rising from my neck all up my face, and managed only a muttered 'pleased to meet you'. And then, to my absolute shame, and for reasons I can't fathom, I held up the watering can and said, 'I'm watering the plants.'

Prof smiled at me and nodded as you would to a small child, and Professor Kapoor whisked him on through the dividing door into what was to be his office.

I sat down at my desk, burning with humiliation and lust and fear and joy and forced myself to calm down using one of Millie's breathing techniques – blue in, red out, repeat. Mercifully they were in there a long while, going through departmental procedures and the status of various PhD students. After about half an hour Professor Kapoor swung the door open and asked me to bring them coffee and I took the opportunity to present myself in a more collected, demure manner which I hope I have sustained to this day. But inside, my goodness, what he does to me is beyond compare.

That's what Prof gives me really, an interior life, a connection to my emotions and heart and soul that I don't get from any other aspect of my existence. He is the essence of me, of the life and love I deserve. The way I feel about him is purer and simpler than I have ever felt about anyone else – even Millie, whom I adore, but who regularly drives me mad with her scattiness and lack of self-control. That's how I know we are meant to be together and, on a good day, I don't care how long I have to wait. In fact, the waiting and the anticipation is delicious and my imagination has an absolute field day creating future scenarios for us in my mind. He makes me happy, that's the truth of it, and my love for him shields me from the pain of being with others who pity me. I smile inside, with my secret keeping me warm, and I pity other women the compromises they have had to make in their relationships with men who don't hold a candle to Prof.

For example, I noticed that over the course of the evening Shona never once mentioned Ian. Imagine not wanting to talk about your beloved and say his name as often as possible? She couldn't shut up about her children's achievements, though (she didn't mention Beth's tattoos so, kindly, neither did I), and, horror of horrors, her oldest son Tom has made her a grandmother to boot. We had to endure picture after picture of a nondescript baby being held up by various family members as Shona trilled on about his daily routine as if it was some kind of a miracle that the child ate and slept. I don't know how I kept the benign smile plastered on my face, really I don't. Emma came too. She has become the most pathetic type of bored housewife – mother of two indifferent teenagers with a golf-mad husband and a heavy hand for pouring Chardonnay.

The only interesting part of the evening was when Tig swung by on her way home from the theatre. I was fascinated by how little she has changed over the years – still the short, edgy peroxide-blonde hair, black eyeliner and leather jacket. The trainers, watch and handbag are now of the super expensive variety, though, and even the fine lines covering her face don't detract from her famously high cheekbones and feline eyes. She is still a beautiful woman, there's no doubt about that, and I wondered if she was still a complete bitch as well.

'Tamsin Iglesias, as I live and breathe!' Millie was quite drunk by this stage in the evening and gave Tig a kind of military salute as she sat down.

'Hi, Mills, girls.' Tig always was a cool customer, not big on showy emotions or the over-the-top gushing that you'd expect from a theatrical type. She was forever having secret affairs with exciting men when I knew her, and not in the least bit interested in settling down or having children. I remember the first time she found out she was pregnant, having had a fling with a famous, married actor. She arranged the termination with all the emotion of taking her car in for a service, a slightly inconvenient but necessary procedure. I was shocked at her pragmatism and the way she refused to entertain any doubt at all about what she was doing. But that's Tig. She's not the sentimental type and that's always been her strength – she just does what she wants to do and doesn't feel guilty about it. Tig has a way of glancing around when she's speaking that makes you feel like she's telling you a secret even when she's sharing something quite ordinary. Her deep, husky voice and laugh are a permanent reminder of how she used to chain smoke Marlboros, always lit with a gold Zippo lighter that she handled constantly. This has now been replaced, at least indoors, by her smartphone. It never left her hand the whole time she was with us, her attention taken unapologetically by constant beeps and alerts, just like Crystal and her friends.

To my dismay, and to Millie's absolute glee, Emma had brought a whole sheaf of photos from what she called our party days and placed each one in the middle of the table in turn, to be exclaimed and marvelled over. There we all were, dressed up in platform boots and flares for a 1970s retro night at the Clapham Grand. There we all were again, in Santa hats, for a Christmas party in Camden. There was Millie, Tig, me and Shona on the deck of a cross-channel ferry on a booze cruise to France (minus Emma who took the picture). And us again, outside the Hyper Marché with Tig in the trolley on top of half-a-dozen crates of wine, swigging from a bottle of champagne. I looked happy, I suppose, although I often found situations of such forced gaiety a strain and part of me would have preferred to be at home with a good book. I was only there because Millie always invited me; I could never have made or kept such lively friends myself. Life was certainly more fun and unpredictable then, but I think it's only really the young who consider that to be a good thing. I suppose being young didn't suit me, if I'm honest. I like to know what's going to happen and I like to feel in control and I don't have a natural silliness or quirkiness like Millie. The one thing I did love about being young was the feeling of having plenty of time ahead, that life was full of opportunities and possibilities. It's difficult to pinpoint the exact moment when 'what could be' becomes 'what could have been' – it's another disagreeable facet of getting older that nobody warns you about and that can only be recognised in retrospect. Thank goodness, in matters of the heart at least, that I am still in the realms of future possibility with Prof.

'And here you are, Mills, back from India with your handsome beau! My goodness, you both look incredible.' Emma held the picture close to her face to fully appreciate their youthful beauty before putting it on the table. I gasped when I saw it, but managed to turn it into a cough, and nobody was taking any particular notice of my reactions anyway. Millie was thrilled by the image and so she should have been. Her fingers traced the outline of Kamal's face and she drifted into a blissful, drunken ramble.

'Looking at this brings back that feeling of being totally happy – you know, when just for a brief time everything is perfect in your life and it all feels *right*, like you have found the truth and even then there is this underlying scary feeling because you know that you will never be this happy ever again. Do you know what I mean?' She looked around the table for signs of agreement and recognition and I copied the wistful smiles and nods, feeling, as usual, that I had somehow missed, through carelessness or bad luck, a huge portion of the happiness and emotional fulfilment that others seemed to take for granted.

I drank in every detail of that photo. It showed Millie at the thinnest she had ever been, with the darkest tan she had ever had – a honey glow that contrasted with her bright blonde curls, white teeth and blue eyes. She had on a coral-colour vest top, faded denim shorts and a patterned blue scarf tied round her hair. She was standing on one leg, clinging onto Kamal's arm with both hands, gazing up at him with a wide, delighted smile, heady with love. Kamal stood barefoot next to her, smiling just as broadly. With his wide shoulders and slim hips, clad in a white T-shirt and baggy jeans, he looked like a member of a boy band. I had forgotten how his skin was golden brown in those days, not the sallow olive it is now, and his eyes flashed with a joyful, playful energy. They were in Mother's garden and the little folding table next to them, set with teacups and sponge cakes, so English in its mundanity, made them look like exotic creatures from another planet, the like of which Harrow had never seen.

Looking closely, I saw a familiar pale hand, my hand, reaching in from outside the picture towards Kamal, like a spectre from the underworld, ready to drag him out of Millie's life. It was with some relief that I realised I was actually reaching for the teapot, me with the boring task, outside the action as usual. I stared hard at that image of Kamal, as if he were a complete stranger, until Emma placed the next picture down on top of it, of her and Millie dressed up to the nines at Shona's wedding. Even then I could still see the top of his head behind it, the Ray-Bans he always used to wear pushed up on top of his wavy black hair. The same pair of sunglasses that he had left at my flat the day he came round to help me carry my new television up the stairs a few months later. The day when everything changed forever because of what we did.

'Oh, wow, do you remember this, darling? Do you remember how cold it was?' Millie pulled me out of my reverie, flapping a photo in front of my eyes.

'I can't see it that close,' I snapped, pushing her hand away.

Millie looked hurt and I could sense that I had killed the mood. I tried to compensate by enthusing over the picture of the two of us on the top deck of a tour bus in New York, wrapped up in woolly hats and scarfs, but she had already turned her attention away from me and towards the more fun people present.

Whilst Millie went about persuading Shona and Emma to do tequila shots, Tig asked me about where I work now and it turns out that she knows awful Martha a little bit from when her gallery provided some art for the set of a production Tig was working on last summer. I was very careful not to express any particular reaction to this intriguing revelation and mined her for information as subtly as I could. According to Tig, at a recent get-together, Martha had told them all that her husband was a bastard who had had his latest affair with the au pair and that she had thrown him out and good riddance to bad rubbish. Tig recounted this with delight, her eyes shining – she always did admire the bad boys. I could feel the red anger rising as she relayed this nonsense and had to swallow down my urgent impulse to defend Prof and set her straight on what really happened with Martha and the architect. I managed to nod nonchalantly and simply commented that there were two sides to every story before I made my excuses (an early start) and left.

'It was nice to see you, Sylvia,' Shona said politely as I put my jacket on, but she didn't suggest meeting up again, which suits me fine. As I opened the door to leave, I could hear them all laughing raucously behind me as they downed their tequilas, but I know that they weren't laughing at me. Millie wouldn't allow that.

Saturday 24 October

It was quite a relief to go to the sanctuary this morning. I don't have to put any effort into socialising with Jonas. We fed the hogs in the usual order, starting with the bottom cage nearest the door, and I let Jonas tell me yet again that we do it like that so that no one gets forgotten. Then we chatted a little about the animals and the garden over tea – I simply didn't have the energy to try and engage him in another dead-end discussion about educational research. In a lull moment, I looked around at the various hedgehog-related posters and postcards on the wall he has accumulated over the years and commented on one I had often read but never really thought about.

'Where is that quote from, Jonas?' I asked. '"The fox knows many things; the hedgehog one big thing". What does it mean?'

'It's by an ancient Greek poet called Archilochus,' Jonas replied at once, comfortably slipping into his English-teacher persona. 'No one knows for sure exactly what Archilochus meant by it, of course – he's been dead a long time – but it's sometimes used as a theoretical term in economics to explain why some people and businesses succeed by being flexible and open to new ways – like the fox, you see – and why others succeed, or fail, by just sticking to what they know and what they do best … like our hogs.

'I've also heard it used to explain why hedgehogs get run over so much more often than foxes.' He took a sip of tea for lubrication, wiped his mouth with his hankie, and continued, 'It's because when hogs have found a route from A to B they will keep on going the same way even if it turns out to be a dangerous road, but a fox will always keep trying different routes and so is safer. The fox learns from experience, you see, whereas hogs don't so much. I think that perhaps it's because they can ball up when they sense a threat, so maybe they don't feel they have to use a lot of energy to avoid danger altogether.'

I listened in stunned silence. It was the most Jonas had ever spoken in one go, and by far the most interesting thing he had ever said.

'That's of no use when it comes to keeping safe from traffic though, of course,' he added thoughtfully after a pause, nodding in the direction of our latest hedgehog in-patient.

'How's he doing?' I asked.

'Not so good,' replied Jonas with a frown. 'I'm taking him to the vet again later, see what she says.'

'So, it's much better to be a wily fox then, Jonas, than a stodgy old hog?' I said brightly, trying to lighten the mood.

He looked at me sternly as if I had missed the point. 'Not necessarily, Sylvia,' he said, picking up the local newspaper, and I knew the conversation was over.

Wednesday 28 October

I dressed around my birthday bracelet this morning, in anticipation of my fortnightly working lunch with Prof. I put it on first, after my shower, and then picked clothes that I felt best complimented its twinkling loveliness. I finally decided on a glossy cream silk blouse, a lemon-yellow cashmere cardigan and a light tan skirt. Caught up in sparkly pleasure, I even dug out a box of colours I rarely use and put on some gold eyeshadow and a very slightly glittery blusher. I daydreamed about Prof all the way into work and felt positively giddy as I took him in his tea and biscuits.

'What time suits you today?' I asked placing his mug on the desk in front of him, subtly shaking my wrist as I did so.

He looked baffled for a moment, then the penny dropped. 'Oh, of course it's Wednesday, isn't it. Yes, Sylvia. I have a student coming at midday, so we can go straight after that. Does that work for you?'

'Perfect,' I said, touching my bracelet and giving him a meaningful smile.

My happy mood was pricked somewhat when I looked at his diary and realised the pre-lunch student was Lola Maguire, but I was determined not to let it spoil my day.

She came breezing in at around five to twelve, dressed head-to-toe in gym gear, with her hair scraped back, eyes bright and cheeks rosy from some sort of physical exertion.

I looked her up and down with distaste as she took a gulp from her water bottle. 'I thought you worked on Wednesdays?' I said.

'Half-term, Sylvia. Ned is with my parents so I have the whole week to work on my thesis. And my fitness.' She said this last bit with a deprecating laugh. At least she realises she needs to lose weight.

'Did you run here?' I was incredulous that anyone would deliberately turn up to a meeting with Prof looking such a mess.

'Well, not all the way. I parked the car a couple of tube stops back and ran from there. And up all these stairs of course.'

I blinked at her, raised my eyebrows dismissively, and turned back to my screen.

She stood there feeling uncomfortable, as was my intention, and I waited for her to speak again, knowing she had something she wanted from me.

'Sylvia, I need your help submitting my abstract to the Rome conference. Carl ... erm, Professor Lomax, said you would register me on the website.'

I continued working as if she hadn't spoken.

'So?' she asked sharply.

'So?' I echoed her.

'So, have you done it?' She was getting annoyed now and her post-run glow was turning into an angry flush.

'It's on my to-do list,' I answered vaguely and she went to protest just as Prof came out of his office.

'What are you doing out here?' he smiled genially at Lola. 'Come on through.' He held the door open and waved her through with a mock bow which made me wince.

I pulled up the Rome website and stared hard at the registration form I had half filled in for Lola. Possibilities came into my mind. I could send it as it was, unfinished, and hope they wouldn't follow it up. I could 'accidentally' send it to the wrong email address. I could make some edits to her abstract to make it nonsensical so they would reject it. In the end, reluctantly, I sent it properly. Prof would be absolutely furious if something spoilt Lola's attendance at this conference and I couldn't risk his wrath being directed at me.

Lola was still in there with him at quarter past one and I was starting to get twitchy. I tried to catch his eye through the glass but he was deep in conversation. The door was finally flung open at half past, a warm sweaty fug leaking from the room as they came out laughing together. 'Sylvia, Lola says you haven't registered her yet for the conference, is that right?' Prof looked at me with a disappointed frown and Lola grinned at me from behind his back.

'No.' I faked confusion and shook my head. 'It's all done. See.' I turned my screen to show them the email confirming her registration had taken place. I had scored a point on Lola and made her look a little silly in front of Prof, but my satisfaction didn't last long.

'Great. You really are a star, Sylvia.' Prof clapped his hands together. 'Right, let's get to lunch.'

I leaned down to pick up my bag and then realised as I went to stand up that he was talking to Lola.

'You don't mind do you, Sylvia? We can do our lunch next Wednesday instead. Lola and I are in the middle of an absolutely fascinating discussion about the school system in Bavaria.' With that they were gone, Lola not even giving me the chance to glare at her as she walked straight out the door ahead of Prof.

'Oh dear, it looks like you've got all dressed up for nothing,' said Margaret, with fake concern as I put my bag back down on the floor and sank, deflated, into my chair.

Saturday 31 October

Imogen Scott and her husband Leonard live in the kind
of huge Edwardian mansion in North London that is
usually divided into a dozen or so flats. It is a house
of dreams. Four floors of warm bohemian homeliness.
Rooms filled with books and cats and textiles from
Morocco and India. The Aga in the kitchen gives the
house character and heart, along with the ancient
wooden table, mismatched chairs and children's drawings pinned on to every wall space. It is exactly the
family home I had imagined myself inhabiting one day,
with a brood of charming children and a handsome,
intellectual husband.

Somewhere along the line I convinced myself that
nobody really has it all – the happy marriage, the
delightful children, the beautiful house, the fascinating
career – and then I got to know Imogen and realised,
with a sting, that some people actually do. And to make
it even more difficult to bear, they are the nicest people
you could ever hope to meet. It would be so much easier
if I could hate them or pity them or judge them for
being small-minded or holding extreme political views,
but they aren't and they don't.

Imogen, an expert in early childhood education, is a fiendishly bright woman with an elfin face and long grey hair. She wears long skirts and clogs and speaks to everyone as if they were her favourite person in the world. Leonard is a famous child psychologist, originally from California. He smiles constantly, and with his white beard and rosy complexion has a Father Christmas feel about him that is rather magical. They wrote a best-selling child-rearing manual in the 1990s called *Love Your Kids and They Will Love Life*, based on their parenting philosophy of treating children as equals, not disciplining them, and including them in all family decisions. It is always fascinating to see how the children of parenting gurus turn out, and Imogen and Leonard's three children don't disappoint – growing up to become prosperous, confident and successfully paired-up adults. Iona and Skye, the twins, are both Mother Earth types with a brood of cherubic toddlers and babies in slings and identikit tall, blond husbands. They make a fortune selling some sort of organic baby food and have a regular slot on daytime TV as well as a huge entourage of followers on social media. Imogen and Leonard's son, Lawrence, is a radio producer on a global news network. He is married to the gorgeous Martin, who is a city broker. They are also super-rich and have a penthouse apartment in Docklands, along with a beachfront town house in Brighton for weekend jollies. At the moment, they are considering having a child via a surrogate, about which the whole family are involved in on-going supportive, sensible discussions. Oh, to have liberal-minded, kind-hearted parents who only want you to be happy! How easy it must be to fulfil yourself and feel comfortable in your skin and in the world.

Walking up the front path this afternoon for their annual Hallowe'en party I allowed myself to imagine for a moment that this was our house, mine and Prof's, with the fading clematis tumbling over the bay windows and the ivy creeping round the door. I stood on the step and marvelled at how the brass lion-head knocker looked so perfect on the creamy yellow front door, enjoying the faint scent from the pots of woody lavender on the porch and feeling the warmth of the unseasonal October sun on my back. I had a shiver of anticipation knowing Prof would be inside. This yearly event, a generous invite extended by the Scotts to all their colleagues and their families, is one of the few occasions I get to see him outside of work. I can't imagine what would otherwise entice me to don a witch's hat and make small talk with people from the department and their children all afternoon. Prof adores Imogen and frequently asks her advice about how to deal with his boys and she treats him like a naughty schoolboy when he is late for meetings or forgets to answer emails.

'Sylvia! We're in the backyard.' It was Leonard, leaning out the side gate, in full zombie get-up with a plastic dagger sticking out the side of his head. 'Come on through, Sylvia.' It is one of Leonard's endearing qualities, the way he uses your name all the time.

I followed him down the side passage and out into their garden which still looked glorious this late in the year, the trees golden and red in the afternoon sun. They had decorated their vast conservatory as a wizard's lair and extended the fun to the tiered patio which was dotted with braziers to keep it warm. The children were hooting and screaming with joy as they discovered secret tricks and surprises around the garden, the adults perched on wicker furniture draped with black sheets, drinking various lurid coloured potions and eating bowls of chilli from a cauldron served up by Leonard. He was in his absolute element, laughing with his sons-in-law as he stirred his creation.

'It's the only time he ever cooks and he won't tell even me what's in it.' A ghostly looking Imogen had sidled up next to me and touched my arm as we both watched her husband affectionately.

'Now, what can I get you to drink?'

I asked for a dry white wine spritzer and scanned the party for Prof. I thought I saw him on the lower patio by the apple bobbing and was making my way there when I got waylaid by Lola.

'Hello, Sylvia, fancy seeing you here.' She smiled falsely, adjusting her black cat ears. I felt a prick of annoyance at how much her costume suited her, especially compared to the way my witch hat just made me look faintly ridiculous.

'Not that much of a surprise, surely? I do work in the department and Imogen always invites everybody.' I smiled falsely back.

'Yes, but I've never seen you at any other social event, that's all.'

She turned back to the group of post-grad students she was talking to, triumphant that she had dropped her bombshell, knowing full well that I was unaware of the social events she was referring to. This was the only one I knew about, so I had to assume that she had been socialising with Prof without my knowledge. My hand shook as I brought my glass to my lips and my eyes burned into the back of her head as she tossed her hair and laughed knowingly with her group. It was then that I saw Ned halfway up the biggest horse chestnut tree in the garden, climbing out onto a low-hanging branch, presumably after conkers, Prof's boys egging him on from the ground. Instinctively I grabbed Lola's arm and urgently said her name. She spun round, her face furious at the interruption, ready for another spat. Then she saw the danger her son was in and sped up the garden, dropping her bowl on the grass as she went. By the time she arrived he had swung successfully to the ground and was being clapped on the back by the admiring Lomax boys. I couldn't hear her admonishments, but Ned was clearly forbidden to leave his mother's side for the rest of the afternoon and looked thoroughly miserable at the prospect.

'You should thank Sylvia for telling me you were in danger,' said Lola tightly as they returned to the patio and Ned rolled his eyes at me before grunting a grudging 'Thank you', saving Lola the trouble and neatly casting me as the fun-spoiler rather than her.

'You're welcome,' I said and resumed my mission to find Prof. Glancing round I saw Ned poke his tongue out at me and, childish though it was, I poked mine out back.

I finally found Prof in the gazebo at the end of the garden with the die-hard smokers. He was dressed all in black with a trail of 'blood' dripping down the side of his mouth and was having an in-depth conversation about educational inequality with Dr Bastow, Dr Kofi, and a postdoctoral researcher called Patrick, the sort of insipid young man whom Mother would describe as a 'drink of water'.

'But of course, Bernstein would attribute it to the restricted linguistic codes of the working class,' Prof was saying as Patrick nodded shyly.

'No, no, no,' said Kofi excitedly, drawing on his pipe, 'it is the legacy of post-colonialism that has embedded class hierarchies in this country. We will never have equality; it is an inherited bias.'

They ignored me as I came in. I stood next to Prof and tried to follow their conversation, nodding sagely.

Bastow, who was clearly losing the argument, jumped on me in his usual unpleasant way. 'Sylvia, you seem to be agreeing with two completely opposite viewpoints there; can you explain your position?'

'I agree with Professor Lomax,' I said after a moment's awkward hesitation.

'Hmmph.' Bastow snorted with contempt and Prof reddened slightly. He obviously felt the need to reward my loyalty with an attempt to include me in the conversation, or perhaps he just wanted to change the subject.

'So, Sylvia, how are the … erm … hamsters doing?' he asked, indicating his empty glass to Martin as he came into the gazebo carrying a bottle of wine in each hand.

'It's actually hedgehogs,' I said, but he had already turned back to Bastow to resume the debate.

I left the gazebo, feeling momentarily deflated, but I understood that Prof was a little drunk and in full socialising mode. It was hard for us to know how to communicate outside our bubble in the office where the balance worked perfectly and I forgave him for that. In fact, I found it endearing, the way that Prof was being typical of his gender in behaving differently when in a group of other men than he behaved when he was just with me. It was also thrilling that he seemed to sort of know about my hedgehog sanctuary work. This proves he must have had at least one conversation about me with somebody else as I have never told him about that myself. On reflection, the whole encounter reinforced for me that we do have a special relationship and by the time I had reached the conservatory I was buoyant with insight and flushed with love.

Imogen had set out a tempting-looking dessert table covered with plates of homemade cheesecakes, trifle, chocolate cake and individual strawberry tarts. I stood staring at the spread, deep in thought about future garden parties Prof and I might hold.

'Do help yourself, Sylvia.' Imogen's cheerful invitation broke the spell and I realised it looked like what I was longing for was cake.

'Oh no, I'm fine, thank you.'

'Go on, you are allowed to treat yourself sometimes. Can't always be good.'

She was starting to annoy me. I hate being encouraged to eat, especially in public. It was so long since I had allowed anything sweet to pass my lips that the concept of eating a bowl of trifle or a piece of cheesecake was as alien to me as putting a live insect in their mouth would be to most other people. I smiled and picked up a slice of kiwi from the fresh fruit platter, hoping that would satisfy her. Imogen gave me a curious look and was about to say something when two of her grandchildren dressed as little devils, ran up and started greedily reaching for the chocolate cake. Imogen laughed and told them to wait while she put it in bowls for them and disappeared back into the kitchen.

I took the opportunity to slip out the side gate and make my way home. I always try to leave social gatherings in that way, under the radar. I can't stand all the protracted goodbyes and pretence that people are sad you are leaving. Nobody cared if I was there or not, except Prof, of course, although he was in his cups, and perhaps Imogen, but she was busy with her family. Once on the pavement I stood for a moment listening to the jovial party sounds going on behind the house that now seemed thousands of miles away – a different planet full of normal people with partners and children and grandchildren and proper lives. I was overcome with an urge to go back. Maybe one of the families would take me home, assimilate me into their world like a stray dog that becomes a treasured family pet. Maybe I could just become one of the Scott family and live with them in their beautiful house? But I knew I couldn't go back in. I took off my witch's hat and shoved it in my bag as I made my way resolutely down towards the tube station, feeling a wintery snap of cold begin to bite as the afternoon sun faded away.

Sunday 1 November

I arrived at the sanctuary early this morning after a restless night going over and over my interaction with Prof yesterday at the party, agonising over whether I should have said more or less or stayed longer or gone earlier. I tortured myself with thoughts of Lola in her cat costume and tried to banish images of them chatting and drinking together from my mind. It was not quite half past eight and the light was still weak as I walked up the side way and opened the back gate.

Jonas was already up and about, tending to his garden, and I knew he would have been out there since dawn. I paused and watched him for a moment, digging over an empty bed, stopping to rub his back after each couple of spadesful, and wiping his face with a large grey hankie. It was impossible not to feel affectionate towards Jonas, seeing him like that, and to feel sad that the physical decline that is slowing him down will gradually take him away from his garden and his hedgehogs altogether. He is such a harmless old man, even if he drives me mad with his lack of opinion or conviction about anything. Perhaps that's what happens as one gets older, although it seems to have worked the opposite way with Mother, whose (largely negative) opinions and convictions about everything and everyone seem only to strengthen with her advancing years.

Watching Jonas made me reflect on how hard it is to look after Mother as she shows no vulnerability at all and is terrified of being pitied. She is always dressed formally and immaculately, as if on her way to one of the Queen's garden parties and any offer of help, a proffered arm for example when crossing a busy road, is swiped away in annoyance. She talks in disparaging terms about 'old people' as if they are a different, weaker breed than her, who have lazily and carelessly allowed themselves to age. Jonas, on the other hand, has a quiet dignity about him in the way he cares for his plants and the animals, the way he seems to calmly accept his fading importance in the world. You could pity Jonas – he wouldn't care – and he accepts all offers of help willingly. He is a man with nothing to prove, who wants only to spend the final part of his life doing what he likes doing, as close to the rhythms and consolations of nature that it is possible to be in the suburbs of South London. And where Mother chose to take father's passing as a personal insult about which she is still, more than twenty years on, furiously indignant, Jonas seems to have taken the love he had for Paula with him, cherishing the people and things she valued and honouring the life they built together. They looked after each other and now their daughters look after him, taking it in turns to bring him dinners and do his washing and keep the house clean. It has been Carrie's turn this week. Not a natural nurturer, Carrie is happiest riding her vintage motorbike round various music festivals with her tattoo artist boyfriend, but she tries her best to look after Jonas on her weeks, bringing round takeaway curries and ironing the collars of his shirts. Harriet and Katie are much more conventional, with their husbands and kids and four-by-fours, but I know Jonas loves Carrie's wild spirit, even though she's not much of a housekeeper.

I looked round for Igor, knowing he would be close by, and spotted him lying among the last of the cabbages, head on paws, watching Jonas with interest. He suddenly flipped onto his back, rolled left and right and did an enormous sneeze, before jumping to his feet and snuffling round where Jonas was digging, trying to get his attention.

'What do you want, boy, eh?' Jonas scratched Igor's ears and the dog lent into him in ecstasy.

'Do you want me to take him for a walk for you?'

He wasn't at all surprised to see me there so early. 'That'd be grand, lass. Carrie didn't have time yesterday.' He smiled as he wiped his face again.

I put Igor on his lead and we made our way down the hill towards the park. I was nervous about letting him off when we got there in case he ran away and I would have to return to Jonas empty-handed, but he pulled and pulled so I undid the catch on his collar and let him dash across the grass and chase the squirrels into the trees. The park was quiet, only a couple of serious joggers passed me as I walked down the central path. Tempted by some movement or scent that was beyond my limited human senses, Igor swerved sharply to the left into a small copse of birch trees. I followed after him, anxious to keep him in sight. On the other side of the trees there was a little clearing, the right-hand side of it separated off by two big rhododendron bushes, and it was there that I thought Igor had gone. I got as far as the first bush and then I saw them – a young couple lying on a bed of coats, making love. The sight was so visceral, so private and so intense, that I stood rooted to the spot, transfixed. They didn't notice me; they were in their own world. He was moving on top of her, she with her arms flung out above her head and then grabbing his black hair and pulling his face towards hers. I couldn't turn away. I wanted to, but I couldn't. I stumbled backwards. A sharp emotional pain seared through me as if I had been electrocuted or burnt; it started at the back of my neck and shot down my arms to my fingers. My whole body trembled as I stood there, transfixed, watching them express their physical love, or perhaps just lust, for each other and I had to force myself to turn around and creep away, shamefully, silently, like a despised, dirty animal. When I was a few metres away I started to run and didn't stop until I reached the path, where I found Igor lying next to a bench eating an apple core that someone had dropped like it was manna from heaven.

I tried to compose myself on the walk back to Jonas's, but I was shaken up. Most of the time I put sex completely out of my mind, turning over the television channel if a steamy scene comes on, or skipping certain passages in books. My fantasies about Prof are more romantic than carnal. Him proposing on a dinner cruise down the Seine, say, or us dancing to Frank Sinatra on a starlit balcony at our wedding. I don't ever imagine actually consummating our love, although that would obviously be part of our married life together. A tipsy Millie recently started telling me about a new sexual position she and Kamal had been trying and I shut down that conversation straight away.

'I don't want to know,' I told her firmly, putting my palm up.

'Don't be such a prude, darling. You have had sex in your life,' Millie had said, laughing at me, putting my reluctance to discuss her private life down to me being uptight and squeamish. That is part of it, I suppose; it has been seventeen years since I have been intimate with a man and I do feel rather uptight about the whole subject. The bigger issue, of course, is that the last time I did have sex all those years ago was with Kamal, a fact I would rather die than ever have Millie find out.

By the time I got back to Jonas's place in Hartland Road, my discomfiture at being privy to such an intimate act had begun to turn into indignation. I found myself telling Jonas what I had seen and how disgusting it was that young people had no shame any more.

'Don't you agree,' I said, 'and wouldn't you have been shocked?'

Jonas clearly didn't share my pique, he carried on calmly planting his daffodil bulbs and said with a chuckle, 'They weren't bothering anyone else, so what's your problem? They must have been cold, though.'

I was quite taken aback at his laissez-faire attitude – I would have had Jonas down as a stalwart of traditional values and moral behaviour.

'I just think there is a time and a place and that was neither,' I stated defiantly as I passed him another bulb from the sack.

'You have to take your happiness where you can in this life. It's over too soon and you're a long time dead.' Igor leapt up then and started digging energetically in the dirt at this, as if he understood the sentiment and wanted to ensure he had made the most of his morning.

'Well, that's a cheerful thought. I must say, Jonas, you do surprise me sometimes.' I wasn't going to back down. The possibility of agreeing with him frightened me; it would feel like stepping off a cliff that I had been clinging on to for a very long time.

'And you me, Sylvia.'

I puzzled at this and looked at him for clarification but he was engrossed in his task and didn't offer any further explanation.

The awkward moment was forgotten when Igor's urgent barking indicated a visitor standing on the other side of the gate, clutching a cardboard box.

'Is this the hedgehog sanctuary?' the man called.

Jonas shouted back to him and waved him in. He was a tall, skinny man in his late teens or early twenties with a shaved head and fretful eyes, dressed head to toe in the sort of expensive sports clothes that aren't intended to be worn at the gym.

'My dad was breaking up rocks for the foundation for our new shed and he killed the mum by mistake.' He was quite flustered and clearly upset by what had happened.

I took the box from him and carefully laid it down on the lawn. Opening the top flaps revealed a litter of three tiny hoglets on a red cushion, squirming and wriggling, seeking the comfort and safety of their mother, who was no longer there. They were about the size of apricots and their little pink bodies were covered in white prickles which were still soft.

'Hoglets? This late in the year?' Jonas was astounded and peered intently into the box. 'They're young ones too,' he said, rubbing his beard with concern.

'Are they too young to survive?' I asked, glancing at the man's anxious face.

'We can have a go with them,' said Jonas. 'We can get them warm, get them feeding and give them a go. They might be all right, but probably not that tiddly one.' The smallest hoglet was already less active than its siblings and Jonas touched him lightly with his little finger.

'Sylvia, you set up the warm box and I'll get some milk. They are going to need feeding every three or four hours round the clock for the next few days.'

The young man looked relieved to have passed on the responsibility and stood watching us galvanise into the action required to try and save the baby hedgehogs.

'Thank you for bringing them in, you did the right thing, lad. You can go now,' Jonas patted the man's shoulder and walked him to the gate. 'Give us a call in a couple of days if you like.' Jonas always offered, but nobody ever did ring again. Whether they didn't want to hear potentially bad news, or that life had taken them on and away from the momentary wildlife emergency they found themselves involved in, I don't know; perhaps a bit of both.

The little one had died by the time Jonas had prepared the first feed. He picked it up gently and stroked its tiny body and said kind things before burying it in the earth beneath the runner bean poles.

'That one wasn't meant to be,' he said, firmly wiping his eyes as he picked up one of the others and started feeding it with a pipette. 'Have we got that box nice and warm with the heat pad for them, Sylvia?'

I nodded and put my hand on his back. 'I'll make us a nice cup of tea, shall I?' I said, falling back on the British answer to every upset. I made my way to the kitchen, circumnavigating Igor, who was sitting in the middle of the garden path, staring sadly at Jonas.

Tuesday 3 November

I watched with distaste while Lola was in with Prof this afternoon, flicking her hair and laughing her wide-mouthed laugh. She had come in in her usual manner, all busty and windswept and disorganised, ignoring the withering look I gave her over the top of my tortoiseshells.

'Professor Lomax is busy. You'll have to wait,' I said coldly, indicating the plastic chair outside his office door.

To my horror, Prof then dashed out of the inner sanctum with a massive smile on his face, and actually held onto her arm as he said, 'Hello, you' (hello you!), helped her off with her coat and carried her bag and files into his office. It was as if he was some kind of lackey and I feel utterly humiliated for him. God knows what sort of sob story she has been spinning him about needing his help and support and about her incredibly stressful life and terribly vital research, but he is on the verge of making a fool of himself and I can't bear to see that happen.

I knew something was up when Prof and Lola both came out of the inner sanctum together after their meeting (which again had overrun by at least twenty minutes).

'Great news, Sylvia,' Prof announced grandly. 'Lola has had her paper accepted for the Rome conference so, with the thumbs up from the faculty finance committee that she got, she is all set to go. It is such an achievement at this stage in your career, Lola – the panel are extremely selective about who is allowed to present their research. You should take it as a great honour they have included you in the programme.' Prof looked fit to burst with pride. Lola at least had the humility to put on a falsely fearful face as if she didn't want to go at all but Prof just beamed at her. 'Don't look so worried. You'll be great. These are exciting times for you, young lady. Sylvia, can you organise the travel and hotel arrangements for Lola out of the research budget, please?'

And he went back into his office, leaving Lola and I in an embarrassed, stunned silence. Lola looked at me expectantly and I told her curtly I would email her the appropriate forms and then looked straight back at my computer screen. If she was expecting any sort of congratulations or words of encouragement from me, she would be waiting a long time.

'Sylvia, can I tell you what I need now? It's so much quicker than waiting for an email from you, replying and waiting for you to contact me again.' She emphasised the word 'waiting' each time she said it, making a pointed reference to the tardiness with which I communicated with her, but I pretended to be oblivious.

'I do apologise if the university procedures for arranging conference attendance are not efficient enough for you. Perhaps you would like to make a formal complaint to the faculty board and they can review their decision to fund your trip to Rome?' I removed my glasses and stared at her while she squirmed.

'No, I'm not saying that. Of course not. It's just that it would be easier to tell you now which days I want to travel and so on as it is coming up so soon.' She trailed off, losing confidence in her position.

I pushed a pad and pen towards her across the desk. 'Write it down and I'll see what I can do.'

She looked at me warily, taken by surprise by my sudden helpfulness, then picked up the pen and wrote a long list of requirements, dates and times. When she had finished she held out the paper to me and I took it gingerly, as if it was covered in germs.

'Well, thank you,' she said as she backed towards the door.

'No problem, always happy to help,' I said, waiting until she had turned into the corridor before scrunching the sheet into a ball and dropping it in the bin.

I then went straight to our travel operator's website and booked Lola on different flights to and from Rome from those I had booked for Prof. He won't want to be bothered with her during the journey – he likes to use travelling time to catch up on work. I had to book her into the same hotel as it is an international chain that the university always uses, but I was at least able to put them on different floors. Prof needs his space to think and write and reflect, and there has to be a respectful boundary between students and their academic superiors. I was tempted to email Lola a note about expected conduct, but I wasn't convinced she wouldn't run to Prof with it – and for the first time I was not entirely sure how he might react to my protectiveness. This made me feel uneasy, as if something was going on that I didn't know about, something that might be dangerous to Prof professionally or personally. I couldn't put my finger on it, but it wasn't sitting well with me. I felt restless and committed to my duty to protect him from that woman.

Jonas called at around seven, asking if I was all right as I hadn't gone to the sanctuary after work as I usually do on a Tuesday. I had completely forgotten, I was in that much of a state. I apologised to Jonas and told him I was unwell. He wished me better and there was an awkward moment where I wanted to get off the phone but he seemed to be waiting for me to say something. I said goodbye curtly and it was only after I hung up that I remembered I hadn't asked him about the baby hogs.

Wednesday 4 November

It is 3.34 a.m. and I have just done something slightly crazy, but also rather thrilling. I have booked myself onto a flight to Rome the day after Prof and Lola are due to arrive and have reserved a room in a little albergo around the corner from their hotel.

I will book two days annual leave tomorrow, directly through the university's Human Resources department, so Prof won't even know I'm not going to be in the office. Margaret will be away next week at her daughter's wedding in Florida, so she won't know I'm gone or ask any awkward questions when I get back. I will take my phone and laptop so I will still be in contact with Prof if he needs me for work-related matters: he just won't know I am actually in Rome as well. I need to be there to keep tabs on Lola. I don't trust her, and I don't want her making things awkward for Prof or being too demanding of his time. I want to be there just in case things go wrong or she needs warning off. This is an important conference for him, especially as he has been asked to give the keynote speech, and it's vital it goes well. I feel like a weight has been lifted from me. I think I will be able to sleep now.

Wednesday 11 November

I didn't tell Millie or Mother or Jonas that I was going away, which has given the whole trip a surreal dimension. I made my way to Gatwick airport in the middle of the night, feeling a little like a fugitive. The taxi driver was exceptionally chatty as always seems to be the way when you long for quiet.

'Where you off to then, love?' he asked, ready to dispense expert knowledge on whatever destination I pronounced.

'Rome,' I replied, my deep-set politeness not allowing me to ignore him.

'Italy, yeah?' I assumed he didn't actually require an answer so held my tongue. 'I love all that stuff, the Romans and that. Never been to Rome meself but I love Italy. Me and the wife went to Madeira for our 'oneymoon; lovely it was, all that pasta and chianti.'

I let him go on detailing the food, accommodation and day trips that he and his wife had enjoyed on the Portuguese island, not having the heart or the inclination to correct his geography, and gave him a larger tip than I intended, possibly out of guilt. As I went through the usual lengthy security procedures I couldn't help furtively checking over my shoulder from time to time for the remote possibility that Prof or Lola had drastically changed their travel plans.

I began to relax on the flight over and thought about the last time I was in Italy, several years ago, and how it had prompted a brief, and in retrospect rather misjudged, change in my behaviour towards Prof. Crystal had been doing the Romans at school and Millie had the brilliant idea that we should all go to Sorrento and visit Pompeii to make ancient Roman life come alive for her. Kamal had to stay behind to look after the deli, thank goodness, but I had to share a twin room with Mother, who was at her absolute fussiest during the whole trip, complaining about the food (the food!), the heat, the Italians ('Well, I suppose it is their country, Mother …'). What annoyed her most was the fun Millie was having. She and Crystal had a wonderful time eating their way through gallons of gelato, marvelling at the architecture and the petrified bodies. Mother was unimpressed and said she found the whole site rather gruesome, as if she were fully expecting a visit to a mass grave to be a pleasant and uplifting day trip. I was somewhere in the middle – fascinated by the history, but hating the crowds and the touristy feel of the place. Wandering around there by moonlight, hand in hand with Prof, listening to his wise musings on the nature of love, death, and the fall of the Roman Empire – now that would have been different. After a couple of hours of aimless drifting we hired a tour guide to throw a bit more of a shape at the day. I say we, but it was Millie who hired him. I knew she wouldn't be able to resist as soon as I saw him approach us with his clipboard and headphones. He stood out from the other more serious, conventional guides like a beacon. He was young and bubbly and, most compelling for Millie, was styled like a rockabilly, albeit a super clean and tidy Italian-style rockabilly, with a quiff, check shirt and perfect turn-ups in his ironed blue jeans. Millie loves quirky people and she loves gregarious people and Fabio was the whole package.

'Ladies! Beautiful ladies, let me show you around Pompeii – I will show you everything.'

He flashed his splendid smile at Millie and so began the flirting they both revelled in for the rest of the day. Mother couldn't have looked any more sour, but he made it fun for Crystal who was equally smitten and it was nice to change the dynamic for a while. He turned his attention onto me while Millie was taking photos of Crystal outside the gladiator barracks.

'Bella Sylvia,' he said, gazing at me with concern, 'where is your husband today? He shouldn't let such a beautiful lady go on holiday alone.'

'No husband, Fabio, and I'm not alone, I'm with my family,' I replied briskly, although I could feel the familiar blush rising up my neck and was ridiculously flattered by his oozing charm. We locked eyes and I recognised his suggestive look with a nostalgic jolt.

Mother broke the moment with an enormous, possibly fictitious, sneeze into her handkerchief and Millie and Crystal reappeared full of busy chatter about some ribald ancient graffiti they had seen.

The frisson between Fabio and me was immediately forgotten by him, but had awakened a tentative feeling of sexual confidence in me that had been dormant for a long time. I decided to bundle it up and preserve it and take it out again when I was with Prof. It dawned on me that this was what was needed to take our relationship further. If Fabio could find me attractive, then surely Prof could too? I just needed to flirt with him more. I carried this delicious idea around with me for the rest of the holiday and devised potential scenarios whereby I could engender the same look of unbridled lust from Prof as I had from the, admittedly more practised and less discerning, tour guide.

Back in our hotel room after dinner, Mother commented spitefully that, as a married woman, Millie should behave with more decorum around young men and that she had put on a vulgar display today in front of Crystal. I sprang to her defence.

'For goodness' sake, Mother, it's just a bit of harmless fun. Millie would never be unfaithful to Kamal. She adores him, for some reason, and they are very happily married.'

'Hmmph,' Mother said. She rummaged in her mini suitcase for her nightie and ignored me while we both got ready for bed. She turned off her bedside light before me and, as mine didn't work, I lay there in the darkness listening to her snuffling and then light snoring. I was just falling asleep when I heard the door to Millie and Crystal's room next door close and some whispered conversation. I jumped up to check everything was all right and, as I opened the door, I saw Millie standing by the lift, repeatedly pressing the call button.

'Mills, what's wrong?' I must have surprised her as she almost jumped out of her skin.

'Nothing! I-I just … Crystal's got – got a headache so I was going to see if they sold aspirin in the hotel shop downstairs.'

'You should have knocked at our door; you know Mother never travels without a full medicine kit in her case.'

'I didn't want to wake you; your light was out.' We stood looking at each other for a few moments in an awkward silence.

'Well, as long as you're both all right.' I backed into my room and slipped into bed. As I drifted off to sleep I thought fondly that only my eccentric sister would have felt the need to wear her red high heels for a trip down to the lobby.

We got home early in the morning the following Monday. I could have taken the day off and caught up on sleep before returning to work, but the thought of another day without seeing Prof was unbearable. It was grey and drizzly and the commute was grindingly familiar and yet I was fizzing with excitement, feeling sure that my new-found confidence would alter the course of my relationship with Prof into a more romantic direction.

I had showered as soon as I got in and spent a long time choosing what to wear. I wanted to send subtle messages that I was open to advances without looking cheap. In the end, I plumped for a peacock-blue cocktail dress with a lowish neckline with a black jacket and black mid-height heels. I added some multi-coloured dangly earrings that Millie had given me for Christmas, but it looked too barmaidy so I took them off. I blow dried my hair upside down with the volumising attachment I hadn't used since the nineties and was quite pleased how glamorous it looked, even without the blonde highlights I used to have. Make-up wise I was bolder than usual. Smokey grey eyeshadow and a red lipstick as well as mascara and eyeliner. I halted at the mirror in the hall, though, and wiped off the lipstick with a tissue, not quite brave enough to wear that classic symbol of sexual receptiveness. I promised myself that I would wear it on our first date after he had left Martha for good.

I arrived at work early and sat watching the clock move slowly towards nine o'clock when I knew Prof would arrive as he had a meeting at 9.30. At 9.08 he burst through the door in his usual bonhomie manner. He did a double take as he walked past my desk and my heart leapt.

'Oh dear, Sylvia – caught in the wind were you?' he said, holding his hands widely to each side of his head and, laughing, he grabbed the agenda I had printed out for him and disappeared into his office.

Margaret, who was still a temp then, and who sat opposite me, stifled a giggle and I turned back to my computer screen, staring but not seeing anything through a blur of embarrassed tears. I had overdone it with the hair and Prof had not even had the chance to see my figure in the dress. I quickly checked his diary. Damn it. Now he would be in that meeting until lunch and then over at the central campus for the rest of the day for a symposium, only returning for a PhD supervision meeting at 6.00 by which time I would have left.

The next day I tried again with a 1950s style black and white polka dot dress that Millie had given me, assuring me it was vintage, and a pair of heels I had last worn at Shona and Ian's wedding. This time I kept my hair in its normal style, but wore the red lipstick. I knew Prof would be in the office all day and I had planned several reasons to visit him at his desk such as forms that needed his signature that I 'forgot' to put in his pigeonhole and so on. As a final flourish, I spritzed myself with Chanel and tried to reimagine the frisson

I had felt with Fabio. I arrived early again: I wanted to be seated serenely at my desk when Prof came in, with my hair just so, not faffing around with my coat and bag. He stormed in at around 10.00, complaining that his train had been delayed and cursing the weather and the fact that he had lost his umbrella. He didn't look at me at all, not even a cursory glance, as he shook off his mac and hung it on the coat stand before throwing open the door to his office and slamming it behind him. The outer office reverberated with his bad mood and Margaret looked terrified as she crept up to his door with an expenses claim that needed to be signed for another academic.

'Don't disturb him, Margaret,' I commanded as she lifted her knuckle to rap on the door.

'But I have to get this signed off. Dr Bastow is furious that he hasn't been reimbursed for his trip to Vienna.' She looked close to tears, but after yesterday's sniggering I felt no pity whatsoever.

'He'll bite your head off,' I warned, turning back to my screen and leaving her to contemplate which irascible academic she wanted to upset least.

'I can't understand why Professor Lomax didn't sign it yesterday; I put it on his desk when I left last night with a Post-it note saying it was urgent, and then here it is on my desk again this morning, unsigned.' Her bafflement was quite endearing. Surely it wasn't that difficult to work out who had removed it?

Jane O'Connor

'Well, perhaps Professor Lomax doesn't take kindly to being told what to do via Post-it notes written by a temp?' I said this last word like it was a disease.

'I didn't think, I didn't realise ... what shall I do Sylvia? I've offended him and made him angry.'

I thought she was going to start crying. Her pasty face crumpled beneath her thick make-up and she was trembling with the realisation that, in her ignorance of academic hierarchies and courtesy, she had made an unforgivable faux pas and now had to face the wrath of a huge, scary Professor. Margaret is the type of woman who never makes mistakes because she never takes risks. Everything in her life is ordered and simple and under her control. She has her husband and her grown-up daughters and her shoe-box house and her catalogue clothes and her Weight Watchers diet and her two weeks in Spain every June at the same hotel – and she never, ever puts herself in a position to be criticised by anyone for anything. It was quite amusing to see her rocked like this. Such a small mistake, really (that she hadn't even made, of course), but she was falling apart before my eyes. I shook my head as if there was no way back from this and sighed deeply.

'Leave it on my desk, Margaret. Go and get some fresh air and I will take it in to him when I take in his tea. I will try and explain how sorry you are and how you are still learning about how things are done at the university.'

'Oh, thank you, Sylvia.' Her gratitude was totally disproportionate. 'Thank you so much. I didn't know. Please explain it to him.' She grabbed her coat and flew out the door, probably to go and have a cry in her car.

It felt good to be reminded of how important Prof was, and how much of a powerful and imposing figure he cut in the perceptions of other, more ordinary human beings. My privileged position as his personal assistant means that some of his specialness rubs off on me by association. I am his gatekeeper. I decide who can see him and when, and I can put calls through or decide not to. I am held in a grudging respect by colleagues and students alike for that and they cross me at their peril. I always have Prof's best interests at heart, of course. I mean, who did Margaret think she was leaving Prof a note of instructions? I wasn't going to allow that, even if she hadn't laughed at me the day before. It also gave me a perfect opportunity to go in to Prof's office so he could have a proper look at my appearance. I carefully reapplied my lipstick at my desk, using a compact mirror, and set about making Prof's morning two-bag cup of tea. I put a couple of Hobnob biscuits on the saucer and tucked the unsigned form under my arm so I could knock and then open the door.

'Come in,' Prof said, and nodded as I placed his tea and biscuits in front of him and then went back to the manuscript he was reading. I stood there for a few moments, watching him read and he turned back towards me and took off his glasses with a questioning, rather irritated look. 'Was there something else you needed, Sylvia?'

I explained about the expenses form and how Margaret had forgotten to give it to him to sign and how scared she was both of him and of Dr Bastow and Prof found the whole scenario amusing and was grateful to me for saving the day.

'Well, I can see why she might be terrified of old Robert "The Bastard" Bastow, but me, Sylvia?' He smiled and shrugged in the most attractive manner. 'Tell me, what's frightening about me? I don't frighten you, do I?'

It was the first time he had ever asked my opinion of him and, along with the dress and the anticipation of beginning a romantic involvement, I was speechless for a moment and overcome by adoration of everything about him.

'No, you don't frighten me Professor Lomax, quite the opposite.' I said it quietly, and I needed him to understand what I meant.

'Hmm, what's the opposite of frightening?' He was being playful with me and I was desperate to keep the conversation going, both in tone and topic, but I realised that it had strayed off the mildly flirtatious and into the territory of ridiculous.

What is the opposite of frightening? I couldn't think what to say then and I still can't think of what would have been a good answer now, six years later, even though I often go over and over that conversation when I'm alone in bed at night. I smiled weakly and considered saying he made me feel safe but that sounded odd and was far from true. He made me feel desperately unsafe, but in a good way, like my heart only carried on beating because of him, that he had the power of life and death over me and that was how I wanted it. But I couldn't say any of that. He didn't comment on my dress or seem to notice my perfume and make-up. I stumbled in my heels on my way out of his office, unaccustomed as I am to wearing them, and unnerved by the exchange. He looked at my feet quizzically.

'Not your style to wear high heels, Sylvia. Are you trying to impress someone?' He laughed at his own joke and I composed myself as best I could and returned to my desk with my heart pounding. Surely there had been advances made there? Surely our relationship had started slowly sailing towards more intimate shores?

I began wearing ever more daring clothes to work after that, although I kept the heels mid height. And I wore the perfume every day too.

I was getting more and more confident around Prof when, one Friday, after the Faculty meeting, I heard Dr Bastow and two other men from the department talking about me. I was making coffee in the kitchenette and they didn't know I was there as they stood waiting in the outer office to see Prof. They were joking around, discussing the physical merits of female colleagues in the way that men do when they don't think any women are in earshot. I heard Dr Bastow say that someone, I didn't catch the name at this point, 'looked like a dog's dinner this morning' and I was racking my brains, wondering who they might be referring to, when one of the others said, 'Carl had better watch out, I think she's got the hots for him' and they all sniggered. I stood rooted to the spot as I realised they were talking about me. I looked down at my low-cut blouse and tight, knee-length skirt and had a moment of horror, a 'reality check' as Crystal would put it. I waited until they had all trooped into Prof's office and then dashed back to my desk, pulled on my cardigan and did it up right to my neck

After that, I kept things much more low-key and subtle, both in my appearance and in my behaviour. The obvious look clearly wasn't working with Prof – he was much too much of a sophisticate and how silly of me not to have realised that. I didn't make that mistake again.

When Prof did finally kiss me at the Christmas party two years later it proved to me that toning myself down and ensuring I always looked classy and demure rather than overtly sexy had been absolutely the right decision.

Thursday 12 November

I was horribly disappointed with my first impressions of Rome. I know I'm not here for a holiday but I did expect to feel at least slightly awestruck by the eternal city. The airport was sterile and the graffiti on the endless grey walls surrounding the tenements on the way into town was a depressing sight out of the train window. I certainly wasn't expecting a curled cheese sandwich, with a complimentary bag of out-of-date peanuts for my first Roman meal either, and the price of it! I nibbled at the edge of the bread and put the peanuts in my coat pocket in the unlikely event that I would be hungry later.

With the help of a map bought at a tourist kiosk I eventually found my guest house, and without too much jumpiness. I knew Prof and Lola would be at the conference centre for the whole day, so there would be no chance of me being spotted out and about. It's called Villa Rosa and is a sweet little place with a pink frontage in an old part of town. The room has big dark wooden furniture, bolster pillows on the bed and a traditional Juliet balcony. I felt quite special and that I was on something of an adventure as I unpacked my small case and placed my journal on the nightstand.

In contrast, the conference venue is a big, soulless hotel in the centre of the commercial part of the city. It was easy enough to walk in past the bored-looking reception staff as there are plenty of people coming and going to attend different lectures and talks. I knew Lola was presenting her research in the afternoon (the graveyard slot after lunch – that's where they generally put the rookie academics) and I located the room without much trouble once I had made sense of the conference plan on the wall by the lift. I was nervous about slipping into the room unnoticed: I knew it would be small as she is not an internationally renowned or established researcher so I timed it so that I entered with a group of loud Australians and took my seat at the back next to the door where I hid behind a large Italian lady and the conference programme.

Prof was there, of course, providing moral support for Lola, I suppose, but it still took my breath away to see him – to be so near and to have put myself in such a dangerous, vulnerable position. It was thrilling too, though, to be honest. My heart was pumping ten to the dozen and I kept getting the urge to laugh out loud. I felt alive and tingly, the way I only ever feel, have only ever felt, around Prof. He was sitting on the front row and didn't look round once. He was very focussed on Lola and nodded his head throughout her presentation.

It looked like he had slicked his hair back somehow with wax or gel, or maybe he was just hot; it was quite stuffy in there. She was passable, I suppose – what she lacks in intellectual rigour she makes up for with enthusiasm (that is one of Prof's phrases, actually). I slipped out during the applause at the end before the questions started because I thought Prof might look round to see who was asking what.

As I was waiting for the lift another name on the conference schedule caught my eye – Dr Michael Landers from Lola's previous university. The name rang a bell because he had been the supervisor for Lola's Masters dissertation, the one that had caused such a stir and excited Prof so much. He was presenting at the same time as her and wouldn't have quite finished yet, so there was no chance Lola and/or Prof would be there. On the spur of the moment I decided to pop into his allocated room down the corridor and see how popular he was and whether Lola had been the bigger draw as they were presenting on a similar subject. I think he must have been late starting because he was still in full flow as I went in. I wasn't so worried about where I sat this time, for obvious reasons, so took a seat quite near the front and arranged myself as a model of attentive listening, looking for all the world as if I was already well acquainted with what he was talking about.

I was surprised at how frail Dr Landers looked. It is surely only in academia that people can go on working until they drop. He stood at the front of the room in a crumpled beige suit and polka-dot neckerchief, gripping the lectern with one hand as if he would collapse if he let go. A shock of thick white hair stood up straight from his head and he had a hearing aid in one ear which he fiddled with constantly with his other hand. His voice was rather shaky as he went haphazardly through his presentation, forgetting to move on to the next slide at the right time on several occasions.

It went on longer than I had expected – he must have been given an extended slot as he has more kudos than Lola – and the longer I sat there, the more uncomfortable I started to feel, and not because of my interloper status. I am no academic expert but even to my unschooled ears it seemed as if Dr Landers was presenting exactly the same research findings as Lola, albeit in a more structured format and with different emphasis. Very curious indeed. I took a copy of his paper as I left and also took a couple of screen shots of his presentation on my phone camera. It seems as though something is amiss here, and for the first time I sense that there might possibly be a way of rocking Lola's boat and forcing Prof to take off his rose-tinted glasses about her. I will file away the information and let it cogitate until I decide what to do next. If she is a fraud, then I will be able to alert Prof before he makes a complete fool of himself as her champion and we can get rid of her out of the department and our lives once and for all. I felt like I was walking on air all the way back to the hotel. I am so pleased I decided to come here. Fortune favours the brave, as they say.

I'm going to lay low, now, until Prof's keynote speech tomorrow morning – I can't miss that. I will sit right at the back out of sight and just let his amazingness waft over me. I love listening to him speak and it makes me so proud to see the reaction he gets from his peers. There's also the conference dinner tomorrow night at a luxury hotel overlooking the Coliseum. You have to be a delegate to attend and I can hardly go on my own, but I will lurk covertly in their hotel lobby at seven o'clock so I can see if they leave together.

Friday 13 November

I am sitting outside a little coffee shop in the Piazza Navona, sipping an espresso, admiring a magnificent fountain, and feeling giddy with love and admiration for Prof. It was worth coming all this way just to hear him talk. He is so knowledgeable and inspiring, his keynote speech this morning was an absolute triumph!

The main conference room of the hotel where they have weddings and the like had been set up like a theatre with rows of gold and pink chairs all facing the lectern at the front. Prof stood up there with the gravitas of an emperor, with a huge screen behind him, showing his slides. I felt a prickle of pride as I recalled how I had prepared them for him the day before he left. He shifted from one slide to the next using a handheld device connected remotely to the computer, allowing him to be in total control of which quotes and images supported what he was saying. It was super-slick, very professional, and extremely impressive.

His keynote speech was about the theory of a French sociologist who explored social class and education through the notion of having a sense of belonging, or not, at school or university. The theory is that when people do not feel comfortable in an educational institution they tend not to succeed. Prof compared it to being like a fish out of water and he used the example of his own difficult experience as a working-class boy who went to an esteemed red-brick university to illustrate this metaphor. Prof explained it all so beautifully and that last point resonated with me very strongly. I frequently feel like a fish out of water, not because of my social class, but due to being a single, childless woman in a world filled with couples and families. I know that wasn't the point Prof was making, but he inspires me to think beyond his words, so gifted is he as an intellectual and as a public speaker.

He was quite flushed when he had finished and I suspect he would have liked to have left the stage there and then, but he had to stay to give the audience the opportunity to ask questions, as is the way of these events. This was the trickiest part for me too. During his speech he didn't look closely at the audience and I knew he wouldn't. He tends to pitch his presentations just over the audience's heads (literally and figuratively) and doesn't fix his eye on anything in particular. Question time is a different story, though. This is an opportunity to properly take in the group of people who have been listening to you and, effectively, have a conversation with them. By the time I remembered this it was too late for me to get up and walk out. It's my fault for being so caught up in the moment that I forgot I was there 'undercover', as it were. I sat there, staring down at my programme, slouched in my chair in the second to back row, praying silently that no one sitting near me would ask a question. It was thrilling, though, being so close to Prof, listening to him talk and for him not to have any idea of my presence. I felt like his guardian angel, willing him to do well, on hand to save him in an emergency if necessary, but invisible to the naked eye. The very best bit was when he used an idiom I know he got from me when he was faced with a challenging counterargument from an intense Norwegian academic.

'Well, that puts a spanner in the works,' he commented, diffusing the tension wonderfully and baffling the non-native English speakers. He even got a slight laugh.

The worst part was having to listen to a pair of arrogant young academics behind me quietly scoff and criticise Prof's research for being old hat and too simplistic. They also mimicked him when he addressed the audience as 'guys'. I'm sure that was by accident but it did sound a bit flaky and I stung for him. I turned around and glared at them at one point, mainly so I could see who they were. I recognised one of them immediately as Dr Dominic Carson from the Institute of Social Research at one of the newer universities in the Midlands and assumed his sidekick was from the same place. A few anonymous emails to their vice chancellor from 'female students' complaining about sexual harassment should put a spanner in their works for a month or two, and put a large dent in their pomposity.

The other slight annoyance was the presence of Lola in the front row, showing her approval of everything Prof said like a nodding dog and bursting into rapturous applause at the end as if his presentation had been dedicated to her personally. I would have liked to stay and watch him leave, but I was worried he might see me, so I slipped out while everyone's attention was on another question.

Walking out through the as yet empty dining hall I noticed a small table in the corner set with individually labelled plates for those delegates with specific dietary requirements. Knowing about Lola's nut allergy, I paused for a moment and, out of curiosity, looked to see if she had requested a separate meal. She had, and there it was, a sticker saying *S.Lola Maguire* on a plate of soggy-looking pasta salad covered with cling film. My hand went to the packet of peanuts from the train which were still in my pocket and I turned the foil bag over and over as I stared at her name. The loud rattle of a trolley bursting in from the adjacent kitchen made me jump and I scampered out of the room and rushed past reception. Once outside, I shot down a side alley and leant against the wall until my rapid breathing had returned to normal. I wouldn't have done that. Of course I wouldn't. I opened my eyes to see two refuse collectors watching me warily as they dragged a massive metal bin towards their lorry. 'Sorry. I'm sorry,' I shouted at them and ran to the other end of the alley and out onto the main road where I joined the crowds of ordinary Romans going about their day and made my way haphazardly back to Villa Rosa.

A long bath and a short sleep went a long way towards restoring my equilibrium, and I drifted into a different part of town for a coffee a couple of hours ago to kill time until the conference dinner this evening.

Saturday 14 November

I am so small, so hurt, so lost. I want to disappear. I want the world to swallow me up and make me not have to exist any longer. I am angry too, so angry. That vile woman. She has stolen Prof from me. She has manipulated him and seduced him and made him want her. She couldn't just leave him alone. Why did she come to us, why did she have to come and ruin everything between me and Prof? He is *mine*. I have waited for him for fifteen years and looked after him and loved him and made myself perfect for him. No one could ever care about him more than me. How dare she come into our lives and spoil everything and take him away from me. I can't stop crying, I don't know what to do with myself. I am totally and completely undone and it will never be right. What a scheming little strumpet she is, stealing my love, making him want her, taking him away from me. As soon as I saw him see her tonight in that blue chiffon dress I knew she had him under some kind of spell.

Poor Prof didn't stand a chance. He was waiting in their hotel foyer for her. I was watching from behind a stand of postcards in the gift shop. I know that look.

The eyes give everything away – that's why I always try not to look directly at Prof if I can help it, so he can't see that look of longing and surrender and downright admiration in my eyes – and that's how he looked at her. I felt utterly sick with dread and as if I were falling into a huge, bottomless black pit with nowhere soft that I could ever land. I followed them out the front door at a safe distance and relocated to the far side of the top step behind a pillar. From here I watched them wave down a taxi, he with his hand on the small of her back. Just before they got in she looked at him and they both laughed and then he kissed her on the mouth, twice.

I took a photo of the second kiss on my phone from my hiding place because part of me can't believe it is true and I want hard evidence to remind myself of this pain to give me the courage and strength to do whatever I will need to do next. I need to protect us from this woman, this interloper, this hateful Jezebel. I had to hold myself back from confronting them, but I knew I mustn't; they can't know I'm here. As the taxi turned the corner, I ran down onto the street, pulled the bag of peanuts from my pocket, opened it and threw them after her, a gesture that drew surprisingly little attention from the well-dressed passers-by.

I hung about in the hotel lobby for a couple of hours and then, when the receptionist kept staring at me unpleasantly, I went and sat in the bar, nursing a small glass of aqua libra. The time dragged and it seemed to take forever to get to midnight, when I knew the event was scheduled to end. I hadn't taken account of Roman time-keeping, though, and it was nearer two when the barman shook me awake, telling me he was closing up for the night.

I ran into the lobby, feeling disorientated and panicky, but all was quiet. I had obviously missed them coming back. The urge to know if they were spending the night together was overwhelming and I pressed the lift call button decisively. I alighted on the third floor and walked silently down the carpeted corridor until I was standing outside Prof's door. I stood motionless, my ear pressed against it, listening for any sounds from inside, but it was completely silent. I went back to the lift, up to the eerily identical seventh floor, and repeated the procedure outside Lola's room, but again, nothing. I took the stairs back down to the third floor and crouched outside room 320. After several minutes of hearing only the hum of the low-wattage lights on the corridor walls, I thought I heard a small sound, like a rustle, from inside. Before I could stop myself, I had knocked loudly on the door and then, in a panic, I ran and hid behind a large artificial fern at the end of the corridor. The door flew open and Prof stood there, dishevelled, in his dressing gown with his hair sticking up, rubbing his eyes in the dim light. He looked up and down the corridor and I held my breath in terror as he called out, 'Yes? Is anyone there?' Then he tutted loudly at the silence and shut the door. I felt relief wash through me. Surely he was alone; he had almost certainly been asleep. I was about to return to the lift when the door to 320 opened again and I leapt back behind the fern. A scrunched, pale face peered out beneath a mess of tangled blonde hair.

'There's no one here, Carl. There's nobody at all,' said Lola, looking up and down the corridor, and straight past the fern.

Sunday 15 November

After my horrendous discovery of Prof and Lola's tryst on Friday night I got a taxi back to Villa Rosa in a state of shock. After writing it all down in my journal I lay motionless on my bed, going over it in my head. Then at first light I got up and spent furious hours pacing the streets of the deserted city, trying to decide what to do. The most obvious course of action was to report them to the university. Relationships between PhD supervisors and students are severely disapproved of by the Faculty. However, they are not actually forbidden, so divulging their extracurricular activities to the Dean would achieve little more than to severely damage Prof's professional reputation – something I couldn't bear to be responsible for. As the first eager tourists started emerging from their hotels around 8 a.m., a much better idea occurred to me, a way of getting rid of Lola whilst ensuring minimal damage to Prof. It was such a perfect plan that I couldn't help emitting a wild little shout of triumph beside the Trevi Fountain, which I happened to be passing, much to the amusement of a group of young people sitting having a smoke after a hard night's clubbing, and I rushed back to Villa Rosa to get organised. After the initial exhilaration came the realisation that there was a lot to do and it was going to take some guts to see my plan through, but I am nothing if not determined in my dedication to ensuring Prof and my future happiness.

I took the metro and then the Leonardo express to Fiumicino Airport early this morning, although my flight wasn't scheduled to leave until mid-afternoon. I didn't want to hang around central Rome any longer than I had to, and risk bumping into Lola and Prof, lovingly sharing a Cornetto at a romantic street-side café.

By the time I got to the airport the anxiety that I might run into them had started to subside. I had booked Prof onto a late-afternoon flight, as he had requested, and I had arranged for Lola to fly home in the early hours from the less-convenient Ciampino airport. I bought myself a coffee and sat watching the passengers come and go, each caught up in their own unknowable stresses or excitements. I had the letter with me in my bag and put my hand on it every now and then to reassure myself that I was about to take back control. Once I had decided what to do yesterday, it had been a rush to find a print shop and a stationer's, and my limited Italian and lack of knowledge of the area ensured it was even more of a challenge to get everything I needed. The open post office that I finally found, in a peculiar non-touristy area of the city, had an enormous queue, which mystified me as the street outside seemed completely deserted. I had to tussle with the woman at the counter after she had weighed the letter and put stamps on it to stop her putting it straight in the sack of post beneath her desk.

'No, no, no!' I shouted, pulling it back from her until she finally let go with such an enraged look on her face that for a horrible moment I thought she was going to spit at me. I wasn't ready to let it go just yet. I needed to be sure and think it through one more time. I could post it anywhere, now it was stamped, and I had in mind that the airport would be the perfect place as most delegates making their way home from the conference would pass through there.

I stood in front of the post box for a moment, then I pulled the letter carefully out of my bag. I touched the front, where the familiar address was printed on a label, and felt the satisfying prick of each corner before placing it in the slot. I hung on to it for just a second, teasing myself, really, but I knew I would drop it in. I couldn't resist. Light as air, I wandered aimlessly around the departure lounge, smiling at strangers like a simple-minded child. The childlike delight continued as I allowed myself to be shepherded onto the flight by the glamorous cabin crew and ordered myself a celebratory gin and slimline tonic. I gazed out of the window as we took off and watched the extraordinariness of Rome blur into yet another urban conurbation, and then to invisibility, wondering with interest, rather than melancholy, if, when we die, the whole world recedes from view like that.

Drinking gin, thinking philosophical thoughts, international air travel – I was deeply satisfied with myself. This was me as the sort of woman Prof should be in love with, the best version of me – a sophisticated, fascinating, astute older woman who makes younger women seem as boring and insipid as a plate of plain pasta.

I excused myself, climbing over the legs of two sweet teenage girls, and walked along the gangway to the toilets at the end of the cabin. It was on the way back that a head of familiar blonde hair, two rows in front of mine, caught my eye, and when the head turned to speak to the air hostess I was sure that it was Lola. I practically leapt back into my row, pushing roughly past the girls, and slunk down low in my seat, my heart pounding. It couldn't possibly be her. She was booked on a different flight, from a different airport. How could she be here? I peeked up again and had a frustratingly limited view of the top of a fair crown. No matter how I twisted or turned I couldn't see any better, until finally the not-so-sweet girl sitting next to me gave me a mouthful of abuse in angry Italian, along with the international hand gesture for 'stop'. The rest of the flight was ruined. I was terrified that Lola – if it was Lola – would get up and go to the toilet and see me. I hid behind the in-flight magazine and allowed myself furtive glances over the top every time I sensed someone walking past. When the plane landed I waited until last to disembark and then found, to my dismay, the entire flight waiting in lines to go through passport control and there was nowhere left for me to hide without looking thoroughly suspicious. Thankfully, I only had hand luggage, so dashed straight out towards the exit as soon as I had been checked.

'Excuse me!' A shrill voice stopped me in my tracks and I looked round sharply. 'I think you dropped this.' My passport was being held out to me by a stout old woman with a concerned face. I snatched it off her, mumbling my thanks, and continued on my harried way to the escalator down to the tube.

I got home around six o'clock and turned the heating on in the freezing flat. I called Jonas straight away, to find out how the hoglets were doing, but he wasn't answering his phone, so I unpacked and went directly over to Hartland Road with a bottle of grappa as a peace offering. I found him in the garage, feeding one of the little creatures in the gloom of the single overhead strip light, with the electric fire on full. I felt a stab of guilt that I had left him to do the round-the-clock feeds on his own. Taking a deep breath, I delivered my rehearsed apology.

'I'm sorry, Jonas. I haven't been well and then something came up at work.' He continued on with the feeding as if I wasn't there. 'How are they?'

I took a step towards him and he looked up at me sadly. His light blue eyes had dark rings underneath them from exhaustion and the skin on his face was grey and baggy. He shook his head.

'I haven't been this tired since Carrie was a baby – she didn't sleep through the night until she was two years old, that one. I was a young man, then, though. Paula thought it was colic, then it was teething, then I think she just got in the habit of it. She was lonely at night, didn't want to be on her own in her cot, even with the light on and her teddies and all. She's always had a strong imagination, that one; she used to frighten herself when we left her on her own, that was what it seemed like. Paula took her into our bed in the end, even though that was something we said we'd never do – a man and his wife need some space together – but that was what she needed, you see, that did the trick. She slept good as gold after that. It calmed her down, made her feel safe again. She went back in her own bed after a few weeks, never another murmur from her. You have to give them what they need, don't you, that's the trick with the little ones. That's what my Paula always said. She was kind, Paula was, and patient. She was a lovely mam to our girls.'

I stood awkwardly in the fusty garage as he reminisced, squinting at the clock on the wall. I was trying to work out whether Prof had landed yet and fretting about whether he would be seeing Lola again

tonight and whether it *had* been her on my flight and, horror of horrors, whether she had seen me.

Jonas put the animal down at last and placed the pipette in a glass on the table. Talking about Paula seemed to have shifted him into a more upbeat gear and he became quite animated, telling me that the hoglets – he'd named them Spud and Sprout – were doing well, better than expected. He went on to recount, in great detail, their increasing milk consumption, growth, funny antics and so on.

'That's good, I'm pleased,' I told him with a thin smile. And I was, in a way, although the plight of two baby hedgehogs had become somewhat eclipsed by the magnitude of the events in Rome and my swirling inner torture at the prospect of having lost Prof and our future together to a breezy, blousy interloper.

I helped Jonas carry the hoglets' box down the path and into the house so he could continue with the night feeds in the comfort of his sitting room. I offered to make him a sandwich and a coffee before I went, which he politely declined.

'I'll be off, then,' I said, but didn't say when I would be back. I couldn't commit to anything until I knew what was happening with Prof. I suspected Jonas was waiting for me to offer to help with the hoglets, to take some of the responsibility off his shoulders, perhaps even take them with me for a night or two, but I just couldn't. I was waiting for his request and had prepared my excuse, but he never asked.

I got into my coat and scarf and had a final peer into the box. Spud and Sprout had curled up together and were sleeping peacefully, their little white prickles rising and falling with their breath. Jonas had given them their lives again and I felt a brief surge of happiness that was quickly tempered by the intrusive, appalling image of Lola in her long blue dress, holding the back of Prof's head as he kissed her.

Thursday 19 November

The letter from Rome arrived for Prof this morning. It was strange seeing it again, as if it had nothing to do with me and was from another dimension altogether. I was trembling with anticipation, though, as I placed it on his desk with the rest of his post. I overcame the urge to put it on top and placed it second from bottom of the small pile, as if it was nothing special or important. He came in as normal, all jovial and full of good cheer. I watched him through the glass partition as he set about opening his mail with the long, silver letter opener he always used, and I managed to coordinate bringing in his tea as he was reading the missive from Rome. I really needed to experience his reaction, not just see it. I wanted to be there as the realisation hit him that Lola was not all she seemed, that she had made a fool of him, that he had been tricked into having feelings for her. He frowned as he read the letter and put his glasses on as he held up the two photos and looked carefully at them. Then he read the letter again and turned it over as if there might have been something on the other side that he had missed. I was just leaving the room when he called my name with such intensity that I started a little and had a momentary feeling of panic that maybe, somehow, I had left an identifying mark on the paper. I turned and smiled helpfully in response, raising my eyebrows a fraction to indicate that I was expecting a question.

'Where did this letter come from? Do you know? Did it come this morning?'

I told him it had and that it had arrived in the regular university postal system.

'Why, is there something wrong?' I asked with a hint of concern and the slightest suggestion that he was behaving oddly.

'I'm not sure,' he muttered as he looked back at the photos. 'Will you contact Lola Maguire for me, please, and ask her to come and see me later today?'

'Oh, I think Lola teaches all day on a Thursday,' I replied innocently, as if I cared about disrupting Lola's schedule.

'Just tell her she needs to come in and see me, please. Urgently. Can you also ask Maurice Lowe from academic misconduct to come and see me as soon as he is free.' I knew from his tone that I was dismissed and I flew back to my desk to email Lola and Maurice, feeling giddy with excitement. I had set loose a typhoon that was about to spin out of control and take Lola with it. Far, far away.

The rest of the day was beyond my wildest dreams and I am sitting here sipping a divine glass of Frascati with Puccini playing in the background, replaying it all in my mind and feeling like the proverbial cat who got the cream. The plan that I put into motion in that hot, crowded post office in Rome came together perfectly. Firstly, Maurice Lowe came rushing up to Prof's office. What an unpleasant, officious little man he is – but just the type you want when you need someone on your side to be completely immovable about university policy and procedures in cases of plagiarism and the like. He and Prof had a deep conversation for about half an hour, during which time Prof asked me to photocopy both the letter and the screenshot photos, adding unnecessarily that he knew he could trust me to be discreet. I took the opportunity to remind him that I am not one for office gossip, and, because he looked so stressed out, I squeezed his hand gently as I took the papers, just in a supportive way. It was well judged and he looked at me with such appreciation I thought I might faint with glee, but I managed to keep a serious face as I headed towards the print room.

Maurice hurried out importantly with the photocopied sheets as if he had been waiting for a scandal like this his whole life and, to my delight, Prof flopped down on the chair in front of my desk – something he has never ever done before. He took his glasses off, ran his hand across his face and then put his glasses back on before looking at me wearily.

'We've got a problem, Sylvia. As you may have seen from the letter, an academic from the Rome conference, who chooses to remain anonymous, the coward,' he said, shaking his head in disdain, 'has evidence indicating that Lola Maguire may very well have plagiarised work from her previous supervisor, Michael Landers, and passed it off as her own.'

I did a sharp intake of breath as if it was the worst crime I had ever heard of and responded with the usual range of disbelief statements and questions, none of which Prof answered. I was so tempted to stick the knife in further and say I had never liked her and thought there was something flaky about her, but I held back and Prof stared out the window behind my desk for a few seconds with a crestfallen expression on his face that pained me a little bit, before getting up and going back into his inner sanctum.

It all went quiet then for the next few hours until Lola arrived, in an absolute spin, at around four. She was a dishevelled mess. Her hair was all over the place and her heaving bosom just made her look fat in the patterned tunic she was wearing. She had rushed putting her make-up on and her eyeliner was smudged across one eye and perfect on the other, giving her the look of a badly painted, cheap doll. I was just about to greet her with a cool, 'Good afternoon, Lola' when Prof threw his door wide and held it open for her as she rushed in. They were still in there when five o'clock rolled round, but I was hardly going to leave and miss the show. I had strained to hear the conversation, but all I got was her high-pitched pleading in a raised voice, and echoes of the stern telling-off tone Prof uses for errant students and underperforming faculty members. Maurice joined them at around ten past five, clutching some official-looking document and she came out five minutes later with a puffy, tear-stained face and mascara all down her cheeks. Oh, she looked such a sight. It was balm to my soul!

That should be the last we see of her then, and good riddance to bad rubbish. It's so lucky Prof has me looking out for him. I 'totally have his back', as Crystal would say. The damage that woman could have done to his reputation is unthinkable and to have had Prof humiliated in his professional circles would have been unbearable for him, and for me.

'Salute' to me for being a clever girl. I am off to bed now with a satisfied smile on my face and a feeling that justice has been done. I just hope this hasn't put Prof's recovery from his divorce back. Learning he couldn't trust one woman was bad enough, but two – that could put him off for ever. He may never be prepared to put his faith in us and the wonderful life I know we will have together. No, I won't think along those lines, not tonight. Tonight is a happy time.

Friday 20 November

A quiet day at work today. Prof was rather subdued and spent the day in his inner sanctum, working on his book. He even had lunch at his desk, which is unusual for him. He asked me to send students away if they didn't have an appointment and to reschedule any non-urgent meetings. I was more than happy to fulfil my role as his protector in such ways. Even given the slightly depressed energy in the office, I definitely feel that things are back to normal and that it will just be a matter of time before Prof bounces back and we can resume our developing relationship. With any luck, we will be a few steps further on than before the whole Lola debacle, given the hand-touching and desk-sitting which occurred yesterday. I am full of hope and joy.

Popped round to Millie's after work to water the plants as they are away in Edinburgh for their anniversary. They have shut the deli too as they couldn't find anyone to run it for a few days, now that their assistant, Katya, has gone back to Poland with her feckless boyfriend. This strikes me as enormously disorganised and irresponsible of them. The money they'll lose over the weekend! I'm just glad they didn't ask me to step in. I would be hopeless anyway, I don't like food that much to want to stand selling small portions of it in plastic containers all day, and the cleaning that needs doing after hours is a most repulsive prospect. Crystal is staying with a friend, apparently; again, I'm relieved she wasn't foisted onto me or I would have had to make up some excuse. I couldn't bear a whole weekend of strained conversation with a moody teenager, permanently wearing earphones and transfixed by her iPad. No, I plan to spend the weekend luxuriating in the knowledge that Lola has gone and treating myself to some beauty treatments and an aromatherapy massage. I really do feel reborn and light as air.

Tuesday 24 November

I don't know where to start. I am destroyed and distraught and in total shock. I need to go through the events of today in my head to try and understand how joy can so quickly turn to pain. I need to work out how I have ended up in this place where I don't belong.

This is how I recall what happened:

Lola and Ned came into the office around four this afternoon so she could return some books to Prof, and he ushered her straight into his inner sanctum and closed the door. I fiddled around with the filing cabinet near the partition wall, hoping to catch the gist of what was being said and never thought to take any notice of Ned who was hanging around by my desk. As Lola came out of Prof's office she looked at Ned and he was holding my phone (my phone!) in his hand, staring at it quizzically.

'Mummy, why is there a picture of you and Carl on her phone?'

The words hung in the air like frozen stones and the whole world turned upside down in the second it took for the implications of what he said to resonate with me and with Lola. I went to lunge towards the boy, but

Lola was nearer and grabbed the phone right out of his hand. Her face passed through so many emotions so quickly it was dizzying. Confusion, bewilderment, disbelief – and then came the anger.

'Jesus, you were there in Italy? Spying on us?' It came out like a question and it came out loud – loud enough for Prof to sense something was up and come to his door. He looked from me to Lola and back again, trying to grasp what was occurring and she took the phone up to him to show him the picture. Her eyes didn't leave me for a second. 'She was there in Rome. She took pictures of us.'

The words were utterly damning. I wanted to howl and scream and beg Prof not to look. I wanted to die right there in that very moment. My life ended. My hands flew to my mouth and I was looking at Prof in absolute terror as he snatched the phone from Lola and held it close to his face.

'Sylvia?' It was as if he had never said my name before, as if I was an alien concept to him. He looked straight at me. 'What is this? Were you in Rome? What …?'

I swallowed, and the only word I could say was 'please'. I said it over and over again, with my hands held out imploringly for the wretched phone. I don't know what I thought it would achieve. In my distressed state, I thought that if they gave me back the phone it would all go away and be forgotten. It was ludicrous, really. I see that now. But no other word would come out of my mouth than 'please'. It was as if we were all permanently locked into this dreadful tableau, a toxic, monstrous situation in which none of us had any idea what to do next.

My immediate instinct was to run away and I went to grab my coat off the back of the door, but Prof wasn't having that.

'No. No, Sylvia, you need to stay here. We need to sort this out.'

I was getting into my coat anyway and going for my bag when he shouted, 'Sit down' and I burst into tears.

Prof has never shouted at me before. In fact, I have never heard him shout at *anyone* before and it was mortifying. He sent Lola and Ned away and told her he would call her in a short while. She didn't want to go. She sensed blood, like the wolf she is, and possible triumph, and she wanted to see me brought down. Ned's eyes were like saucers and he turned his head all sorts of degrees to get a last look at me – the shamed woman – as his mother led him out into the corridor. Prof closed the door behind them, shooing away a bemused-looking Margaret who had just arrived back from a meeting, locked it with his key, and pulled the blind down over the square of glass. Then he turned around to face me with an intense stare and I had to try and explain how I had never trusted her and had my suspicions about her and didn't want for him to be humiliated and that I was only trying to protect him.

He suspected, of course, that I had sent the anonymous letter, damning Lola. I denied it with all my might and he wavered on that one, not knowing what to think I suppose. Without that, all I had done was go to Rome during my annual leave and take some photos of him and Lola on my phone: weird, but not dangerous or illegal in any way, and I could sense him thinking the same thing.

For a moment, I sensed there may be hope, hope that we could move past this, put it down to the menopause or whatever, perhaps even see it as evidence of my excellent instincts about people and my loyalty to him. Perhaps even laugh about it one day when we were together. For a moment, it seemed like life could continue, there would be a reprieve. And then he swiped back to the previous pictures on my phone and saw the screen shots of Dr Landers' presentation that I had posted to him.

The look on Prof's face as he realised the awful truth will stay with me for ever. I can't bear to think about it any more. I want to crawl into bed, go to sleep and never wake up.

Thursday 26 November

I have now been officially suspended from my duties at the university pending an investigation into gross misconduct. Not because of going to Rome and following Prof and Lola, not even for finding evidence of Lola's plagiarism, but because I didn't present this information to Prof in a reasonable manner and because I pretended not to have anything to do with it when the evidence landed on Prof's desk. It's a complicated case and the university aren't quite sure how to proceed, but they want me out, that's for sure. They just need to find a way to fire me.

I am in agony being away from Prof. I can't see him or speak to him or even email him. I have written him countless letters, trying to explain why I did it, and trying to make him see that even though it has gone utterly wrong it was all done for the right reasons and that my actions turned up important information about Lola that he needed to know. But I daren't post them, even to his home address.

Millie and Kamal are back from Scotland, thank goodness, and Millie is being an absolute rock for me. She doesn't know the whole story – she has no idea how

I feel about Prof, for example because I never let on to anyone how much he means to me. It's as if saying it would make it somehow untrue, or I might be laughed at or teased – and I couldn't bear that. She knows I have been suspended though, over a plagiarism charge I made against a student, and although she has no idea about the details, she is completely on my side as I knew she would be. It's comforting just being around Millie at such a difficult time. I find just watching her pottering round the kitchen or doing her embroidery calming and wish I could be looked after by her for ever and not have to go out and face the world any more. I miss the way we used to be, Millie and I, before she met Kamal. Every time I think of what has happened with Prof my stomach twists and I feel like I'm going to be sick. I can hardly eat a thing, no matter how hard Millie tries to tempt me. Last night, as we were sitting watching the news, she brought in a tray of fruit and cheese which she placed beside me with a look of anxious concern.

'Could you just try to eat a little bit of something, darling?' she pleaded, prompting Kamal to throw down his paper in disgust and storm out the room.

Millie winced as he thumped up the stairs. 'Don't mind him, he's just stressed out about the shop,' she said, as she started cutting up the fruit for me. 'He doesn't mean to be so rude.'

I allowed myself to be subsumed into Millie's care and took a nibble of apple, feeling enormously grateful for her love. Lewis called round to see Crystal at about half past nine and Millie told him it was too late and she was in bed already, even though she was actually crouching behind the living-room door with her finger held against her lips.

Saturday 28 November

This dreadful day began with me receiving two letters. The first one I opened was an official letter from the university terminating my employment and the second was the following devastating missive from Prof:

Dear Sylvia,

You will have had official notification by now from the university secretariat informing you of the termination of your employment as my Personal Assistant and as an employee of the university.

I am extremely disappointed by what has happened and feel very let down by your behaviour. I understand that in some way you may have thought you were trying to help me, but surely it is clear to you now that I do not, and never have, required help of this type from anyone. It was entirely inappropriate of you to follow me to Rome and set out on an ill-advised attempt at espionage to try to discredit Lola Maguire. For your information, results of an internal and external investigation into plagiarism indicate most strongly that Dr Landers copied Ms Maguire's work and not the other way around. Unfortunately, Dr Landers is in the early stages of dementia and made a mistake when writing up what he mistook for his own research, when it was actually the work Lola had done for her Masters thesis. He then presented this as his own at the Rome conference, having completely forgotten the origin of the paper. As you can appreciate, Dr Landers is most distressed by all this. It is an inglorious way to end what has been a stellar career and we in the academy are regretful of the circumstances of this whole affair. I would consider an apology from you to be appropriate and I include details of Dr Landers' postal and email addresses at the bottom of this letter.

It is with relief that I can report that Ms Maguire is now re-registered on the PhD programme and is progressing well again with her studies. It is to her credit that she has managed to pick herself up and continue with her research and she is enjoying the full support of the department and of myself as her supervisor.

Please note that I will not be able to provide a personal reference for any future jobs you may apply for, but do feel free to contact the Human Resources department who will be able to confirm your length of service at the university.

May I suggest, Sylvia, that if you have not already
done so, you consider seeking some professional help or
counselling to support you in the coming months?
I wish you luck with your future endeavours.
Best wishes

Professor Carl Lomax

I didn't know what to do with myself after reading Prof's letter, so I did what I always do when I feel completely lost – I went around to see Millie. My dire luck was that she wasn't at home. Kamal opened the door, looking really edgy and cross. I had obviously caught him at a bad time, but that still doesn't excuse the vitriol with which he spoke to me.

'What do you want now?' he said nastily, as if it was the tenth time I had knocked on the door that morning.

'Is Millie in, or is she at the deli?' I asked, desperate to speak to her.

'Neither.' He shook his head. 'They've gone Christmas shopping. Katya is back, she's in the deli today.'

We stood looking at each other while I waited for him to invite me in, which he did, eventually, gracelessly, just by stepping back from the door and allowing me to walk past him into the hall. I had tears in my eyes by now and looked up at him imploringly, needing a kind word or at least some civility and he responded in the cruellest way, with the most unkind words spitting out of his mouth in a horrible whisper.

'What is it you want from us, Sylvia? Eh? You skulk around on the edges of our lives, but nobody wants you here. I'm telling you, Millie is sick of you pulling her down with all your problems. Crystal can't stand you and neither can I. Why don't you just fuck off and leave us all alone. Get your own life, no?'

Almost immediately my upset turned to anger. I could feel it rising from the depths of my being, all these years of hurt and deceit and bitterness, all because of him. And he had the gall to speak to me like that, as though it was my fault, as though it was I who was the interloper in Millie's life, rather than him.

'You bastard!'

The words seethed from my mouth as he put his finger to his lips to try and quiet me, but I wouldn't be quieted, not this time. A tirade of abuse and fury sprang forth as I told him everything I thought of him, everything I had been through, how I was alone because of him, how I was childless because of him, and how appalling it was that he just carried on as if nothing was amiss. How he had everything and I had nothing and now he even wanted to take Millie away from me too.

'Having sex with you ruined my entire life!' I said, screaming this last bit, the awful truth of it finally verbalised. Then I saw the petrified look on his face, which I didn't comprehend at first – until I followed his gaze over my shoulder and into the sitting room where two little old ladies in saris were sitting on the sofa, teacups in hand, staring at me open-mouthed and the only sound was the grandfather clock gently ticking in the hall behind me. I recognised Kamal's aunties straight away and remembered, too late, that Millie had told me they were coming to stay.

Millie and Crystal chose that terrible moment to walk in the front door, Millie chuckling about a cat they had seen, madly chasing its tail in the front garden.

'Hello, darling,' she said to me. 'Why are you all standing in the hall?'

She put down her bags, hung up her coat and kissed Kamal on the cheek. Then she sensed it, the tension in the air, the ugliness of a situation she couldn't grasp. She looked rapidly from me to Kamal with her eyes narrowed.

'What's happened?' she asked, sharply.

I tried to get in first with my explanation, tried so hard to steer Millie away from those blasted, interfering old women who were all over her in a flash, telling her what they had heard, bits of it, disjointed; they clearly hadn't understood it all, but the essence of it was there: that Kamal and I had betrayed her, that we had had sex and we had been deceiving her all these years.

'Is it true? Is it true?' They kept repeating the question to me, to Kamal, to Millie. Crystal had retreated to the stairs and was sitting there, clinging to the banisters like a frightened child, her round brown eyes trying to take in what was happening to her family.

'You see? You see what you have done, you stupid woman?' I remember Kamal snarling at me in the middle of it all. Then he began to cry, he put his head in his hands and sat next to Crystal on the stairs and wept theatrically. She pulled away from him and ran up to her room and the aunties rushed up after her, calling to her and offering comfort. Then it was just me and Millie facing each other in the hall with that damn clock still ticking away behind me, interspersed with Kamal's wretched sobs. She stared at me as if she had never seen me before in her life. Then she turned and threw open the front door.

'Get out of my house,' she said, with her voice trembling.

'Millie, please let me talk to you,' I begged her, but she shook her head and looked at the floor until I finally made my way past her onto the step and then she closed the door in my face as I tried to say sorry. I stood there for a while trying to hear what was going on inside. I could hear muffled voices and crying and shouting and I felt very alone. I don't know what to do any more, I don't know what I have left to live for.

Winter

'Hibernation' is a Latin term which literally means 'to pass the winter'. Hedgehogs are not really asleep during this period, but enter a state of inert torpor in a hidden nest of leaves and grass. If the hedgehog has not had enough sustenance over the preceding months, or if it is woken too early, it may die. The vast majority of hedgehogs hibernate alone, although occasionally a male and female may share a hibernating spot.

There are many things that can harm a hedgehog: slug pellets, garden netting, falling into ponds, cars, dogs and lawnmowers, to name but a few. Even when they are hibernating they are not always safe – we should always check bonfires before we light them and compost heaps before we fork them in case a prickly friend is holed up in there and needs rescuing.

Jonas Entwistle, *The Hedgehog Year*

Friday 11 December

I somehow managed to get back to my flat after the showdown at Millie and Kamal's, although I have no memory of that journey. I must have walked up to Church Road and waited for the bus and got on and swiped my Oyster card, and I must have sat down and looked out of the window so I would know when to ring the bell. I must have alighted and made my way up Princes Avenue and into Tennison Road, but cannot recall any of it. I must have opened the main door with the key, climbed the stairs to the first floor, opened the door of my flat and come in. I must have taken off my coat and put down my bag, walked into my room and written in my journal before lying down in bed and pulling the covers over me. But all I know is being here, in my flat, safe and alone, away from the shouting and the shame and the sickening mess that is my life.

I stand at my window and watch people coming and going from work, or school or the shops, their lives punctuated by normal activities and rhythms, working their way through their days as if an invisible hand were guiding and constraining them. I watch and I wonder like a stranger in a strange land. What stops that man from number 75 from packing a bag, throwing it into his car and driving off into the unknown, rather than rushing up the road to the station every day, toast in hand? Why does that frail old lady pull her trolley down to the minimart at 3.30 every afternoon when she knows the pavement will be blocked by hordes of belligerent teenagers who frighten her and get in her way? Why does the brassy woman who runs the hairdresser's opposite come out every hour, on the hour, for a cigarette that she clearly doesn't enjoy? I can't make sense of any of it any more. I've lost the knack of life, that's the problem. It must be like falling off a horse. They say if you don't get on again straight away you lose your nerve and you'll never be able to pluck up the courage to ride again. But you can live without riding. How can you live without actually living?

The television is great company to me. I can structure my waking hours around its cheerful daytime schedule. Property programmes are my favourite. I get swept up in whether this retired couple will buy the thatched cottage or the barn conversion or if that man and his son really will move to Spain to run a hotel, and sometimes I even forget myself for minutes at a time. Then I remember where I am and that I have no stunning sea view, no partner to plan the future with, no children or grandchildren to come and stay, and no exciting times ahead. But it can help, seeing other people enjoy themselves. I can't be bothered to feel jealous any more, there's no energy left behind it. In fact, I think that if someone knocked on the door and presented me with everything I had ever wanted – husband, children, family, home – I would simply shake my head and close the door, saying, 'Thank you, but it's all too late now. It doesn't matter any more. I can't accept that now. It was never for me.'

I wish I had known that years ago – it would have saved so much wasted effort and heartache. I could have spent the time looking for something else, or building a different life.

'Find a target before you run out of ammunition,' Father used to say to us when we were teenagers. How right he was, but how hard it is to understand that when you are young and full of energy and you believe that the world is a generous place that will give you whatever you want.

I saw Imogen Scott's daughters Iona and Skye on a TV show this morning. They were introduced by one of the gushing hosts as 'earth mothers' (is there any other kind? I have never met a mother from another planet), although their exquisite boho clothes and intricately plaited hair suggest rather more effort and money is put into their appearance than they would like viewers to think. They did a little cooking demonstration of one of the organic baby food recipes from their new book, *Earth Babies*. It seemed to consist of steaming courgettes and peas and mulching them up with a hand blender, but the hosts reacted as if they had just split the atom on live television. The twins kept emphasising how it was 'so easy'.

'It's so easy to buy fresh vegetables from your local farmers' market,' Iona explained.

Skye, nodding enthusiastically, picked up the baton here. 'And so easy to steam and blend the veggies,' she said, beaming as she poked the courgettes with a fork.

Camera on Iona again, head tilted to one side, listening carefully like this was the first time she had ever considered the benefits of cooking a vegetable. She paused for effect and then added smugly, 'I actually grow my own veggies to cook for my children', as if the mothers watching had not already been made to feel guilty enough for failing to buy organic produce from a farmers' market and using it to make their own baby food.

'Me too,' trilled Skye. 'It's so easy and such a fun activity to do with the children. There is a chapter in our book about how to get started. It's really so easy.'

They had a baby with them, whose it was I don't know, but he was sitting docilely in a high chair and obediently ate whatever splodge was being spooned into his mouth. I turned the television off with the remote and sat watching the blank screen for several minutes, listening to myself breathe. When I turned it on again it was competition time and Iona and Skye had gone. Back to their perfect lives with their earth babies and their vegetables and their long floral dresses and their million-pound publishing deal. So easy.

Monday 21 December

I have got into the habit of rising very early. I wake around 4 a.m. and by six I can't lie there any longer. When I hear the first cars going past outside I am up in the kitchen, going through the comforting ritual of making tea. In those moments, I can almost convince myself that my life is as any other, that I have a day ahead, that I have people and plans and a routine and a reason and small pleasures to enjoy. I have none of these things. I just have the tea and the noise of the traffic and that has to be enough.

I try to shower and dress before the sinking feeling really takes hold. Mostly it is a dull ache, a nothingy sort of feeling that lets me drift through time and space unnoticed by anyone else, unnoticed by me, even. I try hard not to pay myself too much attention. I am utterly sick of myself and what I have become. In the mornings, I read through some of Prof's articles or perhaps a chapter or two of one of his books, taking comfort in hearing his voice coming clear and true through the words. I make myself eat some soup and perhaps a sandwich, and then usually find I am able to fall asleep on the sofa until teatime. The evenings stretch out endlessly. I walk a lot, round the streets. It feels a bit odd without a dog to legitimise it, but I like to look in people's windows and catch glimpses of their normality, their cosy living rooms bedecked with Christmas decorations, and their busy kitchens. I like to see what they are watching on television and sometimes I rush home and find the same programme so I can sit and watch it too and feel connected to someone, somewhere else, who I know is sharing the same experience. On Thursday evening, I walked all the way to Dulwich and stood outside Prof's house for an hour. All the lights were out and there was clearly no one in. In retrospect, I am thankful for that. I don't know what I, or he, would have done if he had seen me, and I'm not sure I could have stopped myself ringing the bell if there had been signs of occupation.

Walking back, I started to feel scared. I was sure I was being followed by a man in a hooded sweatshirt. Every time I crossed the road he crossed too and when I stopped to pretend to do up my shoelace he also stopped not ten feet behind me. After a while I could bear the tension no more and I turned to face him, twisting my face into a snarl that I hoped would frighten him off. He didn't even acknowledge me, just walked straight past, head down, texting as he went. I don't know what possessed me but I ran after him tugging at his sweatshirt, asking him, imploring him, 'Hey, were you following me?' He shook me off his arm with a face full of revulsion, shouting, 'Get off me, crazy lady' and carried on walking and texting as if nothing had happened.

When I got home, I sat very still on the sofa in the dark, listening to the noises from the other flats, the other lives going on above and below and to the left and right of me. I heard old Mr Goldberg rustling in his wardrobe on the other side of my living room wall, the children upstairs thundering around, defiant of their mother's shouts, the insistent drum and bass music drifting up from downstairs. I wondered, if I sat there for long enough, perhaps I would simply cease to exist … and that was a comforting thought in some ways. Eventually, I picked up Prof's book on the educational system in post-war Britain and read myself to sleep.

Sunday 3 January

Late December and early January in our family is usually a time filled with celebrations, what with Christmas and New Year and Crystal's birthday on New Year's Eve. Millie always goes overboard with presents and dinners and cakes and parties and people and I hide in the background, waiting for it to be over. I suppose that this year my wish has come true, as I have not been included in anything and have spent the festive season completely alone in my flat. I imagined them all eating the turkey dinner cooked by Kamal, pulling crackers, drinking snowballs and I wondered if they cared, or indeed even noticed, that I wasn't there.

I received two Christmas cards, both on the day before Christmas Eve. One was from Mother, a flimsy multipack type, sporting an insipid nativity scene with a book token inside. It took me a moment to work out why she had written *I hope you enjoy your holiday* in it, and then I realised that Millie must have told her that to explain my absence at the usual family gatherings this time of year. The other was from Jonas and family, with a picture of a hedgehog wearing a Santa hat on the front. *Hope all is well, Sylvia, and that we see you at the sanctuary again soon*, he had put in trembly writing. I stared at the card for a long time thinking odd thoughts about whether the hedgehog was really wearing the hat or if it was photoshopped on and wondering about what might have happened to the hog after the picture was taken and decided it was probably time to go for a walk. As I was putting my coat on I considered going to Hartland Road and seeing Jonas and Igor and the hedgehogs and my heart rose briefly at the thought. But I just couldn't bring myself to do a happy thing or go somewhere I was needed. I feel as if I have a dark blanket wrapped around my head that makes it impossible for me to connect with anyone or anything outside my flat or my miserable thoughts about Prof and Millie.

On Boxing Day my feet took me, unbidden, in the direction of Prof's house again. This time the porch was bedecked with white fairy lights and a huge tree occupied the sitting room window, its red and green lanterns twinkling prettily. I could just make out a figure on the sofa and pictured Prof there, glass of whisky in hand, experiencing the loneliness of the divorced dad at this most child-centred of times. I had to hold myself back from walking up to the front door and ringing the bell. How futile for us both to be so lonely when we are meant to be together, made for each other. I remembered his letter, though, and bit my lip in despair as I turned and made my way back home to face the rest of the festive season alone.

I snatched up the phone when it rang on New Year's Day, thinking it might be Millie, but it was only Mother, ringing to complain about the weather and the shops being closed and her aching knees.

'Did you all have a nice Christmas?' I asked tightly, the 'without me' part of the question left unspoken.

It seemed to take her a while to recall the day, only a week previous, but it eventually lined up in her mind. 'Oh yes, yes it was the usual,' she said dismissively. 'Kamal's turkey was a bit overdone, but the potatoes were pleasant enough. Millie made the crackers herself and they were a disaster. They didn't bang and the hats got stuck in the cardboard tubes. Crystal got a new digital thingy and Kamal gave Millie the most beautiful emerald earrings – they must have cost a fortune. She didn't give him anything, though, not a thing. I didn't mention it, but I thought it was a bit odd. Auntie Bolly came round in the afternoon for tea as usual, so poor Hamish had to go in the garden. He yipped and cried the whole time she was there and I seethed on the sofa while she ate her way through the mince pies. I can understand she doesn't like dogs, but Hamish? Really? He's hardly a Rottweiler.'

I listened in silence as she recounted the entire day, from her own peculiar perspective, of course, waiting for her to acknowledge that I hadn't been there and to enquire after my well-being or my holiday but she didn't.

'Thanks for the book token,' I said in the end, resigned to being of negligible importance even to my own mother. 'I'll give you your present when I see you.' She didn't take the hint and make arrangements to meet, and I was ready to end the conversation. 'Well, Happy New Year, Mum,' I said with finality.

'You too, Sylvia. Let's hope it's better than the last one.' She rang off, leaving me mystified as to what it was she had found so personally disagreeable about the previous twelve months.

Wednesday 6 January

Tea. Soup. Tea. Television.

Monday 11 January

They have been digging up the road outside all day. I don't know why. It's so quiet without the sound of the traffic.

Thursday 14 January

The workmen have gone now. The road is back to normal.

I haven't spoken to anyone since my phone call with Mother two weeks ago. Not a soul. I don't know how much longer I can go on like this. I miss Millie so much and being apart from Prof is agony. My heart is broken.

Wednesday 20 January

A small knock on the door, tentative at first, then more insistent, woke me from one of my extended naps yesterday afternoon. I ignored it at first, thinking it must be for one of the other flats as the intercom hadn't buzzed and I had let no one up. I lay there, listening, and it came again, a slight tentative knock and then a small voice: 'Auntie Sylvia, it's Crystal, are you there?'

Crystal. Of all people, the last person I would expect to visit me ever again would be my niece. It didn't seem possible, and yet here she was. I contemplated whether I should play dead, stay still and quiet until she went away. But it crossed my mind that she might be bringing a message from Millie, or that, in fact, Millie might be standing there with her, and that thought propelled me off the sofa and across the room. The scary thought that an angry Kamal might be there instead of, or as well as, Millie also occurred to me during my short journey to the door, prompting me to keep the chain on as I cautiously opened it and peered out into the gloomy hallway. To both my relief and disappointment it was just Crystal, standing there in her tracksuit and trainers with her swimming bag over her shoulder. She always goes swimming after school on a Wednesday, so with one glance I knew what day it was and the approximate time – it's funny how your brain keeps working even when nothing matters any more.

'Auntie Sylvia, can I come in?'

She seemed genuinely concerned and looked so guileless that I took the chain off the door and let her in. I wandered back to the sofa and she followed me there, making her way carefully around the stacks of books and journals on the floor. Seeing there was no room for her on the sofa, she moved a pile of Prof's papers gently on to the coffee table and then sat down next to me. We stayed like that for a while, her looking at me, me looking out the window opposite, having no idea what to say or do or why she was here and not being able to raise enough energy to start even the most banal conversation. She surprised me then by taking my hand, her warm skin a welcome comfort for my cold fingers. I turned to her and saw that her face was full of concern.

'I don't know everything about what happened, Auntie Sylvia, but I get the gist of it. Mum told me some stuff and how angry she is with you, but I know she can be over-dramatic and over-emotional about things, especially where Dad's concerned. She told me I wasn't to contact you, but that didn't feel right to me. It was weird not having you there at Christmas. You're family. We're family, aren't we? We should be there for each other, no matter what. You shouldn't be frozen out.' She paused and took a breath, steeling herself to say the next part. 'You slept with Dad, right, ages ago, and then Mum found out and went mad?'

I nodded sadly, waiting for the recriminations, but none came. Instead Crystal squeezed my hand gently. 'I get it. Stuff happens. And Dad's no angel, I see the way he stares at Katya sometimes in the shop, when she wears her mini skirt. That's just the way guys are, isn't it?'

'Not all of them,' I said softly, thinking of Jonas and his devotion to Paula. 'And your dad wasn't all to blame, Crystal; he was so young and he was adjusting to a completely new life in a foreign country. It was both of us. It was a stupid, stupid mistake.' My voice cracked and I bit my bottom lip to stop myself crying in front of my unexpectedly kind and understanding niece.

She shuffled along the sofa towards me, close enough for me to smell the chlorine from the swimming pool on her damp hair. She put her arm clumsily around my shoulders and said, 'It's OK, it'll be OK.'

'Thank you,' I whispered, leaning into her, and we spent some time just sitting together and looking out of the window, watching the clouds break up and turn into a porridgey pattern against the reddish sky. When it started to go dark, Crystal told me quietly she had to get back for dinner or Millie would start to worry and that she would come and see me again soon. She kissed my cheek and let herself out, then I lay down on the sofa and fell into a deep sleep.

It was just after midnight when I got up and went to my bedside table to get the teabag Prof had given me. I made the tea and sat sipping it, feeling the warmth of the ginger and lemon filling my body. It had retained its flavour after all this time and I am taking that as a clear and comforting sign that Prof still cares about me. For as long as the drink lasted, I felt that I was with him again and that nothing had changed. I needed that reassurance to give me the strength to keep going. I slept again, then, waking around four as usual, and waited for the traffic to begin.

Friday 29 January

I went back to Prof's house again this evening, I'm afraid, for the third time this week. It's as if my feet have a mind of their own, I decide not to go and then I find myself taking my duffel coat down off the peg and winding my scarf round my neck and pulling on my gloves and hat. By the time I have picked up my door keys I have resigned myself to the long walk ahead, as if some higher power is requiring it of me. At least it's a way of burning off calories, I suppose, as I get precious little other exercise these days. A light mist of rain was dissolving the snow on the pavement, along with the hundreds of footprints made by tired commuters on their way home from work. I imagined them all warm in their houses, greeted like returning warriors by their loving partners and children, secure in their place in the world.

The glimpses I caught into front rooms and kitchens as I walked down the suburban streets reinforced this fantasy. Couples cuddling on the sofa, fathers playing with their children, mothers feeding babies, all bathed in the reassuring glow of central heating and togetherness. It was a perfect night for being unseen, though; nobody wanted to go out dog walking or jogging on an evening like this. Making my way towards Prof's neighbourhood, I had the odd sensation of being the only human survivor of some sort of apocalypse. I entertained the idea for quite a while, imagining the freedom of going into abandoned houses, exploring what people had left behind, eating whatever I wanted, being queen of my dominion. But the thought of no Prof was unconscionable, so I shook myself back to reality as I turned into his road. I sheltered in my usual spot behind a wide-trunked oak on the other side of the street and felt quite cosy in a funny sort of way. I could see into the basement kitchen of their large Victorian terrace, where Harry, or perhaps it was Sam, sat eating a bowl of cereal at the wooden table.

They are nice lads, Harry and Sam, tall and dark like their dad, although they both have a slightly sly look about them which they get from their mother. There were piles of papers and books either side of him – signs of Prof taking his research home with him, as usual. He really does work too hard. My heart truly leapt when in wandered Prof in his dressing gown, a navy-blue towelling number that looked a little worn and faded. The sight of it made me yearn to be the person in his life who could appropriately buy him a new one. He ruffled the boy's hair, picked up a couple of papers and grabbed a beer out the fridge before leaving stage left.

Harry/Sam finished his cereal and started fiddling with something gold on the table, perhaps Prof's watch? No, the wrong shape, this was more of a solid object. Maybe some new kind of phone? He put it down and called after Prof, wandering out of the kitchen after him, leaving the dirty bowl on the table. Such a scene of domesticity, although it does pain me that they have no woman to look after them. I should be there, cooking them all dinner, tidying up, bringing Prof his beer. I waited in the rain until all the lights had gone out in the house and then I walked home, happy in the knowledge that Prof has his boys for company and is safe and sound in his bed.

Tuesday 16 February

I am exhausted after today's revelations, completely wrung out. Nothing is as I thought it was, and I am nothing but a fool.

The day started innocuously enough and I took myself to Dulwich picture gallery after breakfast for want of anything else to do. The weather has really turned arctic, now, and London is covered in frost and thick snow. It gives a nice peaceful atmosphere to my daytime meanderings and I rather enjoy the feeling of strangeness and light that covers the streets, untroubled by the need to be anywhere in particular. It took longer than usual to walk there due to the weather, but I didn't mind. I used up a few hours, drifting around the rooms, gazing at the art, wondering why anyone has ever bothered to paint pictures of what people look like on the outside when everything that really matters is hidden inside. A centuries-old triptych of the Madonna and Child held my attention for a long while and I was lost in thought when at around two o'clock the gallery attendant came up to me, the sole visitor, and told me that they were closing early owing to the weather. Her apologetic tone met with my complete indifference as I let her shepherd me out into the corridor.

After hesitating for a moment outside the main door, I pulled my coat tighter round me against the wind and crossed the road towards Prof's house. It had started snowing again and I stood, allowing the flakes to fall onto my face and into my mouth. Common sense told me to go back home to the safe and warm, but to borrow a phrase, I was 'but helpless in the arms of love'. I climbed the hill up to his road carefully, not lifting my feet between steps unless absolutely necessary as I tried to avoid slipping over. I could sense something was different as I approached Prof's house. There was usually little going on in the road in the afternoon and I generally contented myself with walking past his house, noticing the sort of small detail that can tell one much about a person's life if you know where to look. For example, I know when he has had the boys because of the takeaway pizza boxes in the recycling, and I know if Prof's been away for the weekend because there are no empty beer bottles left out on a Sunday night. Depending on when I come, I also know from the curtains what time Prof goes to bed and what time he gets up. But today his bedroom curtains were drawn at three o'clock in the afternoon. My heart lurched as I feared he must be ill and I had to hold myself back from running to the front door and pressing the bell, desperate to go in, look after him and nurse him back to health.

Then I saw two wine glasses and a bottle on the table in the bay window and felt a rising sense of alarm. I looked around frantically for Lola's tatty old Fiat, but I couldn't see it anywhere. She must have come by train, I thought, perhaps because the roads were icy. I stood stock-still, my eyes narrowed, every nerve alive, like an animal sensing a predator is near. I took several of the steps up towards Prof's front door, full of indignation and searing anger – and then stopped myself. What was I going to say? What could I do? I knew I wasn't supposed to be here, that I wasn't allowed to be in contact with Prof. It was the faint sound of laughter from inside the house that spurred me on in the end. It was utterly unbearable to think of him in there with her. I had convinced myself that the Rome tryst was a one-off, a mistake by Prof that anyone could have made and that any burgeoning romance between him and Lola had been sullied and stymied by subsequent events back home. I had to know if it was still going on, had to *see*. I continued up to the top and pressed the doorbell hard. I still had my finger on it when the front door opened and I found myself standing face to face with Tig. She was wearing a black tracksuit and had her cigarettes and gold Zippo lighter in hand, obviously about to step out to have a smoke on the porch. I don't know who was more surprised, me, Tig or Prof who was standing just behind her in novelty *Star Wars* boxer shorts and a grey T-shirt.

It was a moment that seemed to go on forever. I looked to Tig, she looked back at Prof, and Prof stared at me with an unpleasant, hard look in his eyes that I had never seen before. It was as if I had wandered backstage at a genial romantic comedy and discovered the cast members covered in blood, gutting a sheep. Somebody had to speak first and it was Tig, bold as brass, not an ounce of shame in her husky voice. In fact, she sounded amused.

'Sylvia! Fancy seeing you here.' She stepped past me onto the front step, lighting up as she did so, not waiting for me to respond. She at least had the decency to go down to the bottom of the stone steps and have her smoke on the garden path, leaving Prof and me to speak in private. I fully expected Prof to apologise and explain. Instead, he snapped at me in angry embarrassment.

'What is this? What do you want?'

'Why is *she* here?' I indicated towards Tig, although it was pretty clear that she and Prof were having some sort of sordid fling.

'For Christ's sake, Sylvia, it's none of your business.'

'I thought … What about Lola?'

'What about her?' His eyes flashed in such a menacing manner at this point that the thought passed through my mind that he was not really Prof, not my kind, noble, wonderful Prof. Could he be ill? Have had some sort of brainstorm?

'What do you want?' he asked again sharply, pulling me back to the moment.

'I want to protect you, to be with you.' I needed to try and explain why I was there, but my voice sounded as if it was coming from somewhere very far away.

He scoffed loudly and I noticed some specs of spittle on his lips. His face had transformed into an angry red mask. The man next door, who was sweeping snow off his front steps, lingered on the top one, presumably to try and catch the drama. Prof glanced at him then came right up close to me and enunciated horribly.

'Let's get this straight, once and for all. I don't need your *protection*, I don't need your help in any way. I don't want you anywhere near me. How dare you come to my house. I know you've been here before. I have let it go and I think I have been reasonable, but you are becoming an embarrassment. You clearly have problems, but if you ever come near me or my children again I will call the police. Do you understand?'

My head was spinning in confusion. 'But ... Our lunches and the way we talk and understand each other ... And the teabag and the journal. I thought ...'

'You thought what?' he spat. He opened his palms and shrugged his shoulders as if he was searching for the answer to his question. 'That we had more than a working relationship? That you meant something to me? That I wanted to be with you?' His voice sounded incredulous and my temples started to ache.

'But our special kiss, under the mistletoe …' I said, looking straight into his eyes and nodding, trying desperately to find our connection again. He regarded me blankly.

'At that Christmas party,' I continued as he shook his head, bemused. 'You must remember?'

'No, I don't remember, Sylvia,' he said dismissively. 'Why must you make so much of everything? None of it is important. If I did kiss you that night I was probably pissed and you were there giving me the glad eye, as usual. I think I might have even had a snog with Margaret too. It was a party, for pity's sake. No. Big. Deal.' He emphasised the last three words distinctly.

I stared at him, aghast, mortified that Margaret could have had a romantic moment with *my* Prof.

'I don't understand. Why did you give me such a beautiful bracelet on my birthday?' I couldn't make any sense of it. I needed him to explain.

'Well, it was your fiftieth, wasn't it?' he snapped. 'Imogen told me I should give you something special.'

'No, it was my fifty-second. I'm fifty-two,' I said slowly, part of me still not believing that I had really got that old.

'Well, whatever. You need to leave,' he said decisively, and started to close the door.

'I love you.'

I had to say it out loud. Maybe if he knew that for sure then it would change everything, would be enough to stop all the pain and loneliness and misunderstandings. That on hearing those words he would hold me and kiss the top of my head and make me feel right again.

The door opened fully and he went to say something, then he shook his head and shut the door hard. The movement of it dislodged some small icicles on the porch and I watched them fall silently to the ground and lie on top of the snow. All was quiet apart from the noise of the man next door still scraping his top step.

I turned and climbed slowly down towards the path, clinging onto the handrail as I went. It suddenly seemed to be of utmost importance that I look after myself, like a baby bird with a broken wing or a little motherless hoglet. I had temporarily forgotten about Tig and coming face to face with her at the bottom of the steps was a jolt.

'Get a life, Sylvia,' was all she said to me, grinding her cigarette stub out on the frozen ground. Then she turned and went back up to the front door. I watched her ringing the bell and knocking for what seemed like a long while until Prof finally let her in and closed the door again behind her.

As I made my way home in the dark, through the freezing streets, I knew what I had to do. It had all gone on too long and it was over now. There was no point

any more to any of it and there was a release in the
realisation that I no longer had to struggle with it –
that it would soon be over. My feet were soaking and
numb as I walked up to the flats, but I didn't go inside.
Instead I made my way round the back and found the
small key on my set that opened the padlock on the
communal storage shed in the garden. The lock had
frozen solid and I had to hold it in my gloved hands for
a long time before I was able to coax the key to go in
and then turn. Once unlocked, I dragged the door open
and blinked in the darkness trying to identify the bulky
items from their general shapes. The barbecue was right
at the back, put out of the way as nobody expected to
need it again until the summer. Propelled by some inner
strength, I managed to move aside the various pieces
of patio furniture and power tools, pick the barbecue
up and take it out into the garden. I dropped it down,
making its lid clang, and hauled it across the snow to the
middle of the lawn. I was aware at this point that Mr
Goldberg was watching me from an upstairs window.
In no mood for an audience, I turned and stared back at
him, holding up my middle finger until he disappeared
back behind his curtain.

It took four trips up and down the stairs to my flat
to fetch all of Prof's articles and books, and then a final
trip to get the matches and brandy from the kitchen.
I doused his work and watched it burn, throwing in
handfuls of paper at a time, rejoicing in the warmth it

generated and holding my hands close to the flames. The snow around the feet of the barbecue began to fade away, exposing long-hidden patches of grass and a little cluster of indomitable snowdrops. All those words and ideas, meaningless to me now, disappeared up in smoke into the wintery London sky. When there was only ashes left, I took off the bracelet and threw it on top of the smouldering pile, watching as the last small licks of fire reflected on its links and the fake gold started to shrivel and peel off, drifting away on the breeze.

Spring

Spring is when hedgehogs come out of hibernation and join the living world again. Their main aims at this time of year are to feast on the good things in the garden and find a mate.

The Ancient Egyptians venerated the hedgehog as a symbol of rebirth due to its cyclical reappearance, and as a symbol of protection thanks to its spikes. Amulets of hedgehogs and small hedgehog statues have been found on archaeological sites dating back to 1700BC.

The main hedgehog rutting season takes place in May and June. The boar circles round the sow, snuffling and grunting for hours until she finally acquiesces and flattens her prickles so he can mount her. There is certainly verisimilitude in the old joke: 'How do hedgehogs mate? Carefully!'

Baby hedgehogs are called hoglets. They are born blind, with soft white spines after four to five weeks gestation. By eleven days they can roll into a ball. Hoglets stay with their mother and suckle until they have put on enough weight to survive by themselves. She teaches them how to hunt for food and stay out of sight during the day. However, hedgehogs are solitary by nature and once they leave the nest they are unlikely to encounter their mother or siblings again. A group of hedgehogs, rare though that might be, is called a 'prickle'.

Jonas Entwistle, *The Hedgehog Year*

Wednesday 9 March

Crystal drops in now most Wednesday afternoons, just for half an hour or so on her way home, and it is the highlight of my week. I have started baking in the mornings so I have something nice to offer her when she gets here and it gives me something to do in place of reading Prof's work. She teases me that I make all these cakes and scones and brownies and never eat any myself, so I am trying to have a couple of bites to be sociable when she is here and not worry too much about the calories, even if it does make me a little anxious. We talk about her day, her friends at school, her lunch hours spent in the art room, and how awkward things are with Lewis who has now declared his love for her and follows her around like a motherless chick. I have advised her that the kindest course of action would be to sit him down and explain clearly that she doesn't return his feelings, but I know how hard that would be for her. She's not one for confrontations and is soft as butter inside; she doesn't want to hurt him.

'It makes me feel guilty, Aunt Sylvia,' she told me today. 'Like I owe him something just because he has feelings for me. But I didn't ask him to feel that way about me and I don't want him. I mean, I like him as a friend, but I don't fancy him at all, and now it's as if his happiness is my responsibility and I don't want it, it's not fair. Does that make me sound like a mean person?' I could see how much it was upsetting her and I felt an unexpected twinge of guilt for my misplaced devotion to Prof. Then she astonished herself by saying, 'I don't know if I like boys at all in that way, actually.'

I hugged her and told her she hadn't done anything wrong and that you can't help how you feel, or don't feel, about someone else. And that if she doesn't like boys it's no big deal and that the most important part of life is finding out how to be happy and to be peaceful inside and not to waste time always trying to please other people. The irony of me, of all people, handing out romantic advice! But she squeezed my hand and thanked me for understanding.

We don't talk about the awful scene at her home back in November when everything became uncovered, and I don't ask about Millie or Kamal or try to find out more about what happened after I left that day. I think it is easier for both of us to pretend that it never happened, even though it is always there, really – the proverbial elephant in the room.

I don't think Millie knows that Crystal comes to visit me, or if she does, it is certainly not with her blessing. It is curious how I never noticed before how alike Crystal and I are, but by talking to her and getting to know her, I now realise that she is complicated and sensitive and finds life hard. She finds people perplexing and draining and needs lots of alone time to recharge. She overthinks things and her emotions and thoughts scare her sometimes. She tries hard to be what Millie and Kamal want her to be, but inside she feels she is someone different, and that this is somehow wrong. It has not always been easy for Crystal being their daughter. I wish I had seen it sooner. I could have been much more of a support for her, growing up. Another item to add to my list of regrets. How blind I've been about so many things.

Friday 18 March

The phone startled me this morning. I was reading through a recipe I had pulled out of a magazine for a coffee cake I thought Crystal might like when the landline began to ring. It springs to life so rarely that I'd almost forgotten it was there. I picked it up with trepidation, expecting a cold caller, which it was, but not in the usual meaning of the phrase. My heart leapt at the sound of Millie's voice and I hoped that she was calling to say that she was missing me and wanted to start building bridges. How wrong I was. The conversation went like this:

'Sylvia?'

'Yes … is that you, Millie?' (I knew it was her; I was playing for time, waiting for my heart to stop racing.)

'You know it is, Sylvia.' (I can't remember the last time she used my name; she usually calls me 'darling' or 'sweetie'. Each formal 'Sylvia' cut me like a knife.)

'Are you OK?' (I didn't know what else to say.)

'Not really. Crystal tells me she visits you sometimes after swimming. Is that right?'

'Yes, she does sometimes. She pops in, we—' She cut me short here.

'I don't like it, Sylvia. If I had my way she wouldn't be coming again.'

'I didn't ask her to come. Millie, don't be like this. Please. Can't we just talk?'

'No, Sylvia. Kamal and I don't want anything to do with you. I've told Crystal I'm not happy about her seeing you, but she is seventeen and I can't stop her if that's what she wants to do. But I have explained to her that you are not to be trusted and that you have hurt me and her daddy and that you are not welcome in our family. That's all I wanted to say. Goodbye.'

Then she was gone. Realising I was still gripping the recipe in my hand, I let it go and it drifted slowly to the floor.

Monday 21 March

It had started to drizzle as I left the flat this morning and by the time I was at the bus stop the rain was coming down in rods, but I was determined to see Millie and try and sort things out. I had forgotten my umbrella and stood, dripping wet, in my duffel coat and jeans, waiting for the bus to appear out of the deluge. It was oddly warm on board and the windows were steamed up so it was hard to see when we arrived at Streatham Common. I had to lean over the man next to me and rub a clear patch in the window to make sure I hadn't missed my stop. I got off into weak sunshine, the only clue to the torrential downpour being the mist rising off the pavement and the streams of murky water running into the drains. My damp coat clung heavily to me as I walked across the common towards the K&M Delicatessen. I know Kamal always has the day off on a Monday and I wanted to grab the opportunity to talk to Millie alone, apologise again, explain, try to get into some sort of dialogue with her that might move things forward for us. The thought of losing her love for ever is too horrible to contemplate. I'm not sure who I am without Millie. She acts as my foil, my centre of gravity, my emotional reference point. My sister, my friend. I just can't let all that shared history disappear so easily. Not without a fight or without at least trying to find a way through.

It was unbearable that she had sounded so cold on the phone – distant and removed as if I were a light-fingered customer she was barring from the shop. I had to speak to her. I made my way across the wet grass, holding onto the belief that surely there was still some way to connect with her and work this out. I had given her months to reflect, given her space, allowed them both time to talk it out and work through it together. The problem was, of course, that she had only had Kamal's version of events to cogitate on – and God only knew what poisonous lies he had dropped into that story. I needed to see her, alone, and tell her my side of it, try to make her understand what happened and why.

I stopped off at the minimart next to the station and bought a box of chocolates and a card from their measly selection that said *Sorry* with a picture of a huge-eyed puppy next to a ripped-up newspaper. I opened it next to the till to write a message inside but couldn't think of how to word it, so I simply wrote *I miss you, love Sylvia* and put a couple of kisses. I realised how pathetic the card was on the short walk up the parade and shoved it in the bin just outside the deli. I took a moment to compose myself, and then pushed open the door to be met by a furious-looking Kamal standing right in front of me. He shook his head angrily and reached behind me to lock the door and turn the sign to closed before meeting my gaze head on. We stood glaring at each other, with the hum of the big fridge and the buzzing of a bluebottle in the window providing an edgy backing track to the inevitable confrontation that was brewing. The deli smelt stuffy, a spicy, meaty, herby combination that was making me nauseous.

'She's not here, she's gone up into town for a lunch with the girls.' Kamal finally broke the silence, answering my unasked question. I felt a sting of rejection as I realised which girls he probably meant – Emma, Shona (surely not Tig?) – and then I remembered how much I had loathed their company on our night out. The thought that Millie would be recounting our fall out to them was painful, though, and I took another silent body blow from that one.

'What have you said about it, Kamal? Have you explained to her that it was only that one time and it was a mistake? That we didn't mean to hurt her?'

'It's the lying, Sylvia.' Kamal enunciated carefully, as if explaining the situation to a complete stranger. 'It's the lying for all these years that she can't stand. She feels betrayed by you, be-trayed.' He split the word into two distinct syllables to emphasise Millie's distress.

'By *me*?' My voice rose in indignation. 'What about you? You are her husband, Kamal. You made the first move. You were just as much to blame as I was.'

'We weren't even married then,' he said in a sing-song voice, as though it was a secret winning card that I hadn't realised he held. He did a horrible fake smile, even though his eyes were furious.

'Does that matter?' He had wrong-footed me, confused me. 'Does Millie only blame me?' Then, incredulous as the penny dropped, I asked, 'Has she forgiven *you*?'

'Yes, Sylvia, yes.' He was beaming now, like a mad religious zealot who has been absolved of all sins by a magnanimous leader. 'Yes, my wife has forgiven me.'

A banging noise broke the moment as an elderly man in a turban tried repeatedly to open the door, pushing it with his shoulder, not having noticed, or believed, the closed sign. Kamal rushed past me and shouted his apologies through the door, holding up his hand and mouthing 'five minutes'. The man tutted and ambled away and Kamal turned back to me, waving his arms at the door. 'Look, look what you did. You are losing me business, woman. Now go away. I told you before. Go away and leave us alone.'

'I need to see her, Kamal. I need to talk to her. Please tell her I came round.' I was being dismissed and I felt utterly powerless.

'She. Doesn't. Want. To. Talk. To. You. Or. See. You. Ever. Again.' He sounded it out as if explaining to a simpleton. 'Now get out of my shop.' He threw open the door and held it as I walked out into the street.

Then he slammed it shut behind me, making the bell jingle long and loud as I felt the first spots of a fresh rainstorm fall onto my burning face.

I wandered across the common towards the bus stop in a daze. Halfway across I started to feel faint and slumped down onto a bench. I looked down at the box of chocolates I had bought for Millie, which I still held in my hands, and realised how paltry such an offering was in the light of the enormity of the pain I had caused her. Her pain was exactly what I had tried so hard to avoid for so long. That was why I did what I did, and why I could never tell her any of it. I carried it all by myself, so that she could be happy, so that we could continue being sisters and best friends.

Kamal carried it too, I saw that now, but it was different for him. Over the years he had altered it, edited it, made it all my fault, put himself in the position of Millie's protector. I understood now the pure hatred he had for me. It wasn't because I reminded him of what he had done wrong, but because in his revised version of events I was the evil party, the danger to Millie's happiness. I opened the lid of the white-and-black box, lifted the ridged sheet of paper on the top, and smelt the intense sweetness of the contents. I picked up each chocolate in turn and examined its colour and shape, identifying them from the key on the side of the box. I knew which one was Millie's favourite and I ate that first, in two small bites, the caramel and hazelnut making a delightful contrast to the milk chocolate shell. Then I ate the orange and coffee creams in one go each, just to get them out the way, before chewing thoughtfully on the toffees and hard centres. With only the fudge and dark chocolate ones left, there was no point saving them, I reasoned, so I finished the layer. The remaining layer went down with no order at all, the chocolate feeling rough and sickly in my mouth and down my throat so I thought I might gag, but I kept it down.

The nausea I felt from the chocolate drew my mind unwillingly back to the last time I had had a confrontation with Kamal in the deli, eighteen years ago. He and Millie had only just bought the premises then, with her share of the money Uncle Clarence had left us. It was a complete state and needed total renovation, a task they had thrown themselves into with unbounded enthusiasm. That afternoon I'd known Millie was taking Mother to the opticians and that Kamal would be alone in the shop, decorating, and I needed to see him urgently. The unspoken agreement that we would forget our tryst had ever happened – which I would have been more than happy to go along with – had fallen apart for me in the worst way possible and I had to speak to him.

I pushed open the door, narrowly avoiding knocking him off the ladder he was balanced on as he painted the ceiling. He had splotches of white paint all over his hair and overalls and a big smudge across his nose. The radio was on, loud, playing a rock anthem, and he was singing cheerfully along. He froze when he saw me and looked behind me for Millie. Seeing I was alone, he jumped off the ladder and eyed me warily.

'What do you want?' he asked, holding the paint brush in front of him like a weapon. I pressed my lips together and stared down at the planked floor, noticing two splotches of paint that had dripped down from the ceiling. If I didn't open my mouth I didn't have to say it; it would stay a secret inside me and I could hide it forever. 'She's not here,' he said, narrowing his eyes.

I forced myself to speak. 'Kamal, I have to tell you something.'

'What?' He was shaking his head by now, as if he knew on some level what I was about to say and was already objecting to it.

I put my hand on my belly and he looked fearfully from my hand to my face.

'No! No way. No, no.' He came towards me, waving his paint brush as if I were a wasp he was trying to get to fly back out of the window.

'I'm sorry. I don't know what to do.'

He put his hand to his heart in a beseeching gesture. 'It's not mine. Why do you think it's mine?'

His words stung. 'It is yours, Kamal. There hasn't been anyone else. I'm sorry.'

'I don't believe you. I don't want to talk to you!' He put the brush down on the top of the ladder and walked behind the half-built counter, his hands pressed against his cheeks. He muttered in words I didn't understand, kicking the back wall. He turned and pointed at me, his voice rising in panic and anger. 'Don't you dare tell Camilla! Don't you dare ruin everything for us. Sort it out or I will tell her it was all your doing, that you are in love with me and that you hate her and are jealous of her. I will tell her you tricked me and that it isn't mine anyway.' Then he delivered the final blow. 'You will lose her, Sylvia. She will never speak to you again. Ever.'

The nausea overtook me then and I ran out of the shop and vomited down the wall next to the window. When I stood up again, Kamal had shut the door and pulled down the blinds. I tried the handle but it was locked. A well-dressed businesswoman who was rushing past towards the station stopped and put her hand on my arm.

'Are you all right?' she asked, looking at me with concern. I brushed her hand away and stood up straight, pulling a tissue out of my pocket to wipe my mouth.

'Yes, thank you.' I gathered what little dignity I had left and walked purposefully in the other direction and round the corner. My legs were shaking so much that I had to sit down and I made it into a greasy little café where I dropped into a chair at the table next to the window. I sat there sipping milkless tea for hours, watching the world go by, everyone carrying on as usual. I felt safe in there, outside reality and away from the consequences of my actions. It was nearly closing time when I got up to leave. The proprietor had taken away my teacup and was now wiping down the table, whistling loudly.

As I reached for my bag I saw a flash of bright green outside and knew it was Millie, returned from Mother's at last, parking her distinctive old car on the road outside. My instinct was to run to her as she got out and locked the door. She didn't even glance in the direction of the café; why would she? I often think that had she seen me then, had she come in and talked to me, everything might have turned out differently, but of course I can't know that for sure. In all probability, I would have just ended up losing her even sooner. As she walked away from the car, all of her being was aiming for the deli round the corner where the love of her life was making it into their perfect dream. She was wearing a full-length leopard print faux fur coat over cut-off jeans and high gold platform boots. Her hair was in plaits and she had a huge smile on her face. She looked radiant and quirky and fabulous and so happy as she bounced off down the road towards Kamal and their future together. I drew myself back into the doorway of the café and let her pass unnoticed. How could I ruin this for her?

Watching her turn the corner, tottering on the platform boots that nobody else I knew would even attempt to wear, I felt a surge of love and protection for the woman who would, to me, always be my kooky, free-spirited, wonderful little sister. I would have happily ceased to exist or passed my life over to somebody else to deal with as I faced the enormity of the impact my news would have on her. I had no interest at all in continuing in a life that didn't include Millie. I had contemplated carrying on with the pregnancy and pretending the father was somebody else, some random one-night stand, but I couldn't face the prospect of a whole life of lying to her, having to live with a constant reminder of my betrayal, bringing up the unwanted child of a man who detested me. My nausea was a constant reminder of the decision I had to make and somehow, in that moment, it became very simple. I wanted Millie to still love me. I wanted Kamal to not be angry with me. I wanted to just be me again.

Now, nearly twenty years later, after I had composed myself and thrown the empty chocolate box into the bin beside the bench, I got up unsteadily, my head rushing with an unfamiliar sugar high and started towards the bus stop. One of the plastic seats was free and I squeezed myself into it, between a hugely fat young woman with a toddler in a buggy next to her and an immaculately dressed elderly lady with matching hat, shoes and bag. The toddler was eating a packet of crisps. He had crumbs all over his face and in his hair and his mother ignored him as she played with her phone. He had kicked off one of his trainers, displaying a grubby grey sock with a faded superhero motif on it, which made me feel sad for him in a way I can't explain. I forced myself to look away and began replaying the scene that had just occurred with Kamal, shifting my understanding of the situation and the position of us all in it, according to the new light that the horrible spat had shed.

I was brought out of my reverie by the bus pulling up and the woman next to me swearing and springing into action, yanking her child out of his straps and struggling to collapse the buggy. He howled when she took his crisps off him and looked at me in despair.

'I'm sorry,' I mouthed to him. 'I'm so sorry.'

He was startled by my response and started to giggle. His mother glared at me as she swung the buggy onto the lowered platform of the bus and he tottered after her, hanging onto the hem of her voluminous dress.

I found myself getting off the bus a few stops early and heading towards Hartland Road for the first time in months, drawn by some instinctive need for the safety and protection of the sanctuary. I stumbled over a bag of feed as I darted in out of the rain, pulling my hood down and taking in the familiar warm, musty smell of the garage. Jonas had his back to me and didn't look up. He was engrossed in cleaning the spines of a filthy old hog, the radio on quietly beside him.

I went to speak and then stopped, my attention caught by the poster on the wall beside him. It was for an eons-old amateur production of Shakespeare's *A Midsummer Night's Dream* from the school where Jonas used to teach. It was part of the sanctuary scenery and I must have glanced at it a thousand times, but I had never really registered it before and it certainly had never resonated with me as it did today. It was a picture of a radiant Titania in a sky-blue gown, her blonde hair, threaded with flowers, tumbling down her back. She was dancing in a forest glade, hand in hand with her woodland sprites. In the tangled undergrowth around them dark, spikey shadows lurked, waiting in the wings for the chance to spoil her joy. Along the bottom of the image ran a quote from the play; 'Thorny hedgehogs be not seen … Come not near our fairy queen.' The words jolted through me. Was this me? Was this what I had become through my actions towards Lola in Rome and in relation to my beloved Millie – a reviled creature, hell-bent on destroying beauty?

I forced myself to calm down by closing my eyes and pressing my palm against my forehead as I took some deep breaths. Then I went to stand beside Jonas, placing my hand tentatively on his shoulder.

'He looks like he's on his last legs,' I said, taking in the hedgehog's half-closed eyes and flea-bitten face.

'He might perk up, he's just been rudely disturbed out of his hibernation,' Jonas replied, as he methodically worked up and down the spines with a cotton bud, turning the hedgehog round every now and then to a more helpful angle. I stood staring at them in a sort of morbid fascination for several minutes – Jonas being so careful and kind, and the hog in such a dreadful state.

'Where have you been all this time?' he asked, when he finally looked up at me. Then, taking in my bedraggled appearance and tear-stained face he said gently, 'What's the matter, Sylvia?'

I shook my head and bit my lip, staring at the dusty floor.

He put the hog gently back in its cage and washed his hands methodically at the sink.

'If it would help you can tell me about it,' he said with his back still to me.

'I couldn't ... I'm so ashamed. I c-can't ...' I stuttered, my eyes drawn again to the poster, incredulous at its prescience.

'You can if you want to, lass. I'm pretty good with secrets – just ask my girls. I've heard a fair few of theirs over the years, I can tell you.' He turned towards me as he dried his hands, oblivious to the impact the poster was having on me, his earnest offer hanging in the air. I made myself look away from Titania in all her loveliness and nodded my head slowly at Jonas. He had thrown me a lifeline and I didn't know what else to do but take it.

I hung up my coat and we sat down at the table. I started to talk, falteringly at first, muddling things up. I tried to put into words what had happened and how all the bad things seemed to be connected somehow and how my world was falling to pieces and I didn't know how to make it stop. I told him about Prof, about how I had loved him with all my being and how I had thought he was a noble, decent man, but how he is, in reality, selfish and cold. I told him how my heart had been broken when I thought he loved Lola and how I had tried to ruin her life and had, in fact, ruined my own instead. Then I told him how I had made another terrible mistake, many years ago, with Kamal and had kept it secret from Millie for such a long time because I couldn't bear to lose her or be responsible for ruining her happiness.

I explained that Millie and Kamal had only recently set up home together in London then and that she had been away for the weekend, visiting our friend Annabel in Eastbourne. I told him I was having a new television delivered on that Saturday, but the men who delivered it had just left it in the downstairs hall and had refused point-blank to carry it up to my flat. I was worried it would get stolen if I didn't get it upstairs straight away, so I called the only young, fit male I knew at the time, and that was Kamal. He was in the deli as usual, plastering the walls I think, and he laughed and said he would pop round and give me a hand. I remember thinking how lovely it was going to be, having such a wonderful brother-in-law, and how Kamal was like a breath of fresh air in our little family, which was all female since Dad had died. I told Jonas that he turned up just after one and we somehow managed to haul the blessed thing up two flights of stairs, stagger down the corridor to my flat, and dump the box in the middle of the lounge. I remember Kamal's face when I commented that it would have been easier to go up in the lift and how we both laughed when he realised I was joking, because there isn't really a lift in my building. I explained to Jonas that it was then, while we were catching our breath in the aftermath of the joke, that we caught each other's gaze and didn't, couldn't, break it. He moved towards me and I went to step back, but I found myself actually moving forwards, towards him. He put his hands on my shoulders and raised his eyes as if for permission before he kissed me and I didn't say no.

I stared at the wall to avoid looking at Jonas as I recalled how Kamal and I had made love on the sofa and that it was fast, and passionate, and exciting. And then it was over and he was gone.

I told Jonas how I had been mortified and panicked to find out I was pregnant several weeks later and how having a termination was the only possible option I could see.

I told him how my ache for a baby of my own has never gone away. That I have felt guilt and shame and remorse about what I did with Kamal, and about the abortion, every single day since, and how I can see now that it somehow deadened me inside and made me defensive and spiteful towards the world.

I explained how Kamal and I both knew we would never speak of it again.

And we wouldn't have; my darling Millie would never have found out, not about the sex or the pregnancy or any of it, if I hadn't blurted it all out in front of his damn aunties when I was so upset about what had happened with Prof.

I met Jonas's eye at this point to see if he was aghast, but he just nodded and patted my shoulder.

'Tea?' he said, unperturbed as if we had been discussing the weather.

Jonas turned the electric heater up to maximum and returned with the tray several minutes later, Igor at his heels. We sat quietly together for a long time, listening to the rain pound on the tin roof, sipping slowly from the chipped white mugs that we never seemed to get around to replacing.

'And now she knows, Jonas. She has found out in the worst possible way and she won't forgive me.' My voice broke on those last four words and I watched my tears hit the surface of the tea and get swallowed up as if they had never existed at all.

Jonas stared at the electric fire deep in thought as he stroked Igor's head. At last he turned to me and said kindly, 'The way I see it, lass, the most important thing is for you to find a way to forgive yourself.'

Tuesday 22 March

I dreamed about Kamal last night. It was a muddled half-erotic, half-panicky dream where he was running his hands all over me and kissing my neck as we were rushing through an airport to catch a plane. I remember thinking, *Not now, not here, for God's sake*, but he wouldn't stop and I didn't really want him to either. Then I was standing alone as my bag went through the security machine and the X-ray picture came up, not of my luggage, but of a scan of a baby. Then all the airport staff came running over and started pointing and shouting at me in a foreign language and wouldn't give me my bag back, no matter what I said or how hard I tried to pull it from them. I woke up shaking, soaked through with sweat, pinned to the bed with the weight of loss.

It's the backs of babies' heads that devastates me every time. I can cope with their chubby fingers and toothless smiles and bright new eyes. But if I catch sight of the back of the head, where their hair meets the neck and there's that little roll of fat and the whole area is the softest place in creation, that's when I completely unravel inside and have to stop myself from howling aloud like a madwoman. I managed to avoid Millie quite a lot when Crystal was very small and found I could tolerate her better when she was past the baby stage and her hair had curled down to her shoulders. I used to dread it when women on maternity leave brought their babies into the office at the university, especially if they just turned up unannounced. If I knew they were coming at least I could disappear for an hour and feign regret I had missed them on my return. But the unexpected baby visit was a living nightmare for me, involving a clenched stomach, rictus smile and a silent plea for them not to turn the baby with its back to me. At least I don't have to face those situations in my daily life any more.

After my visit to Kamal all those years ago, I was so focussed on convincing not one doctor, but two, that having the baby would destroy my life, and my sister's life, that I begged them to allow me to make it stop, to make it all go away. No, I didn't want any counselling, no, I didn't want more time to think it over, no, I didn't want to consider other options, no, I didn't want to read this or that leaflet. They gave in and signed the form in the end, as I knew they would. What was I to them? One more woman who had made a mistake that they had the power to rectify. At the clinic, I was required to have a pre-op scan, despite my protestations. They explained that it was compulsory, that they have to check exactly how many weeks along you are in the pregnancy before they can do the procedure, so I had to acquiesce. I sat in the waiting room with half a dozen other women and girls, trying not to catch anyone's eye, flicking through a travel magazine until the nondescript receptionist called out my name and I walked through the door and into the medical side of the clinic. The gel was cold on my stomach and I felt a light pressure as they did the sonogram. They asked if I wanted to look, but I refused, and so they turned the screen away as I counted the number of cracks in the ceiling tile above my head and pretended I was somewhere else, far, far away. If I could turn back time to that moment and force myself to look I wouldn't have gone through with it, I know that now. I couldn't have.

'Are you sure?' the nurse said to me. 'Are you absolutely sure?'

I know it was a boy, my baby. The only useful piece of information Mother ever shared with Millie was when she was eight months pregnant with Crystal and wondering aloud, for the thousandth time, whether she would be having a boy or a girl.

'It's certainly a girl, Camilla,' Mother said, putting down her knitting and enjoying her moment of rapt attention from us both.

'How can you be so sure about that?' Millie asked. 'Just because you had girls, doesn't mean I will.'

'No, it's not that,' Mother continued. 'The women in our family only ever get morning sickness when they are having boys and you've had none of that, have you? That means it's a girl. You mark my words.'

Satisfied that her point had been made with maximum impact, Mother picked up her knitting again and continued clack-clacking as a tiny white bootie began to take shape. Millie didn't say anything but I knew she was annoyed that Mother had spoiled the surprise for her because she was right, Millie had never had a moment's nausea with her pregnancy. I, on the other hand, was silently elated. At last I had a tiny bit of information about the child I had been carrying, about what might have been. A boy. My son who never was.

Two days after the termination it was Millie's birthday and we went out for dinner at one of those novelty places, done up to be like a Hawaiian beach party, that were all the rage for a while. I sat at that table with a plastic garland round my neck, listening to the Beach Boys singing about good vibrations, watching her and Kamal kissing and giggling together and I felt like I was the punchline to a sick joke. My abdomen ached as a constant reminder of what had happened and I longed to go home.

Kamal barely even acknowledged me. When Millie went to the loo, he made stilted conversation with Mother, asking her about her new glasses of all things, rather than speak to me. He didn't even ask me how I was. Something changed in me that evening, something tender closed over and an intense panic swept over me, making it seem as if I were watching the world from a great distance with no idea how to find my way back. I sensed myself curl up inside like a frightened hedgehog, waiting to feel safe again – but I never did.

As well as Mother and I, Emma was there and Shona and their other halves and a couple of women from Millie's life-drawing class. Tig had dropped by for a drink early in the evening and then rushed off to meet a new man for a dinner date, a hunk, she had described him as, bringing to mind an image of her sitting in a cosy bistro opposite a great boulder of rock. Emma's screeching, open-mouthed laugh, made her look grotesque to me and I gazed at her husband, wondering how he could bear to wake up to her every morning. Shona talked and talked about her latest project and how important she was at work and how they were going to go to Tunisia on holiday, and I watched her lips move as if they were separate from her body, a part she couldn't control.

Everyone seemed odd and unreal that evening, except Mother, strangely enough, who should have looked the most out of place in that gaudy restaurant. I watched her go through her familiar rituals, rituals that didn't change whether she was eating in a burger bar or the Ritz. Napkin spread on lap, mouth dabbed after every second mouthful, salt and pepper automatically shaken on each savoury dish as soon as it arrived, a little food left on the plate to indicate that she had had enough and was no longer hungry. What I wanted was to go and sit on her lap and have her hug me and smell her lily-of-the-valley scent and feel her soft cardigan against my cheek and have her hand me one of her white cotton handkerchiefs to dry my tears ... and for her to tell me it was all going to be all right. I ached for that love and comfort, although she had never in my life provided me with such affection. I hadn't realised, before then, that it was possible to feel nostalgia for something that had never happened.

Emma had been trying to get the waiter's attention for several minutes, he studiously ignoring her desperate waves every time he passed the table. 'Oh, it does annoy me when they do that,' she said in exasperation. 'They are paid to wait on the tables, for heaven's sake. They pretend they can't see you but you know they can. It's their little bit of power in a rubbish job'

'He probably fancies himself as a musician or something and this is all rather beneath him,' Shona added, and they both laughed in agreement.

I saw Millie bristle at this. Kamal had been a waiter when she met him in Kerala, and, for someone who so embraces a non-materialistic life philosophy, she was disproportionately defensive of his humble beginnings.

'You two can be such snobs,' she tutted. 'There's nothing wrong with being a waiter.'

'Of course not, Mills don't be silly, but this one is particularly annoying.' Emma held up her empty plastic coconut shell which had housed a pina colada and raised her eyes. 'I'm losing my buzz. I'll remember how tired I am in a minute and that I've got two constantly bickering children to look after in the morning.' She looked at Millie's glass and noticed for the first time that she was drinking water. 'Not drinking, Mills? Let me get you a cocktail. It's your birthday, you have to have fun.'

'No, I'm fine, darling, just have a bit of a headache. I'll have something in a bit, promise.' She blew Emma a kiss and turned back to Kamal, draping her arm round his shoulders and listening with intent as he explained to Shona's husband about the problems they were having with the ancient plumbing in the deli.

My mind was grappling with a possibility that I couldn't face and I stared at Millie's glass of water as if in a trance. I was about to get up and escape to the bathroom when the waiter appeared at last, carrying a pink frosted cake with candles and sparklers stuck in the top, and everyone launched into a boozy rendition of 'Happy Birthday'. I sang along and watched Millie giggle and flap like an excited child, blowing out the candles and nearly burning her fingers on the still-hot sparklers.

Kamal stood up then and it was like being trapped in a nightmare. I knew what he was going to say. He thanked everyone for coming and said how gorgeous Millie looked and how happy he was that she was going to be his wife and how much they were looking forward to opening the deli soon. Then he held up his glass and we all toasted Millie. I was holding my breath, waiting for the next announcement, but it didn't come. I took a long drink of my wine and told myself I was paranoid and being ridiculous. Then he stood up again.

'And we have some even more beautiful news!' Millie was tugging at his shirt trying to get him to sit down, but he wouldn't. He was tipsy and getting carried away with the pleasures of the evening. 'We are going to have a baby! Yes, we are so happy.' He was beaming and tears of drunken joy were rolling down his cheeks. He went to kiss Millie but she was already standing up and he missed and nearly fell, righting himself on the back of her chair. Millie was a bashful bright red and glowing with delight.

'Yes, we are. It's really early on,' she said, raising her eyebrows at Kamal, 'and we weren't going to tell anyone for a while, but there it is – I'm going to be a mummy!'

Emma and Shona screamed and jumped up to hug her, welcoming her to their club. Mother's face showed little emotion except the slight disappointment with which she greeted all news, good or bad, but when Millie looked right at her she did at least have the decency to smile and nod graciously.

'What do you think, Sylvia? You're going to be an auntie.' Millie was trying to include me in the general frenzy of excitement and the table fell silent waiting for my answer.

'It's truly wonderful news. Millie and Kamal, congratulations to you both.' I lifted my glass and Millie slowly lifted hers back, her face hurt and confused at my lack of enthusiasm and the insincere tone of my response.

I couldn't help it. I could hardly breathe and I needed to get out of there. Kamal refused to catch my eye, his waiter training standing him in good stead. I waited another twenty minutes until the furore had died down and people were back to chatting about themselves rather than Millie and then slipped out, whispering to Millie that I had to catch the last train, and handing her money to cover my share of the bill for food I hadn't eaten.

'Call me tomorrow,' she said, holding onto my hand, 'please, darling.'

'Of course I will.' I touched her hair and withdrew my hand from her clammy grasp.

I stood outside the restaurant in the cool night air and pulled on my coat, tying the belt tightly round my waist and trying to ignore the soreness across my middle. I knew, then, that I had made a terrible, irreversible mistake.

The next few months were pure agony for me, and then it got worse. Millie was completely swept up in the joyful anticipation of her impending motherhood and all I could do was watch from the sidelines with a growing sense of horror. She wanted me centre stage with her, of course: to accompany her to scans and midwife appointments instead of Kamal so they didn't have to shut the shop, to help her choose the paraphernalia she needed from Mothercare, and to listen to her hopes and fears about the birth. I managed to dodge nearly every request, citing work responsibilities and prior engagements wherever possible. She was hurt, I know she was, but she said she understood and took either Mother or Emma with her instead. Mother was no help really, stunned by the level of care and attention contemporary pregnancy demanded and non-forthcoming about her own experiences. She shifted with embarrassment and claimed not to remember when Millie asked her about our births and infancies, let alone the mechanics of her pregnancies. At least I could plead ignorance and had no relevant experiences to share that she knew of.

The one favour that I found impossible to get out of was decorating the nursery for the new baby in the dilapidated end-of-terrace that Millie and Kamal had hastily bought with a huge mortgage, using the last of Uncle Clarence's money as a deposit. Millie asked me directly if I would strip the dated woodchip wallpaper off the walls, tidy up the plaster, and paint it in a gender neutral creamy white. She also had a stencil of teddy bears that she wanted put up as a border and a pair of bright yellow curtains that needed hanging in the little window overlooking the tangled garden. What with getting the deli off the ground and sorting out the rest of the house, neither she nor Kamal had time to properly prepare the nursery and she wanted it to be lovely for the baby. What could I say? I agreed to come round after work and do a couple of hours every week night while Millie pottered round unpacking and got dinner on, but I insisted I would leave as soon as Kamal got home and would not stay for the evening meal. Not wanting to intrude, is how I put it and Millie appreciated the gesture, hugging me tightly and telling me I was the best sister in the world, just as she used to do when we were children.

Those hours in Millie's box room, scraping wallpaper, painting and stencilling, were quite therapeutic when I could blank out why I was doing it. I found I could get into something of a meditative state if I put a classical music radio station on and focused purely on the job at hand. Even so, I would frequently, with a start, remember the situation I was in and accelerate my scraping or painting with a nervous vigour in order to get the job done fractionally quicker so I could be free of the task.

Millie loved being pregnant. Her hair grew more lustrous and crazily curly than ever and her skin glowed.

She took the opportunity to wear the kaftans she had always wanted to lounge around in, bought on a long-ago trip to Egypt, and talked endlessly about the foetus being the size of a pea, then a walnut, then a satsuma, as though it was an ever-changing list of groceries. She would read me sections from the books on pregnancy she had borrowed from the library, detailing exactly what was developing at each week, and I nodded sagely, throwing in the occasional impressed or surprised interjection as I carried on with the job that was starting to feel like an extended part of the punishment that had begun that evening in the Hawaiian restaurant.

'What do you think he or she will look like?' she asked eagerly one evening as she handed me a cup of coffee. 'It will have the most beautiful colour skin, darling, can you imagine? Like ... Like ...' She gazed round the room, searching for the answer. Finally, her eyes settled on her milky coffee and she laughed in delight. 'Like this,' she exclaimed. 'Like caffè latte. And maybe brown eyes, maybe green. Kamal's are green but his mum and dad's were brown. Or maybe blue like ours?' Millie and I had exactly the same eyes, a boring medium blue, replicated ad infinitum in schools, buses and workplaces up and down the country. 'But it says here that they are always blue to start with. Oh, that will look so pretty, won't it? And then we can see if they change.' She closed the book and looked dreamily out of the window, tears in her eyes.

'Are you all right?' I asked in concern, Millie's hormonal ups and downs being another foreign territory for my usually constantly upbeat sister.

She held the book to her chest as if it held all her baby's wonderful secrets. 'Just so happy, darling.' She grinned at me and I smiled my traitorous smile back at her. Her happy mood went up another notch as she heard the key in the door downstairs and she jumped up, squealing, 'Ooh, Kamal is home early.'

I closed my eyes and laid down my paintbrush, silently counting to ten to calm my rising dread.

'Come and see how far Sylvia has got with the nursery.' Millie was pulling him up the stairs and they both appeared in the doorway, his eager face freezing to stone when he saw I was still there. Millie didn't notice, of course. We never see the things we aren't expecting to see, and he was standing behind her anyway. I met his gaze and he narrowed his eyes at me, skewering me with a look of pure hate. It was over in a moment and then he was responding to Millie's excitement, agreeing with how lovely the colour was and what a nice room it was going to make for their baby. I stood, trapped in the far corner, while they talked, unable to get to the door without pushing past Millie's considerable bulk. So, I waited until they had finished and then said I had to leave.

'Darling, stay for dinner,' Millie pleaded. 'I was going to make spaghetti carbonara. I can do yours without cream, if you like.'

'I really have to go now, Millie' I said, glancing at Kamal who was staring at me blankly. 'Have a nice evening, both of you.'

'All of us you mean,' Millie laughed, rubbing her belly.

Once the nursery was finished I managed to avoid them for a while, until the night when Crystal was born. It was New Year's Eve, and I was on the bank of the Thames with a group from work, waiting for the fireworks when Kamal texted me, presumably on Millie's instruction.

Baby on way, Millie wants you. Come to hospital.

I stared at the message for a long time until the words seemed to jumble up and I could imagine not being able to understand them at all. Then I pressed delete and stood staring at the empty night sky that would soon be an explosion of colour and light. I walked home in the early hours and sat, wakeful, on the sofa until Millie rang, tearful and exhausted at 7 a.m.

'Where were you? I wanted you here. I was so scared, Sylvia, and Kamal was useless. He wouldn't even come in the delivery room. I knew he wouldn't. He's such a coward.'

I blamed the New Year's Eve overload on the phone network and told her I'd only just got Kamal's text and she believed me. I promised her I was coming straight away.

At the hospital I stood in the lift with a heavily pregnant teenage girl in a wheelchair and her po-faced mother. The girl was squirming in her seat, her sweaty hair pulled back in a ponytail, her face contorted in pain and panic. 'Is he coming? Is Brandon coming?' she kept asking, her mother staring at the doors refusing, or unable, to answer.

I moved aside to let them past at the delivery floor and continued up to the maternity ward, resisting the urge to follow them and find out if Brandon was the baby or the absent father, anything rather than go and see Millie.

The lift doors opened at the next floor and an animated Greek family were waiting to go down, holding balloons, bags of presents, and a big blue cake, a joyful mum and her new baby cocooned in the middle of them. I made my way through the party, pressed the buzzer, and was suddenly in silence waiting to be let onto the ward. The door was opened by a flustered nurse who directed me to a room at the end of the corridor. The closer I got, the harder my heart pounded in my ears and I felt as if my bones might fall through my body, leaving me a heaped mess on the floor. I slowed my pace to try and calm my breathing and stopped in front of a pinboard covered with breastfeeding advice and local baby groups for new mothers, which I felt I was not entitled to read, as though I was snooping on the details of a secret club to which I had forfeited any right to be a member.

'What are you doing out here? She's in there, Sylvia.' It was Mother, her sharp tongue bringing me back to reality and making me feel guilty in that strange way she always did.

I could put it off no longer. I walked into the room as if it were a chamber of execution, in which the only way to survive was to pretend to be happy. So that's what I did. I said all the right things and did all the right things. I hugged Millie and insisted on holding the baby, holding my breath whilst she was in my arms so I didn't have to smell her, protecting at least one of my senses from being bombarded with painful baby information. I marvelled at how small her hands were and counted her toes and let Millie tell me her birth story like a shell-shocked soldier returned from the front line. I lied that I had left the card and present that I had forgotten to buy on the bus, being so eager to get here and in such a state of excitement about the baby. Mother eyed me suspiciously at this point, but she couldn't place the origin of her unease so turned her attention back to her granddaughter.

'What do you think of the name?' she asked, stroking Crystal's feet.

I knew one of mother's traps when I heard one and was aware of her general opinion of any names which wouldn't sound at home in a period drama. Millie looked at me anxiously for support and I declared it a beautiful name that suited her completely and how lucky she was to be called something unusual. Millie beamed lovingly at me and Mother rummaged in her handbag for a mint, her usual dismissive response to losing a minor battle. I stayed twenty minutes exactly and then said I had better leave so Millie could get some rest.

'But you haven't seen Kamal.' Millie's face dropped in disappointment. 'He's gone to ring his family and get some coffees. He'll be back any minute.'

'I really must go, Millie. I have to be at a lunch thing. I'll call you this afternoon, promise. Happy New Year and well done.' I rushed out the door, desperate to avoid seeing Kamal and needing the solitude of my flat.

The lift seemed to take ages to arrive, long enough for the proud middle-aged couple also waiting to tell me all about their precious and longed-for IVF baby, who slept on, oblivious, swathed in purest white in an expensive-looking car seat.

I exited the double doors at the front of the building as if I was coming up for air. I put my hand on the wall and stood next to a couple of heavily pregnant young women, smoking forbidden cigarettes as they geared up for the long labour ahead. A glance down at my flat belly excluded me from any part in their conversation, and they turned away blowing smoke back over their shoulders. Through the smog I saw Kamal standing on the other side of the parking bay, talking animatedly into his phone. Before I could escape he had finished his call and was walking purposefully back towards the hospital building. He stopped dead in his tracks when he saw me and then pretended I wasn't there and continued on through the doors. I called after him, determined to at least be acknowledged, but he was gone and the lift doors were closing by the time I got to the lobby.

They went to Gretna Green to get married later that year, just the three of them, with two complete strangers as witnesses. Millie apologised profusely to me about it and said it was easier that way because of their different religions and the complications of getting all of Kamal's family over. They just wanted to be married, she said, and be a proper family without the expense and hassle of a big wedding. I was relieved, of course, if a little baffled. Millie had always talked about having a huge do and inviting everyone she had ever known. I suspect that it was Kamal who persuaded Millie that a secret small ceremony would be best, knowing full well that he may otherwise have pushed me too far.

Friday 8 April

Yesterday, after much procrastination I decided I really did want to go and see Crystal's drawing at the young talent preview evening being held at the W gallery in Wandsworth – one of the smaller galleries managed by Prof's now firmly ex-wife Martha. I knew Millie and Kamal would be there, and perhaps, if I'm honest, that was part of the pull. Coming out of the station into the early spring drizzle, I took a deep breath and reminded myself that I had committed no crime. The gallery was a few minutes' walk away on the edge of a small park – an old Victorian villa with an artisan bakery on one side and a vintage clothes store on the other, part of a row of boutique shops catering for the hipsters in this part of London. The door was ajar and I pushed it open straight into a wooden walled gallery, which took up the whole of the ground floor. A serious-looking young man, all in black with blond dreadlocks, sat behind a small desk just inside the door and handed me a programme detailing the art on show, with a list of prices should I want to buy.

I was early, so only a few people were drifting around and they all seemed to know each other.

Crystal's picture, almost directly opposite the door on the far wall, was easy to locate – one of her usual black and grey, strangely compelling obscurities. It was hung carefully under a small light halfway up the wall. A card to the left acknowledged it as her work and gave some brief biographical details, which I wanted to read. As I was reaching into my bag for my glasses I heard Millie's voice behind me urging Kamal to hurry up. My hands started shaking and I fumbled with the glasses case, swearing under my breath as I dropped it on the floor. That's when Millie must have seen me as she stopped mid-sentence. I turned to face her and she completely blanked me, striding purposely past me towards Crystal's picture, her long red velvet dress trailing on the floor behind her like that of a medieval queen. I stood mere inches away, yet she refused to look at me. Kamal was behind her, shifting from one foot to the other, jangling the change in his pocket, staring at the drawing with an inscrutable expression on his face.

'Millie …' I couldn't help myself saying her name, but the word hung in the air between us as another black-clad youth offered us a tray of vol au vents. She turned, and for a moment I thought she was going to acknowledge me, but she directed her comment to her uncomfortable-looking husband.

'Look at how she fragments the light round the trees. She has such a unique way of seeing.'

Kamal screwed up his eyes in an attempt to better see the light, or indeed the trees, and nodded his head.

'I am here, you know. I can see you and I know you can see me. Can we please stop this?'

Again, Millie ignored me and spoke to Kamal. I stared at her profile, noticing the lines of strain beginning to show round her eyes and fought down a fleeting urge to slap her hard across the face. Looking round the gallery, I saw Crystal talking to the boy at the front desk and headed towards her with relief. She smiled shyly as I approached and congratulated her on her picture. We giggled a bit about the price tag and she introduced me to her friend.

'Has Mum spoken to you?' Crystal glanced anxiously over to her parents.

'No,' I shook my head. 'She won't.'

'I'm sorry.'

'You of all people, Crystal, have nothing to apologise for.' I touched her cheek and she moved to hold my hand.

'It's so sad,' she said, pouting just like she used to do when she was a little girl.

'I know. Your mum is still very angry with me, though.'

'And Dad is as well.'

'Yes.'

'Can I ask you something, Auntie Sylvia?'

'Go on.'

'Are you in love with Dad?' Crystal sounded doubtful at her own question.

'Good God, no!' I couldn't help but laugh and Crystal looked relieved.

'I didn't think you were, but I hear them talking about you sometimes and I can't make it out.'

'I was in love with someone. Not your dad, someone else.' I paused, and then made myself say it, 'But he didn't love me back.' Crystal went to reply just as Lewis staggered in the door as if on cue. He looked a complete mess and had clearly fallen over on the muddy ground on his way to the gallery. My heart lurched for him as I recognised the determined look on his drunken face. He saw Crystal and started towards her, knocking over a stand of leaflets on his way.

'Crystal, baby …' He put his arms out to embrace her and she looked utterly horrified at the sight of him.

'No.' I found myself coming between them. 'No, Lewis.' And I took him firmly by the arm and steered him back the way he had come.

'Get off me! Piss off!' He was angry, but not at all physically aggressive, and I continued guiding him out the door, trying to attract as little attention as possible.

'Lewis, it's Crystal's special night. You need to go home,' I said gently as I got him outside. He crouched down on the pavement and put his head in his hands.

'But she means everything to me.' He looked up tearfully, like a small child.

I pulled a tissue out of my bag and handed it to him. 'She knows that, Lewis, but now is not the time. Don't ruin it for her.'

He sat sniffing for a while longer and we talked a little bit about the hurt of unreturned feelings, like the experts that we both are.

Finally, he stood up and nodded in drunken sincerity. 'No, you're right. I don't want to wreck this for her.'

'There's a good boy, best you go home to bed.' I held his arm as he steadied himself and watched him weave his way back down the road, muttering to himself about how tonight wasn't the right time.

As I turned to go back into the gallery I saw Martha standing in the doorway, arms crossed, holding a flute of champagne. 'You averted a scene there, thanks for that, Sylvia. There always seems to be at least one fuming ex who turns up on opening evenings; it's all rather predictable.'

'He's not her ex-boyfriend. More a thwarted love interest, I think.' I didn't want Martha assuming Crystal was like her, discarding loyal lovers for more exciting offers as and when the mood took her, regardless of the hurt she caused.

'Well, you know what they say – "unrequited love's a bore". You should know that better than most.' She didn't say it unkindly and she toasted me with her glass as she drained the last of the champagne. 'We've all been fools in love, Sylvia, and Carl has a particular way of making women feel special. It's all for his own ends, though, that's what you have to remember. It's how he gets people to do things for him and how he gets to sail through life being everyone's hero, but never actually being there when anyone needs him. He's a child, Sylvia, and I'm sorry you lost your job over him. He's not worth it.'

I stood rooted to the spot as she spoke.

'He broke my heart and destroyed our family, all for a leg-over with the au pair, who he also dumped as soon as she started making demands on him, by the way. He's a shit, Sylvia. A charming, articulate, intelligent, handsome shit – but a shit all the same.'

It had stopped raining by now but passing cars were still swooshing in the ground water and the laughter and chatter from inside the gallery seemed to be coming from a faraway place. I didn't want to hear it, but why would she lie to me? What did she have to gain? I had already been humiliated, lost my job, lost everything. She was looking at me intently and I met her concerned gaze in what felt like a completely truthful moment between the two of us.

I nodded and she smiled and dipped back into the warmth and light of the gallery, leaving me alone on the damp pavement to process what she had said. I could sense the last vestiges of Prof fading away. My gentle, funny, kind Prof, to be replaced by a hard, mean, self-centred man called Carl Lomax whom I barely knew and wasn't even sure if I liked. I wanted to reach out and grab hold of the person I had been in love with for so many years, the one who had made me feel safe and hopeful and who had saved me from disappearing into the bleakest place imaginable. But he no longer existed and I felt for a moment that I might disintegrate right there on the pavement as Prof turned into fragments like the light in Crystal's drawing.

Crystal peered out after a few minutes and pulled me back to reality. 'Auntie Sylvia, has Lewis gone? Are you coming back in?'

My instinct was to slink off home away from Martha, away from Kamal and Millie, back to my own private refuge, but I forced myself to go back in for Crystal, head held high. I told her how proud I was of her and she gave me a lovely hug, then we both had a glass of champagne and she showed me a couple of pictures that she particularly liked. We were deep in conversation about a peculiar collage of London Bridge when Millie appeared at my left elbow like a bouncer.

'When are you leaving?' she asked. 'Kamal and I are trying to enjoy our daughter's special night. It's a *family* occasion.'

She emphasised the word family in a completely unnecessary manner, presumably intended to drive home the fact that I was no longer to consider myself part of theirs. I don't know if it was the champagne or the revelations of the evening or Millie's serious face or her ridiculous dress or a combination of it all, but I started to laugh, really laugh, for the first time in a long time.

Kamal came rushing over, flapping his hands saying, 'What's happening? She's hysterical. You see, she's a madwoman.' And that made me laugh even more.

'Yes, Kamal, I'm mad. Mad, bad and sad. Just like you.' Turning to Millie I said, 'Enjoy your family evening,' then I kissed a bemused-looking Crystal on the cheek, walked out and left them to it.

I got a text from Crystal later, thanking me for helping with Lewis and saying sorry if Mum and Dad had spoiled my evening. I texted back, reassuring her that Millie and Kamal hadn't spoiled my evening at all.

Wednesday 27 April

I was required to go into the university today for a meeting with Human Resources about my severance pay and pension scheme. It felt slightly unreal doing my usual commute in the middle of the afternoon without the usual familiar faces, and I had to buy a travelcard as my season ticket had expired. The scenery from the train window was reassuringly familiar and yet it seemed that I was observing it all on a screen, or that the whole day was happening to somebody else. I had a mild panic as I approached the external door to our building. I had to ring the bell as my security card had been taken from me as part of my humiliating exit interview back in November. The office I was headed for was at the top of the building, so I had to go past the third floor in the lift, but mercifully no one I recognised travelled up with me.

The meeting was conducted by one of the human resources robots in a professional manner, with euphemisms used all over the place to avoid having to say I was fired and that I was never coming back to my old position. The financial aspects were sorted out. I can draw my pension early, thank goodness, and that, along with my savings and the fact I own my flat outright, with no mortgage, means that at least I don't have to worry about money. I was given a standard reference, saying how long I had worked at the university and in what capacity – with no mention of why I had left.

'Now, do you have any questions?' the woman asked perfunctorily, as she handed over the paperwork.

'Yes, just one.' I couldn't help myself, I had to know. 'Could you tell me who has taken over my job? Are you hiring someone new or …'

'As far as I am aware, an existing member of Professor Lomax's administrative team has been promoted into the role of his personal assistant.'

'Margaret Davidson?' I asked tightly, bracing myself for the sting of confirmation.

The woman nodded. 'Yes, that's right,' she said before throwing me another curveball.

'Before you go Miss Penton, Professor Lomax has asked that you be given the opportunity to apologise to Lola Maguire for attempting to, erm, discredit her academic reputation and for your behaviour towards her in general. Would you be willing to do that? If so, Ms Maguire is waiting in the room next door.'

I started to tremble and could feel the familiar blush running up my neck onto my face. How could they just spring this on me? Was this even allowed? I was completely put on the spot and the human resources woman regarded me with a plastic smile, waiting placidly for a response.

'Oh … I suppose so, yes.'

'Come this way.' She bustled out and I followed her down the corridor and into the next room along, a small office with a desk and two chairs, one either side. Lola sat facing the door and I sat down meekly opposite her, feeling like a recalcitrant child, summoned in front of the headmistress. She was wearing thick glasses, her hair was a tangled mess, and she looked tired and fed up, a far cry from the fairy queen of Rome. She looked at me expectantly as I cleared my throat.

'I'm … I'm sorry,' I stammered.

'Is that it?' she asked

'Please accept my apology. I was wrong to follow you both to Rome and I was wrong to try and make trouble for you.' I said it as if I was reading off a list written by someone else.

'I don't understand why you did it. Is it just about this absurd infatuation that you have for Professor Lomax? He told me all about it, by the way. It's pathetic, Sylvia, as if he'd ever be interested in an old one like you!' She let that hang unpleasantly in the air for a moment before adding, 'Or do you hate me for some other reason?'

I didn't answer that. I looked past her out the window as she spoke, watching the JCBs moving jerkily around the building site of the new library.

'This opportunity to study with Professor Lomax means everything to me,' she said, putting her hand on her chest for emphasis. 'I don't know if you know this, but the year after Ned was born my partner couldn't handle it and he left me, left *us*, and I have never been so scared and alone in my life. Have you any idea how hard it is to be a single parent, Sylvia?'

I wasn't sure if I was supposed to answer her question or not, but the pause went on for longer than I had expected, so I acknowledged quietly that I didn't have any idea about that. I restrained myself from asking if she had ever considered that it may be even harder for some people not to be a parent at all.

'It has been a really tough ride for me and my boy. This PhD and the possibility of the academic career I've always wanted has been a dream come true. I never thought good things could happen for me again. And Carl – I mean, Professor Lomax – was so supportive and encouraging that I started to believe it was possible. And then you. You came along and tried to destroy it ... so spiteful and vindictive. You upset me badly and you frightened Ned. He calls you the nasty lady and I have to reassure him that you have gone out of our lives for ever. You behaved in a completely unprofessional way.'

'I am sorry – I never meant to frighten Ned.' I realised with a pang of guilt that I hadn't given a thought to how my actions might have affected him. 'I am truly sorry about that.' I paused, sensing Lola enjoying her status as the noble woman wronged. Still, I had to go on, 'But you were having a sexual relationship with Professor Lomax, weren't you? Maybe you still are? I don't call *that* conduct particularly professional either.'

The victim persona fell swiftly from Lola. It didn't suit her anyway. She's far too canny for that. Her eyes flashed with anger behind her glasses and she pointed her finger at me, saying, 'That is none of your business, it's got nothing to do with you.'

'Well, I've obviously hit a nerve, and for that, again, I apologise. Good luck with your studies, Ms Maguire. Send my regards to Professor Lomax and tell him he needs to buy some more grown-up boxer shorts.'

With that I got up and left the room, Lola's stunned face an image to treasure for a long time. The HR woman was waiting expectantly just outside the door. 'Did it all go OK?' she asked with a vague wave of her hand.

'Yes, fine, thank you,' I said as I swept past her into the waiting lift.

I stopped at the flower sellers at the station on the way home and bought myself a bunch of yellow roses – out of season, ridiculously expensive, but oh so beautiful.

Sunday 8 May

There's a patch of grassy woodland at the edge of the park where we let recovered hedgehogs back into the wild. The garden of one of Paula's friend's backs on to the area and she always puts down food and water for visiting hogs, so Jonas feels reassured that by releasing them here he's giving them the very best chance of survival. Today was the turn of a big old boar that Sophie had named Guy. He had been with us since early November when a couple of local Scouts had found him close to death in the smouldering ashes of their annual bonfire. I didn't think he'd make it – his spikes were singed, his feet and nose horribly blistered and he was struggling to breathe – but Jonas worked his magic and we all marvelled at how he pulled back from the brink and came back to life over the following weeks and months. It was quite an occasion for us, letting him go, and Sophie and her little sister Natalie had joined us to see Guy on his way. We crouched in hushed silence, watching as Jonas pulled open the front of the box, and he came slowly out, snuffling around in the long grass, eventually wandering off in the direction of a pile of fallen branches.

'That's him, then,' Jonas said, leaning on a tree stump to help himself up. 'He'll be right. He's a strong lad, that one.'

'Goodbye, Guy, and good luck,' Sophie whispered, giving him a solemn wave while Natalie blew him a string of kisses.

'Yes, good luck,' I echoed quietly as he disappeared back into his own world. 'Do you think they ever remember being at the sanctuary or think about us again once they've gone?' I asked, turning to Jonas.

'I don't reckon so,' he said, pulling on his hat. 'They're too busy trying to stay alive to ponder on the past.'

'Maybe they dream about us when they have their long sleep in the winter?' Sophie said hopefully, taking hold of her grandad's hand. Jonas chuckled at that. 'Maybe, sweetheart,' he said. Natalie took Sophie's other hand and I took hers and we made our way back to the car where Katie was waiting to take us home.

After Katie and the girls had gone I found myself still at Jonas's, pottering around, tidying up the hanging baskets and sweeping the patio, reluctant, I suppose, to go back to the empty flat. Jonas was sitting on the bench patiently throwing Igor's rubber chicken over and over again, telling him he was a good boy and scratching him behind the ears when he brought it back.

'Do you ever feel lonely, Jonas?' I asked, leaning on my broom and watching the game.

'Aye, lass, sometimes,' he replied after a few moments thought.

'How do you bear it, though? Losing the one you loved?'

I knew it was too much to ask, really, but I couldn't stop myself. I needed to know if there was an answer, a secret coping strategy that he could share with me to make it all less painful. I regretted my impetuousness as he took off his glasses and wiped the corner of his eye, the game with Igor momentarily forgotten.

'I'm sorry, Jonas, I didn't mean to upset you,' I said, coming to sit beside him, not knowing what to say to make it better. Igor popping up in front of us, chicken in mouth, broke the tension perfectly and Jonas blew his nose and started to laugh.

'What a rum bunch we are, eh, Sylvia?' he said as he grabbed the toy and played tug with the dog. 'You, me, Igor, the hedgehogs. Even Jack and Jill. We're all lost and broken in our own way, washed up together in this little corner of London, clinging on for dear life.'

'Looking after each other,' I said, and we shared a knowing smile at the sheer ridiculousness of it and the sadness of it, and because we both know that Hartland Road is as much a sanctuary for us as it is for the hedgehogs.

After we had given the hogs their last feed, Jonas went into the house to get us a couple of blankets and we sat on the garden bench late into the night, with Igor asleep across our laps, chatting quietly and watching as the sky blurred over and the stars began to appear. Walking home through the deserted streets I hesitated for a moment at the turning that would take me towards Dulwich. I stood there, waiting for the familiar flutter of excitement or the ache of longing to compel me to make my way to Prof's house, but I felt nothing of the sort, so I kept on going, straight back to my flat.

Saturday 21 May

Crystal came to help out with the hedgehogs today as she often does now at the weekend. I used to bring her here sometimes when she was little and foisted on me for babysitting duties while Millie and Kamal were busy in the shop. She used to love drawing the hedgehogs and feeding the animals, but she lost interest when she became a teenager and preferred hanging out with her friends. Now, though, she has a new-found enthusiasm for helping us in the sanctuary, and we like spending time together in a way we never have before. Jonas is delighted, because we are so short of volunteers, especially young ones, and Crystal has a lovely, gentle way about her and isn't afraid to get her hands dirty. I'm very proud of her, actually. We seem to have turned another page in our relationship since the night at the gallery. Millie and Kamal no longer loom so heavily between us and this seems to give us room just to enjoy each other's company.

Saturday 28 May

An emotional day today, in so many ways.

I went to Jonas's by myself this morning as Crystal had some coursework to finish. Walking down to Hartland Road I heard the hum of lawnmowers and the smell of cut grass and noticed with joy the first signs of spring turning into summer. Daffodils are turning brown and tulips and bluebells have begun springing up in front gardens. The warmth of the day made it seem impossible that it had ever been so cold or that anything bad could ever happen again. When I arrived, Jonas made tea in the two new mugs that Crystal had made for us in her ceramics class.

We sat with our drinks, warm on the bench at the back of the house looking out at the garden buzzing with bees and new life and I felt more relaxed and companionable than I had for a long time. Jonas sensed it too and he patted my knee. 'It's all changing for the better, lass. The hogs are out of hibernation and summer's on its way.'

He offered me a toffee out of a crumpled white paper bag and I shook my head out of habit. Then I found myself taking one anyway, luxuriating in the sweetness of it as I rolled it round my mouth. Igor, deeply asleep in the forget-me-nots, suddenly jumped up from his slumber and stared unblinking at the side gate, indicating that someone was coming, but it was half a minute or more until Jonas and I heard the motorbike's mellow growl and saw it slowly pull up in the driveway.

I watched a figure in black leathers get off the bike and kick down the stand, and wondered who on earth it could be. I knew Jonas's youngest daughter rode a motorbike, but this person was too large to be Carrie. Someone bringing hedgehogs to the sanctuary on a motorbike would be a first, but stranger things had happened. I got up and went over to investigate our mysterious visitor. I reached the gate at the exact moment Neil pulled off his helmet. He grinned at me sheepishly as he rubbed his hands over his damp hair. The smell of him, sweat and leather, was quintessentially masculine and he undid his black jacket to reveal a white T-shirt and silver St Christopher necklace that I recalled he used to wear when we were teenagers. He stood there awkwardly as I gaped at him through the wrought-iron bars and finally said, 'Millie told me where to find you. Can I come in?'

Jonas was getting curious by now and shouted out, asking who it was. 'It's nobody, Jonas, he's just leaving,' I replied, removing my hand from the gate and taking a step back.

Neil reddened and fiddled with his necklace. 'I'm sorry, Sylvia. Let me explain. Please?'

The memory of that evening he left me in the restaurant all those months ago flooded back and I felt the anger rising at the humiliation and upset he had caused me. I bit my lip and took a deep breath.

'No need for apologies, Neil. I'm afraid you have had a wasted journey. Goodbye.'

I turned to walk back to Jonas, dignity restored, a small victory won. Hearing the clank of the gate opening I spun round in disbelief. Surely he had not just let himself in after I had asked him to leave? In fact, it was Crystal, coursework obviously abandoned for the day, shyly edging round Neil to get into the garden and politely asking him if he'd like to come in.

'I'm here to see Sylvia,' he persisted and walked in with Crystal, who looked at me with exactly the same quizzical expression and arched eyebrow as Millie would have done. Jonas introduced himself and the two men shook hands.

'Well, I need to see to the hogs,' Jonas announced abruptly, heaving himself up from the bench. He tottered momentarily and Neil stepped forward, grasping his arm to steady him. Jonas nodded his thanks and set off towards the garage, asking Crystal to come with him to help with the cleaning out.

'So, this is what you like to do,' Neil said, glancing around approvingly, taking in the disorderly vegetable patch, blooming herbaceous borders, and various animals in hutches and runs that characterise Jonas's garden.

'It's a hedgehog sanctuary,' I said indicating the garage. 'We look after sick hedgehogs and baby ones – hoglets.'

I felt silly. Exposed. Why had he come here? If it was to laugh at me and add more spice to his story of the sad old spinster who used to spy on him then I was not going to give him any more grist for that particularly unpleasant mill. But there was something gentle and honest about his manner that made me sense that wasn't why he had come.

'That's so cool. What a great thing to do. My little boy would love it here. He's always wanted a pet but his mum hates animals.'

I ignored the flutter of gratitude I felt at his approval and shifted the conversation back to its essence. 'What is it you want, Neil?'

'May I sit down?' He pointed at the bench and I nodded, although I remained standing, holding on to the power position that Prof always aimed to achieve with his extra-high desk chair.

He sat down and leant forward with his elbows on his knees. He ruffled his hair again and then sat bolt upright and looked at me levelly. 'This isn't easy for me. But I needed to come. It was unforgiveable of me to leave you like that at Stones. I would like to explain what happened.'

'There's really no need.' I wanted to end this awkward situation. I didn't want to be pitied or patronised or to have to make him feel better for being badly behaved.

'No, there is a need, Sylvia. What happened was that my daughter's friend called me on my mobile as I was on my way back from the bathroom. I don't know if you remember the layout of that restaurant, but I was right near the front door at this point and our table was way at the back.'

I looked at him, bemused, and he shook his head. 'This isn't making any sense I know, just hear me out. Holly, my daughter, she has panic attacks, Sylvia. Really bad ones. She thinks she's dying; she can't breathe, she shakes all over. She's delicate, you know? She's a fragile girl. She's grown up without her mum and I've done my best but … Anyway, she tries hard to have a normal life. She works in a clothes shop and she goes out with her friends, but sometimes she has a meltdown and I have to get to her and look after her and take her home. And that's what happened the night we were having dinner. She had been with her friend in a tube train that had broken down and they'd been stuck in a tunnel for twenty minutes. I know it doesn't sound that traumatic to us, but she was in a terrible state and her friend called me and told me to come and I just dashed out so I could get to Oxford Circus and look after her. I didn't have your number to text or ring.'

'But you had time to pay the bill?' I wanted to believe him, but this part didn't make sense.

'I literally shoved a fifty-pound note in the waitress's hand as I ran past the front desk and said it was for table twenty-three, and to say sorry. Didn't she tell you that?'

'No, she just said you had paid the bill and left.'

'I did think about coming back afterwards, or calling the restaurant after I had calmed Holly down and got her home and safely into bed, but it was so late by then, I assumed you would have left.' I waited for him to continue, not knowing what to think.

'I'm sorry it's taken so long to get back into contact. I had to go to Japan the day after and then work went crazy. I asked Mum to talk to Millie next time she was in her shop, but she doesn't go to Streatham very often, only when she's visiting her brother.'

He was rambling now, which I took as a good sign. In my experience, people who lie tend to be economical with what they tell you, as the less they say, the less chance there is that they will expose themselves.

I sat down next to him on the bench and he visibly relaxed.

'Am I forgiven?' he bit his knuckle in the most endearing way and I found myself laughing.

'Am I forgiven for spying on you?' I asked playfully.

'What, that? I was flattered, Sylvia. I should have asked you out at the time. I was too busy perfecting my "too cool for school" image – and that was my problem:

I was actually terrified of girls.' I laughed again and he took my hand. 'Will you let me take you out again? I *will* stay for the whole evening this time. Promise.'

The invitation hung in the air as Crystal appeared out of the garage and ran towards us shouting, 'Jonas has collapsed! He's on the floor.'

Neil sprang into action immediately, leaping over to the garage in two or three huge bounds. By the time I got there he was already leaning over Jonas, putting him in the recovery position and instructing Crystal to call for an ambulance.

'What's happened?'

I stood back, horrified at the sight of Jonas prostrate on the grimy floor, his body convulsing every few seconds, his eyes half closed, mouth drooling open.

'He's having some sort of fit. Is he epileptic, do you know? Or a diabetic?' I was grateful that Neil was taking control of the situation.

'No, not that I know of.' I racked my brain for any clues. 'No,' I answered more firmly this time, 'I would know if he was.'

Crystal looked at me imploringly after she had made the call. 'Is he going to die, Auntie Sylvia?'

I took her hand and held her close to me. 'Let's hope not, sweetheart. The ambulance will be here soon.'

Neil continued ensuring Jonas was safe and spoke reassuringly to him until the ambulance crew arrived at the gate. I ran to it, cursing myself for not thinking of having it opened already, wasting another few seconds when Jonas was in such a terrible state. The professional urgency of the medical crew spun the scene into a surreal yet familiar trope: the oxygen mask, the barked questions, the stretcher.

'I'll go with him in the ambulance,' I stated. 'Crystal, can you stay here and hold the fort until I get back?'

'I can't, Auntie Sylvia.' She looked pained. 'I promised Dad I would help in the shop this afternoon. He has to go to the wholesalers.'

I glared at her and was about to tell her what I thought of her priorities when Neil interjected, 'I can stay and look after the dog and look after things here. You go.'

I had no choice, I had to trust him. Igor was cowering under the hedgehog cages in the corner of the garage and Neil said, 'He'll be fine. You go with Jonas.'

I phoned Katie from the ambulance and she met us at the hospital with Sophie and Natalie in tow. They must have been pulled out of a dance class as they were dressed in pink tutus and ballet shoes, faces anxious for news about their grandad.

'Thank you, Sylvia, for coming with him. Is there any news?' Katie squeezed my arm and we sat down on the plastic seats outside the treatment room.

'They think that he's had some sort of stroke. They are running tests now to find out for sure.'

'How bad is it?' She held her huge handbag to her chest, like a shield.

'I don't know, Katie. The doctor will be out soon. She's assessing him. Have you rung your sisters?' She shook her head. 'Do you want me to?'

She nodded slowly and handed me her phone for the numbers.

I didn't get back to Jonas's until late afternoon. Carrie and Harriet had both been miles away when I called them, and Katie's husband, Mike, was on a stag do in Prague. I couldn't leave her and the children to deal with it alone. Eventually, Carrie dashed up the corridor in a fluster, having ridden back from a music festival in Dorset, and I slipped away with a small wave to Katie as they were hugging outside Jonas's room. As I was waiting for a bus in the car park I saw Harriet pull into a parking space in her Range Rover and run over to the main doors, locking the car over her shoulder with an electronic fob as she went.

The bus came almost straight away but took a torturously slow route back to Sydenham, seemingly going up every side road to pick up non-existent passengers. A large, elderly woman got on at one stop and sat right next to me, squashing me against the window, although almost every other seat on the bus was free. She launched into a monologue about her bunions playing her up and the cost of raspberries, which were her favourite fruit, and I let her go on, smiling and nodding every now and then. I recognise loneliness when I see it.

I turned down the side path to Jonas's back garden with bated breath, but surely Neil wouldn't still be here? And then I saw the motorbike and my stomach jumped.

I opened the gate and glanced around the garden. He was nowhere to be seen. Maybe he had gone, after all, but left the bike here for some reason? I went into the garage but he wasn't there either. I would have to feed the hogs at five, I reminded myself, and tidy up the garage for the night before going home and getting my journal and the other things I needed so I could stay here for a while. I stood in the garden and called for Igor. Nothing. I sat down on the bench wearily and closed my eyes, clueless as to what to do next.

Igor's cold nose pressing into my hands brought me back to the moment and I opened my eyes to see Neil standing in front of me with a concerned expression on his face. 'I took him for a walk. I hope that's OK? His lead was in the garage.'

'That's great. Thank you. And thank you for staying,' I was touched at his kindness and the fact that he had given up his whole Saturday to help us. 'You can go now, Neil. You must have somewhere you need to be.'

I wanted to release him, was embarrassed by his generosity, but it came out sounding unpleasant. He flinched and picked up his jacket from the other end of the bench where it was still sitting from this morning.

'How is he?' he asked as he zipped it up.

'They think it was a stroke. They'll know more in the morning. His daughters are there now,' I replied.

'I was happy to stay, you know. It wasn't a problem.' He rubbed Igor's head and the dog responded by licking his hand and pushing against his leg.

'You've made a friend there,' I commented and smiled at Neil, trying to recapture something of our earlier rapport.

'I'll call you,' he said decisively as he turned and went out the gate. I watched him put on his helmet and kick-start his bike, turning it carefully in the narrow passage before roaring off. I listened as the noise of the motorbike faded away – and then realised that he hadn't asked for my phone number.

Sunday 29 May

I was woken at midnight by the ringing of my mobile and I snatched it up, expecting it to be Katie with bad news about Jonas. When Mother's brisk voice came on the line it was something of a relief, momentarily at least.

'Why are you calling so late, Mum? Is everything all right?'

'No, it most certainly is not.'

Mother was furious and I sighed as I struggled to sit up on Jonas's saggy sofa and locate my glasses on the coffee table. 'What's happened?'

'The man next door has been playing his music for hours at full volume. I can't get to sleep. You have to come and tell him to turn it off.'

'Have you called the police? Have the other neighbours complained? Is he having a party?' My mind was sorting through possibilities as I tried to avoid the trip across town to come to her aid.

'No, it's not a party, and no, the others haven't complained. I haven't called the police. He is doing it to get his own back at me.'

I was sitting up by now, looking out at the moonlit garden, trying to get my bearings on the conversation and feeling a growing sense of unease. 'What do you mean "get his own back"? For what? What did you do?'

'I reported him and his vile family to the social services and the immigration office and I told him so.'

'Dear God, Mother, why did you do that? What happened?'

'His children were very rude to me and so was he. They were running all over my garden.'

'You haven't got a garden, Mum, you live in a flat—'

'Then they pulled down all my washing and threw it in puddles.'

I was wide awake now and standing bolt upright. 'What are you talking about? That was something that happened years ago, when we lived in Harrow.'

'I know what I saw, Sylvia. They are a bad lot, I tell you, and he is the worst of all.' Her voice was rising to a hysterical pitch.

'Mum.'

'Yes?'

'I can't hear any music.'

She started to cry then and I told her to stay exactly where she was and I would be there as soon as I could. I dashed round getting back into the clothes I had only taken off an hour ago and splashed some cold water on my face. I needed to call a taxi, but I had no number, no internet connection, and, paralysing realisation, no cash on me. I had to ring my sister. I had no choice and I braced myself as I dialled her landline, knowing she turned her mobile off at night. Eventually it was answered by a sleepy, cross-sounding Millie. I cut straight to it.

'It's me. Mother is having some sort of confused episode; she's in a terrible state. We need to get over there.'

She arrived in her Mini less than twenty minutes later, a mac pulled over her purple onesie and her hair in a scruffy ponytail on top of her head. I was waiting for her outside Jonas's, having left out food and water for Igor in case he woke up before I got back, the spare keys Katie had given me tucked in my jeans pocket.

She unlocked the door for me and I climbed in gingerly, trying not to look her in the eye. As soon as the door had closed she sped off without a word and we drove all the way to Mother's mansion block of flats like that, in strained silence. When we got there we stood outside the front door, each looking expectantly at the other.

'Well, open it then,' Millie said.

'I don't have a key, Millie, I thought you did.'

She shook her head in irritation and pushed the doorbell for the flat. We waited several minutes until a light eventually came on in the shared hall. Millie peered through the peephole and whispered, 'She's coming,' in a way that reminded me of when we had been up to mischief as children. Much unlocking and unbolting ensued before the door opened and there stood Mother, resplendent in her pink dressing gown and slippers, with a gracious smile on her face.

'Oh, hello girls, how nice to see you. Do come in.'

'Mum, are you all right?' I placed my hand on her arm and she looked at it in bemusement.

'Yes, fine, Sylvia. Thank you. And yourself?'

'You rang me earlier about the man next door, you were upset and frightened. Do you remember?'

'No, not me.' Mother chuckled. 'What a silly story.' She glanced at Millie and tutted as she looked her up and down, taking in her unkempt hair and messy nightclothes. 'Goodness me, what a mess.' Millie pressed her lips tightly together and managed not to respond. We got her settled in bed again and I took Hamish for a quick walk round the block while Millie checked the flat was safe. There was nothing else to do.

'I'll ring her GP in the morning,' Millie said, as we walked back to the car. 'She's going doolally. Just what I bloody well need.' It struck me as an unforgivably selfish thing to say, but I suppose there is a part of me that feels the same. 'We'll have to do something about that dog as well,' Millie continued. 'She can't look after him properly in that flat.'

The journey back was another silent affair, until we turned into Jonas's road.

'Why are you staying here anyway?' Millie's curiosity had got the better of her. 'Don't tell me you've shacked up with the crusty old sod.'

I shook my head with a look of mock horror on my face and we both laughed despite ourselves. 'No, not that.' I told her what had happened and she said she was sorry and that Jonas sounded like a nice man. The tension between us seemed to have dissipated a little and I put my hand on hers.

'I really am so sorry, Millie. I miss you.'

She stiffened and sniffed. 'Not as much as you miss Kamal, though, hey Sylvia?'

'I don't miss Kamal. What do you mean?'

'I saw the card you gave him, Sylvia. "*Sorry ... I miss you, love Sylvia.*" It's pathetic. I mean, really pathetic. You can't let it go even now.'

My mind raced as I tried to make sense of what she was saying.

'That card was for *you*, Millie. The one with the puppy on it. I put it in the bin outside your shop the day I came to see you and you had gone out to lunch. Kamal must have got it out the bin after I left.' My voice rose in disbelief. 'Good God! Why would I send him a card like that? Please, believe me, Millie.'

She stared straight ahead at the shadowy road, her eyes following a fox that had darted out of the bushes opposite.

'Millie.' I tried one more time but she was once again immovable so I let myself out the car and walked up the front path. I turned round as I unlocked the door and saw her staring sadly after me, but seeing me turn she looked quickly back to the road and pulled away.

Crystal and I have been managing the sanctuary between us for the last couple of weeks, with Katie popping in when she can to help. I have been sleeping on the sofa in Jonas's living room and using the downstairs shower. I have never been upstairs in his house and it would seem presumptuous, somehow, to go up there without his permission. Igor sleeps up there, though, on Jonas's bed, according to Katie, where he has always slept. I can understand that. No one likes to sleep alone. He clatters down the stairs early in the morning when nature calls and I let him out and sit on the bench drinking my tea, listening to the birds singing and watching the garden come to life.

Crystal has her exams, but comes by in the evenings and helps me feed the hogs. I spend the days tending to the garden, walking Igor, and dealing with any new arrivals at the sanctuary. I try not to think actively about Prof, or Millie, but they swirl around in the space just behind my conscious mind, forever trying to break back through, jostling to take the central position. Weeding helps, so does looking after the animals. Repetitive, necessary, nurturing work that engages my hands and some level of concentration. At night, though, when there is nothing to distract me and Igor is asleep upstairs, they stride onto my psychic stage and demand my attention.

One of them steps forward first – usually Millie. I think it's because I am so much more used to communicating with her in a free and open manner, and because she is generally wearing brightly coloured clothes that contrast with Prof's subdued suits. He stands behind in the shadows, hand on chin, listening carefully as she rages at me and tells me how, of all the people in her life who she thought might hurt her, I was the last one she would ever have suspected. She shakes her head, asking 'Why?' over and over again, her bottom lip trembling, as if she were five years old and I had stolen and broken her favourite dolly. Then her eyes flash and she begins to hurl insults at me. I am a slut, a cow, an evil, jealous, pathetic, old hag. I ruined her life because I couldn't bear to see her happy. Her whole marriage has been a sham because of me. She doesn't know the man she married and it is because of me. Then she cries, huge shuddering sobs that gradually subside into silent tears and we stare at each other as if we are strangers in a strange land, a land where love and loyalty and sisterhood don't mean anything and nothing is true or real or solid any more.

Then it is my turn to speak. I tell it from the very beginning. I explain to her over and over again how

I didn't mean it to happen. How it was just that one time on the sofa in my sitting room with the curtains closed against the afternoon sun and the television he had just carried upstairs for me on the floor beside us in its cardboard packaging. I tell her that that was the last time I had sex, so strong was my self-disgust. Eighteen years ago. I tell her how I've gone over it so many times in my head and I still don't really know how it happened.

We didn't speak, not one word. We stood looking at the space where the TV was going to go and he suddenly stepped forward and closed the curtains. She hates to hear the next bit, but I tell her how he looked at me with this inquisitive hunger and I let him kiss me. And then I tell her how it all happened really quickly, and then he was gone, out the door and down the stairs and back to their shiny new life together.

I remind her that they had not long moved in together and that they had so many plans for their lives, that there was an aura of magic and potential and pure love emanating from them that made everyone around them feel happy too – and sometimes she smiles here, because she is remembering that feeling, the taste of it, the thrill of it. I try to explain that it was as if I got swept up in their joy and somehow thought I was part of it.

The next part is hard to say, but I press on, because I want her to understand. I tell her that it was as if having sex with Kamal was a way of me placing my stamp of approval completely on her choice of man. She generally scoffs here, in an angry fashion, and I tell her that I know that sounds ridiculous now, but it's the only way I can explain it to myself and it is truly how I felt.

I emphasise to Millie that I never wanted to take him away from her, I just wanted to not be left out. I explain how it was like the instinct to warm your hands in front of a cosy log fire, that I was drawn to the comfort of it. Then I realise I haven't given her the whole truth and I have to be completely honest because there is no other way for us to move forward,

And the truth is that he was beautiful then as well, there is no denying it.

She sometimes gives another small smile at this point, allowing her own memories of the young Kamal to envelop her. I add details and describe his smooth brown torso, soft black hair, sensitive, intelligent face. And he was young, only twenty-five – seven years younger than Millie, ten years younger than me. I remind her that I used to tease her about her toy boy, but I knew she secretly loved it.

I tell her that we didn't speak. I remember that. Not one word. I tell her how I lay there on the sofa afterwards, 'undone' as the Victorian ladies would say, wondering if it had actually happened at all.

When the shock had worn off, the self-revulsion and shame rolled in to take its place. And then the fear. An animalistic fear that seemed to crawl out of the floor and seep out of the walls and sofa, surrounding me, entering me, becoming a permanent part of my very being. The fear that I was going to lose her, lose her love and lose my place of safety in the world.

I tell her how I got up and opened the curtains to a cold grey sky and sat watching the pigeons landing and taking off from the roof opposite for hours, wanting more than anything for it not to have happened. Then I tell her that, seven weeks later, I found out I was pregnant and that I did what I had to do because I loved her so much.

At this point, there is silence for a moment or two and then Millie backs away, rather theatrically, into the gloom with her hands covering her face. The space is empty for a few beats and then Prof moves forward and looks at me expectantly. It always takes me by surprise, because it seems like he is from another story, another part of my life completely, but I am beginning to realise that it is all connected, that he is a continuation of the first story and I can only explain myself to him in light of all that happened before.

As I watch him watching me, I feel the familiar longing for his touch, his attention, his love – everything I never had from him – and I wonder again how I can feel such loss when, in retrospect, what we actually had was so little. I try to take a mental step back from him and see him for who he really is: a middle-aged, divorced, unfaithful, averagely successful academic with a charming manner and a selfish heart. How can I not have seen that? How could I have made such a fool of myself? I feel hot with shame as I force myself to confess that I thought I was in love with him and all the ways in which I tried to demonstrate that love. And he looks at me in a slightly bored way and I notice him discreetly checking his watch several times as I pour out my heart.

I have tried to imagine him reacting differently to my confession, throwing his arms around me and kissing me passionately or wiping a tear from his eye as he realises that true love has found him at last, but even in my fantasy world such a response seems ludicrous now. When I have finally finished and he is required to speak, he fiddles nervously with his tie and smiles in what he probably thinks is a concerned way, but which comes across as wholly patronising and dismissive.

'OK, I see,' he says briskly, searching for words to bring the whole uncomfortable interchange to a close. 'Well, it's probably for the best you have ... erm ... moved on, Sylvia. Good luck with the future.' He puts out his hand to shake mine, thinks better of it, and changes it into a quick wave as he disappears off my mental stage as if he is being pursued by invisible hounds.

'This is the truth,' I tell myself as I sit in the darkness wrapped in Jonas's patchwork quilt, feeling the different textures of the squares that his wife sewed together with such care. 'This is the truth of the man.'

After Prof has left, a long time after, sometimes Neil appears, wandering onto the stage wearing his leathers and motorcycle helmet. 'Take that off,' I tell him. 'Let me see you and then we can talk.'

To my relief, not once has Kamal appeared for a psychic showdown. I have nothing to say to him and nothing left to explain.

Friday 10 June

The first thing I did this morning, before I had even had a cup of tea, was grab the pad of writing paper and Parker pen from Jonas's bureau and write Millie a letter. I allowed our imaginary conversations to take form on the paper and told her everything that I could remember and every reason why. Once it was down, I didn't dare read it through in case I changed my mind. I put it in an envelope, found a stamp in my purse, pulled my coat on over my pyjamas and ran over the road to post it in the pillar box opposite. I felt slightly giddy as I glided back to the house and let myself in, thankful that no one in the road had seen me in my nightclothes and anorak. I briefly considered penning a similar apology and explanation missive to Prof, but the idea clanged and stalled as soon as I pulled out the writing pad and I realised it would be a mistake. I wasn't sure what to apologise for, and couldn't think how to explain my behaviour in a way that he would understand.

The early mist cleared as I showered and dressed, and as I pulled on Jonas's battered gardening gloves and threw open the back door, the sun appeared from between two clouds and transformed the garden into glorious Technicolor. Igor rushed out for his usual exploration of any new scents and trails that had been left on the lawn overnight, then followed me into the garage in the hope I might drop some hedgehog food on the floor that he could hoover up.

Disturbing hedgehogs first thing in the morning is akin to walking uninvited into a stranger's house when they are engaged in a secret and underhand activity. They stay still and watch you with beady little black eyes, their prickles rising up and down with their breath, or they shuffle into their bedding and hide, with just their snouts poking out for air.

'Morning, hogs,' I greeted them cheerfully and, their cover blown, they gradually began emerging from their bedding and coming forward in their cages, propelled by the expectation of filling their bellies.

I did the usual checks and gave the necessary medications to those that needed it before cleaning out each cage and then giving them fresh food and water. Absorbed in my task, I didn't realise I had company until I turned to the door to empty out the last water bowl. Standing just outside the garage entrance was Neil and, next to him, holding his hand, was a beautiful dark-haired little boy of about three.

'I hope you don't mind. I told him about the hedgehogs and he wanted to come and see.'

Igor ran up to them and nuzzled Neil's hand as I gathered myself and got over the shock of his unexpected visit.

'I didn't think I'd see you again,' I faltered. 'I didn't think you wanted to, after last time. I thought you were cross at having to stay here and—'

'I was happy I could help. I didn't want to be in the way. How is Jonas?'

'Not good at all.'

We stood looking at each other in commiseration, me not wanting to expand with the little one there.

'And who is this?' I said brightly, smiling at Neil's son who was gazing around at the hedgehogs as though he was in a magical wonderland.

'This is Rikuto. Say hello, Riki,'

'Hello.' He waved at me and then hid behind Neil's leg.

'Would you like to see the hedgehogs?' I asked him, and Neil translated unnecessarily as Riki was already nodding and pointing at the cages.

'You know, in Tokyo they have hedgehog cafés where you can drink coffee and look at hedgehogs in pens. If you manage to make one uncurl and show its face, you get your coffee for free,' Neil mused, peering into one of the cages at a tightly curled hog.

'How extraordinary! The poor little things. I think I'd rather pay for my coffee,' I replied, thinking how much Jonas would love that nugget to add to his eclectic hedgehog fact file.

'Needlemouse,' Neil suddenly said, staring at one of Jonas's posters.

'I'm sorry?' He had lost me entirely.

'The word for hedgehog in Japanese, *harinezumi*, it translates literally as "needlemouse".'

'"Needlemouse",' I repeated, turning the words over in my mouth. 'How perfect!'

He smiled, pleased at my response and repeated it to Riki in a sing-song voice, making him clap his hands together in delight.

We spent the whole day together in the end. Neil helped me pick sprouting broccoli and leeks from the vegetable plot and Riki played with Jack and Jill and planted sunflower seeds in flowerpots. We had a picnic lunch on the lawn, which Neil had given its first mow of the year, struggling comically with Jonas's ancient push-along. The smell of cut grass combined with the scent of the early sweet peas growing up the fence in the most sublime manner as the warmth of the sun brought the garden to life. As we sat eating our food, fielding off Igor's attempts to help himself to the sandwiches and watching Riki dig for worms in the herbaceous border, I remembered what it was to be still inside.

When Katie rang an hour later I knew what she was going to say and I was ready for it, but I was still grateful that Neil was there to sit with me as the news sank in.

Sunday 12 June

Katie and Carrie came to the house today and went upstairs to choose an outfit for their father to be buried in. I sat downstairs petting Igor, who was blissfully unaware that everything had changed, and wondered what was going to happen next. I felt strangely ambivalent about my own circumstances. I didn't care whether they wanted me to stay or go. I was only worried about who was going to look after the animals and the garden.

'What shall we do, then?' Katie asked as she finally came downstairs with a dark suit folded over her arm. Carrie followed behind her holding a white shirt and polished black shoes – their formality a stark contrast against the rainbow-coloured tie-dye dress she was wearing. I stared at the clothes in amazement, wondering where they had found them as I had never seen Jonas wearing anything other than baggy cords and a tatty cardigan.

'It's his wedding suit,' Katie said, seeing my expression. 'He lost quite a lot of weight in hospital and I'm sure it will fit him again now.' Carrie let out a sob and sat down heavily on the other end of the sofa, the shoes and shirt dropping to the floor.

Katie hung the suit on the picture rail and stood next to Carrie, holding her head to her hip and smoothing her hair.

'Shall I go?' I suddenly felt awkward and unsure of why I was there witnessing their grief.

'No, Sylvia, please stay. You've been so kind. I don't know what we'd have done without you these last few weeks.'

'You must be desperate to get back to your own life,' Carrie said earnestly, wiping her nose on a tissue.

'No, not really.' They both looked at me in surprise. The idea of not having a life worth returning to was clearly an alien concept to them both. 'I mean, I haven't got a job at the moment. I'm at a bit of a crossroads, you see, and I'm not sure what I'm doing next. I don't have any firm plans.'

They glanced at each other and Carrie's eyes brightened. 'Could you ... would you ... stay? At least for a while, until we sort out what we're going to do with the house and the sanctuary and everything.' Katie said it as if she could hardly believe this was even a possibility.

I thought for a moment and then said with certainty, 'Yes, I can do that, but I will need to have my mother's dog, Hamish, here with me, if that's all right. She's not able to look after him any more.'

'Of course,' Katie said, nodding. 'Are you sure you'll be able to manage?'

'Yes, I know I will. Crystal will help me when she can. And I'll look after Igor too.'

Carrie burst into fresh tears. 'I thought we were going to have to take him back to the dogs' home,' she sniffed. 'Thank you so much, Sylvia. We will pay you, of course.' She looked at Katie for confirmation and she nodded, leaning down to put her arms around me. Carrie joined in with a side hug and then Igor jumped on us, joining in the game, making us a mess of tears, laughter, dog and cushions.

Tuesday 14 June

The taxi journey from Mother's flat to Jonas's house was one of the longest journeys of my life. It was extraordinary the level of adoration and care Mother lavished on Hamish, especially in comparison to the rather offhand manner with which she had always dealt with the well-being of me and Millie. I suppose her little dog had been a safe repository for her love – he couldn't answer back or change or disappoint her. She fussed and fretted about leaving Hamish in my care all the way across London. And when she couldn't think of any new points to remind me of, she started again at the beginning and went through them all again.

'You do know he won't eat fish, don't you?'

'Yes, Mother.'

'And he is not to get wet under any circumstances. He is extremely susceptible to colds.'

'Yes, Mother.'

'And he needs his brown blanket in his basket. When it's in the wash he will tolerate his blue one, but then he doesn't sleep as well.'

'Yes, Mother.'

'And you won't allow the other dog to bully him, will you?'

'No, Mother. Look, we're here now,' I said with relief, indicating to the cabbie to pull up outside Jonas's. I sensed Mother was about to say something disparaging about the house and gave her a warning look as I picked Hamish up and paid the driver.

'Here we are! Your new home, Hamish,' I said brightly as I let us in the front door and set him down in the hall. Hamish snuffled around with interest, freezing when he came face to face with Igor who was standing motionless on the threshold of the kitchen. Mother and I both held our breath. This was the moment of truth, when the dogs would decide between themselves, by scent alone, whether they would get on or not. It was not a relationship that any human could influence and the outcome of this meeting would determine if both or only one of them would be staying. It was a tense minute or so as Hamish growled quietly while Igor stared at him, twitching his nose.

'You see! They're not going to get on,' Mother wailed, ready to throw in the towel as she went to scoop up Hamish.

'Wait, Mother,' I said, blocking her gently with my arm. 'Give them a chance to find out about each other.'

We stood watching them continue their mutual cryptic appraisal until suddenly Igor made a decision and his tail began to flap. Hamish's stump started wiggling then too and they ran circles round each other yapping with delight. I manoeuvred past them to throw open the back door and they tumbled out onto the patio and did joyful laps of the garden. Even Mother was smiling by then, and I was pleased for her that she didn't have to worry about Hamish any more. I will look after him for her.

Saturday 25 June

I was at my flat this morning, going through my accounts with a rising feeling of possibility, when Katie rang and invited me over for lunch with her and Harriet. 'Sorry for the short notice, Sylvia, but we are here and child-free and we thought it would be lovely if you could join us. Carrie might be popping by later too.'

It was perfect timing and I happily agreed and caught the bus over to Forest Hill.

Katie's house is small but homely, and the white and yellow kitchen has French windows that open out onto a garden filled with the plastic paraphernalia apparently needed to keep children occupied in the summer.

'We'll eat in here if that's OK,' said Katie, laying the Formica table with a checked cloth. 'There's so much junk in the garden. I can't face tidying it all up only for them to get it all out again when Mike drops them back.'

I glanced at her in confusion and she bit her lip. 'Mike and I have separated,' she explained. 'He has them every other weekend and we are sorting out how the holidays are going to work. He has taken them to see their grandparents today – I mean *his* parents. Oh, you know what I mean.' She sat down and stared at the floor. 'I never thought this would be me,' she said sadly. 'I thought we'd last, that Mike and I would make it. That we'd have a marriage like Mum and Dad's.'

'Well, those are few and far between,' said Harriet, returning from making a phone call and ready to bolster up Katie with brisk support. 'Now, what needs doing? Shall I start on the veg?'

We sat round the table, companionably peeling and chopping and talking and I felt quite at home in the most unexpected way.

'Of course, Harriet hit the jackpot with her hubby,' Katie suddenly announced with a mischievous smile as she carried the veg over to the sink. 'You should see her and Rob together, Sylvia – talk about love's young dream.'

Harriet blushed slightly, but she looked pleased. 'Well, middle-aged dream, perhaps. But yes, we are very happy and he is wonderful, and a fantastic dad as well. I've been lucky this time round.'

I raised my eyes in interest and Harriet took the cue. 'I was married before, you see, when I was much younger. It was a complete disaster, Sylvia, and I was an idiot.'

I waited for her to continue, intrigued that such a together person as Harriet had an unexpected blip in her past. 'What happened?' I asked finally, unable to hide my curiosity.

Harriet told me all about how she had fallen for an egotistical actor called Daniel when she was just eighteen. How Jonas had loathed him from the start, how her mum had cried at their wedding when Daniel told her Harriet belonged to him now, how he had controlled her and frightened her and taken away all her confidence. How she had finally left him and trained to be a lawyer as she had always wanted to do.

'I moved back in with Mum and Dad so I could go back to university,' she said. 'I was twenty-nine and I had nothing. I was the oldest in my year by miles and I almost didn't go back after the first day. "I'm too old," I said to Dad. "It's too late for me now," and he promised me that it wasn't, that age didn't matter, that I could still follow my dreams and do whatever I wanted to do. He gave me courage and he believed in me. Everything I am now, and everything I have now, it's all because of him and Mum.'

I stared at her transfixed and moved by her story.

'And he was a rubbish actor as well,' Carrie said dismissively, helping herself to a handful of chopped carrots ready for the pot. None of us had noticed her slip in the kitchen door while Harriet was talking and she grinned cheerfully as she sat down at the table, her bangles jangling.

'Where did you spring from?' Harriet was delighted to see her and gave her an enormous hug as Katie came over to join us.

'We got back earlier than we expected from Cambridge. Great festival – lots of customers for my reiki. Did you find the ring?'

'No, not yet. I can't think where he must have put it.' Katie tutted and turned to me. 'We have gone through all Dad's personal stuff and the whole house and we can't find Mum's wedding ring anywhere. I don't suppose you have any idea where it could be?'

For a horrible moment, I feared I was a suspect, but I quickly realised there was no trace of accusation in Katie's tone and I felt ashamed for underestimating their trust in me.

'I'm sorry …' I shook my head. 'I've never seen it and he never mentioned it to me.'

'Of course not. Why would he?' said Harriet, firmly back in the present after her unpleasant trip down memory lane. 'It's just so upsetting because we wanted to pass it down to one of our daughters.'

'Hey, hey, hey! Slow down, lady. I want to wear it as a nose ring first!' said Carrie winking at me as Katie threw a tea towel at her.

'The other thing we need to sort out is selling the house,' said Harriet, when the laughter had died down, and three pairs of hopeful light-blue eyes turned towards me.

Harriet dropped me off at the house around five and I lingered for a while on the pavement outside, looking over the old place with affection. The afternoon sun showed up the missing tiles on the roof, the peeling paint on the window frames and the deeply unfashionable pebbledash. The dilapidated state of the house used to fill me with dismay, but I had come to realise its charm over the last few months and it was beautiful to me now, in its own special way. As I stood watching, the pair of swallows who return every summer flittered to and from their nest under the bathroom window, and the wind chimes hanging from the porch jangled happily, its metal tubes clanging together in the breeze. It had been a birthday gift, long ago, from one of Harriet's children and I remembered Jonas showing it to me in bafflement, having no idea what it was and having not wanted to ask. I had put it up for him, crossly as I recall, annoyed at being held up by such a petty task as I had some article or another of Prof's at home that was waiting to be read. But Jonas's smile when he saw it had been worth the delay.

'Well, I never,' he'd said, stroking his beard in awe as I clambered back down the ladder. I'd left him there gazing at it, lost in his own thoughts as I pulled on my coat and said goodbye. And here it still was, twinkling and tinkling – welcoming, comforting, familiar.

I went down the side passage and let myself in via the gate, breathing in the mingled scent of grass, vegetables and flowers. I unlocked the back door to let the dogs out, sleepy after their naps, fascinated as ever by the delights of the garden, and left them to snuffle round and explore while I went to check on the hogs. They were ready for a feed, their shy little faces peeping out of the hay and I saw to their needs as methodically as Jonas and I had always done together, starting with the bottom left cage and working my way round.

'This way we don't forget anybody,' I said out loud, echoing Jonas's much repeated words on the system.

When I had finished I made a cup of tea and put two biscuits on a plate – one for me, one to share between Igor and Hamish. After my break I wandered round the garden, drawing up a mental inventory of what needed to be done. I noticed there were a lot of weeds springing up in the strawberry patch beside the garage and decided to tackle that first. I went to the shed to find some suitable tools and selected a fork and a trowel from the ancient collection hanging on the wall, along with Jonas's trusty kneeling pad and gardening gloves.

Having fended off both the dogs, who were desperate for a game, I had just started digging out the dandelions when something bright caught my eye on the handle of the trowel. I took the gloves off and pulled my glasses out of my pocket to have a closer look. Holding the trowel up, I could see quite clearly that, where the wooden handle joined with the little metal spade, there was an extra band. A band of gold.

I turned it over in my hands and saw that Jonas had unscrewed the two parts and put the ring in between them before fastening them back together – it must have been there for years. It had been Jonas's lovely secret connection to his wife and it made me laugh with joy. I sat back on my heels and ran my fingers around the smooth warmth of the band, thinking of how Jonas had used this tool countless times as he worked in the garden and imagined how close he must have felt to Paula as he dug up the weeds and planted seedlings in the ground. I went straight into the house to ring Katie clasping the trowel to my chest, the dogs running ahead of me, sensing my excitement. I couldn't wait to tell her that the mystery of their mum's wedding ring had been solved in the most wonderful way. How delightful it is to have friends to share good news with at last.

Summer

The hedgehog is often referred to as the 'gardener's friend' because its diet contains so many plant-eating insects. It is particularly during the summer months, when crops and flowers are at their peak, that we are most grateful for their help. Hedgehogs haven't always been so positively regarded, though. Indeed, in sixteenth-century England there was a pernicious belief that hedgehogs were witches in disguise and that they stole from farmers by drinking milk from their cows at night. A three-pence bounty was placed by the English Parliament on the head of each hedgehog that was caught and killed, leading to thousands being slaughtered across the country.

Another erroneous myth about hedgehogs was relayed by Pliny the Elder in the first century in his *Historia Naturalis* and was even repeated by Charles Darwin, who really should have known better. The scholarly Roman described how hedgehogs would climb apple trees, knock the fruit down, roll on the fruit to impale them on their spines and then carry them off to hide underground. All nonsense, of course, as hedgehogs can't climb trees and nor do they store food in their burrows or carry it on their prickles.

Hedgehogs may have been misunderstood in the past, but the truth is that they are precious and harmless (unless you happen to be a slug). Just because they are not easy to stroke and live a secretive sort of life doesn't mean they are not worth loving. They are just being hedgehogs. And they don't all have fleas.

Jonas Entwistle, *The Hedgehog Year*

Friday 21 July (One Year Later)

I sat motionless on the tube train as it made its way overground towards King's Road station, transfixed by the two French girls who were sitting opposite me and chatting in a way that I knew without a doubt meant that they were sisters. They were engaged in a never-ending conversation about life, just like Millie and I had once been, until it did end, and I still miss that connection even though it has been over a year since that final, awful scene in the car. It is a testament to the skills and patience of Crystal as a go-between that we managed to organise Mother's move to a residential home and sort out and sell her flat without ever having to meet or speak. Texts from Crystal would specify the exact times between which I could go to Mother's and choose the furniture I wanted to keep or inform me of the need to arrange a visit to the solicitor to sign the power of attorney papers. We have a rota for visiting Mother now: Mondays and Fridays for me, Sundays and Wednesdays for Millie, with Crystal free to pop in whenever she feels like it – which admittedly isn't often, but at least she doesn't have to worry about who she might bump into.

Mother is mercifully unaware of the rift between her daughters, just as she is increasingly unaware of anything that isn't food-or tea-related. The carers try to keep up her fastidious personal appearance, dressing her in her twinsets and arranging for a hairdresser to come and give her a blow dry once a week, but she is disappearing in front of my eyes. Every time I visit it seems she has shrunk further away from the world of people and places and things, further into her own skin, her own essential being. She is unexpectedly timid and gentle in her dotage.

I had been warned that, with old age, people become more extreme versions of themselves with no social filter and, deeply acquainted with Mother's acerbic tongue and judgemental attitude over the years, I was dreading hearing what she really thought of me. She isn't that way at all, though, she is more like a frightened little girl who just wants me to sit holding her hand while she nibbles on biscuits, the crumbs clinging to the grey hairs on her top lip. I have ached to talk to Millie about her and share the experience of seeing our once formidable mother slowly fade away. But it was made clear, through Crystal, that there was to be no contact, even after my letter, and, although I have never fully accepted it, the loss of her has become familiar to me and stings a little less as time passes.

This evening, though, I knew Millie and Kamal would be there. My wonderful, talented niece had had a painting accepted at a prestigious London art fair and tonight was the opening night – an invitation-only, black-tie event. All of London's art crowd would be there, along with a thrilling selection of actors, musicians and politicians.

I agonised over whether to go. Crystal had handed me the gold-embossed invite and stated, matter-of-factly, that she wanted me to be there and she wasn't prepared to choose between me and her mum.

She has spent hours at Jonas's house over the last year, sketching and painting the dogs and the garden and the hedgehogs. The picture on display was one I hadn't yet seen, but I knew it was a bright watercolour of Igor lying amongst the potted geraniums on the patio and that it was on sale for a considerable sum. Crystal has already been approached by an illustrators' agent for children's books and no one is more stunned than me at the turn her work has taken in such a short time from adolescent, angst-filled black-and-grey wastelands, to whimsical animal portraits. When I asked her about it, she simply shrugged and said she was bored with being miserable and wanted to paint happy things, and I nodded in complete understanding.

The train trundled to a stop and I alighted onto the platform, looking furtively around me like a criminal, expecting Millie and Kamal to appear from behind every pillar. I could see the enormous marquee in the park and feel the buzz of the approaching attendees from three streets away – men, dapper in their formal dress, with the sort of high-maintenance women who spend their whole lives preparing their bodies, hair and faces for these kind of events.

'This is for Crystal,' I said to myself, determined to remain calm. 'I have every right to be here.'

I smoothed down my green satin dress as it was pulling a little over my hips; along with the rest of me, they've started to fill out in quite a pleasing way over the past year, and took a deep breath. I was glad I had also worn the expensive cream and olive pashmina Millie had given me for my fiftieth and wrapped it around myself protectively as I entered the reception area. The usual squad of black-clad, trendy art students were manning the desk and a Chinese girl with lilac hair ticked my name off a list while continuing an animated celebrity-spotting conversation with her friend.

I took a glass of prosecco from a passing tray-bearer and entered the main space, which had the grassy humidity of all marquees, mingled with the unmistakable smell of money. The art was displayed in a confusing maze of booths, some much larger than others, reflecting, I supposed, the level of esteem for each artist or group of artists. I grabbed a guide from the first stand and searched for Crystal's name on the list at the back. I was about to head off to the far-left corner where her picture was hanging when a round of applause alerted me that something formal was happening. I turned to the right and saw the patron of the art society, Sir Donald Bewley in blazer and cravat, standing with open arms, ready to begin the proceedings with a speech.

'Welcome, one and all. It is a pleasure to see so many familiar faces here on this delightful summer's evening for the twenty-fifth annual Art Society Show. We have an outstanding range of talent on display tonight and I do hope you will enjoy some old favourites as well as discover some rising new stars. And, of course, I hope you have brought your credit cards.' He paused at this point to allow the polite laughter to rise and then fall and went on to detail the high-profile guests who had graced us with their presence. 'Finally, this year we have also invited leading academics from all the London universities, in the hope that we can begin to share ideas across disciplines using the visual arts as inspiration. I look forward to hearing and having many interesting conversations and wish you all a wonderful evening.'

The crowd clapped and then dispersed to explore the exhibition and find friends and I was left standing alone, clutching my glass, feeling utterly exposed. I had already been nervous about bumping into Millie and Kamal, but the possibility that Prof could also be here had completely unnerved me.

'Hello, Sylvia,' said a woman's voice and I looked up to see Martha in a slinky black tuxedo, standing in front of me in her absolute element. 'Isn't this great?'

She lifted her glass to indicate the entire marquee and everyone in it.

'Yes, wonderful,' I replied, desperate to ask her the question, but not wanting to seem like I cared. She answered it anyway.

'Carl is here, you know, with his student shag. Have you seen him? He looks like a pathetic old letch.' She sniggered and took another swig from her glass.

'No, no I haven't.' I felt disorientated, as if the rules had changed in a game I didn't know I was still playing.

'Look! There he is, the swine,' she trilled affectionately and then to my horror she tried to wave him over. 'Carl, over here, someone for you.'

I saw him then; he was leaning down in rapt conversation with a stunning young woman in a long yellow dress and wasn't about to be interrupted.

'Is that his girlfriend?' I started in surprise.

'Hardly.' She threw her head back and laughed at the thought. 'She's the new Bond girl.' She paused for effect, but she could tell by my blank expression that I didn't recognise her. 'No, he's with that one,' she said, indicating with a long red talon as Lola went storming up to them with a fierce smile on her face and inserted herself firmly between Prof and the actress. She was wearing the very same blue chiffon dress she had had on that night in Rome, but it looked different here in a marquee in London – less striking, somehow, more fussy. 'Apparently, she's preggers,' Martha whispered to me behind her hand, delivering her prime piece of gossip with delight. 'I hear it's been an absolute scandal at the university and she's had to put her PhD on indefinite pause to protect his reputation. Bit late for that, if you ask me! Can you even *imagine* Carl doing the nappies and sleepless nights again? He was hopeless enough the first time round.' She chuckled at the thought, and I simply nodded and absorbed the news without surprise, feeling nothing but a strong sense of pity for Lola as she glared angrily at Prof.

'Oh dear, trouble in paradise.' Martha raised her eyebrows and her glass to me with a wicked smile and wandered off in search of more fun.

I still find it hard to believe that I wasted all those years on the arrogant philanderer who is Carl Lomax. I have forgiven myself, because I can see now that I was in love with the idea of Prof, rather than the man himself, and that I needed that fantasy of love to protect me from the pain of being lonely. Perhaps it is the same for Lola? It shows how far I have come that I actually think it is a crying shame that she's giving up her studies – she really is incredibly clever. I genuinely hope she finds a way back to herself in time. She has coped admirably being a single mother to one, and I have no doubt she will be able to do the same with two if Prof leaves her in the lurch at some point, which, unfortunately, I suspect he probably will.

I watched as Prof ignored Lola, as he had ignored Martha's beckoning, despite her repeated attempts to join in the conversation. It was only when the actress decided to go and talk to somebody else – a presenter I recognised from morning television – that Prof acknowledged Lola was there and absently put his hand on her back as he scanned the marquee. He looked past me several times as if I were invisible and I continued to watch them from my spot five or so metres away, feeling like a camouflaged wild animal photographer. I considered raising my hand or walking over, but I didn't want to be reminded by his response of his opinion of me and the way I had behaved last year. A bald man in a flamboyant pinstriped suit tapped Prof on the shoulder and he turned and greeted him with a hearty handshake, allowing himself to be led away to see some piece of art or another. Lola remained where she was, cutting a lonely figure, awkwardly sipping from a water bottle and trying to be interested in the minimalist line drawings nearest to her. I briefly considered going over to talk to her, but I didn't want to be the cause of any more upset and I was not at all sure what to say after our last unpleasant meeting at the university.

The marquee was really filling up by then, with people wandering and chatting, the art an excuse to get together and see and be seen. I was different, being on my own and on a mission to locate a specific picture, and

I had to politely push my way through the well-heeled crowds to get to the area where Crystal's painting was hanging.

I felt quite emotional when I saw it. It so perfectly captured the peace and homeliness of Jonas's garden and the magic, as well as the sadness, of last summer when everything began to change. I smiled as I recognised Igor's expression of utter bliss as he basked in the sun, eyes tightly shut against the light, his fur muddy after rolling in the flower beds, scattered with geranium petals from where he had bumped against the pots.

'What do you think? Have I got him right?' It was Crystal, looking radiant in a bright red mini dress, her hair cropped round her ears, tilting her head to one side and looking anew at her creation.

'Crystal, you look beautiful! I love your hair.' I kissed her on the cheek and she beamed with a confidence I had not seen in her before. 'It's perfect,' I said, turning back to the picture. 'You are really so very talented.'

'I couldn't have done it without you, Auntie Sylvia,' she said, 'and the sanctuary. And Jonas, of course.' Our eyes met in a moment of mutual sympathy.

'I made something for you,' she said, pulling a small black velvet pouch out of her purse. 'I hope you like it.' She watched me closely as I opened the little bag and pulled out a silver chain with an exquisite hedgehog charm attached. It was made out of clay with tiny shards of metal as prickles and beady jet eyes. I laughed with delight as I held the necklace up and let it spin in the light.

'It's adorable, Crystal. I love it,' I exclaimed and let her help me fix it round my neck. 'I think it's the nicest present I've ever had,' I said happily as I touched the charm again and felt its wonderfully familiar shape.

Crystal beamed, then tapped my elbow in warning, and I looked to the left to see Millie and Kamal approaching. Kamal was frowning at the exhibition map and pointing the other way as Millie dragged him forward, having spotted Crystal. They were nearly upon us by the time Crystal stepped forward, revealing that I was standing behind her. Millie's delighted face froze and Kamal glared at me.

'Look, it's here, Mum, Dad.' Crystal took control of the ghastly situation by channelling their attention onto her painting and they exclaimed with enthusiasm as I had done. Kamal clapped her on the back and told her how proud he was and Millie gave a detailed commentary of every aspect of the composition and the colours she had used as if it was the work of an old master. Crystal was pink with delight by the time they had finished and they had a group hug which stung in ways I still couldn't quite articulate. I wondered for a moment if I really was intermittently invisible this evening as I stood to the side of them with my now empty glass in hand.

'Can you show us what other paintings you like?' Millie asked, putting her arm through Crystal's and grabbing Kamal's hand.

'Aunt Sylvia is here,' Crystal said, pulling her arm from Millie and putting it around me. It was a bold move and Kamal and Millie looked equally perturbed at the encounter Crystal had forced between us.

'Yes. Hello. How are you?' Millie's clipped tone was painful to hear and I answered in a similarly formal way. 'Fine thanks, Millie. How are you?'

'We are fine. We are all fine, thank you, lady. Goodbye,' Kamal turned and attempted to herd his women off but Crystal wasn't ready to go.

'Come on, guys. Hasn't this gone on long enough?' she said pleadingly, looking from one to the other of us. 'I love you all and I'm sick of being in the middle. It wasn't all Auntie Sylvia's fault. Can't you just forget the past and move on?'

Kamal started shaking his head, but Millie's eyes brimmed with tears and she reached out for Crystal's hand and then, miracle of miracles, very tentatively with her other hand, for mine. I gripped it tight and felt a surge of loving energy flow between us.

'I'm sorry,' I said quietly.

'I know you are,' she said in a shaky voice.

'Dad?' Crystal urged.

'No, no, no!' Kamal said, waving his finger in the air.

'Kamal, I think it's time,' Millie said slowly. 'I know things can never go back to how they were, but maybe Crystal is right and there is a way to work things out. Let's at least talk about it. She's my sister. I miss her.' She looked at me shyly and I nodded in agreement.

Kamal reddened and sighed, clearly sensing he was being outnumbered. 'OK, maybe. But not here, not now,' he said leading them away. 'Come on, let's see the rest of this show.'

As I watched them go, Crystal turned and smiled at me and I held up crossed fingers, finally daring to hope that there might be an end to this dreadful falling out.

I stood alone, looking at Crystal's painting for some time, reflecting on the juxtaposition of a sliver of Jonas's humble life being present at an event like this until I felt the need to leave. I wanted to be outside in the night air and out of the stuffy tent full of people I didn't know. I made a quick phone call and then wound my way back to the welcome area, pausing to take in a few of the exhibits that caught my eye.

The grassy area between the marquee and the road was busier than I had anticipated and I pulled my pashmina round me protectively as I made my way to the kerb. I turned automatically at the raised voices of a couple arguing and realised that it was Lola and Prof. She was shouting that he hadn't been paying her any attention and he was desperately trying to placate her by shushing, which seemed to be enraging her further. They both saw me then and looked at me with the confused recognition that occurs when you see a familiar face in a completely unexpected context. I put my head down and hastened my pace past them, not wanting any part of their public display of non-affection.

'Auntie Sylvia, are you going?' Crystal ran up to me and I saw Millie and Kamal waiting for her just outside the marquee. 'I saw you heading out and I wanted to thank you for coming.' As I hugged her and thanked her again for the necklace, I heard the familiar throaty rattle of a motorbike drawing up on the kerb next to us.

I hitched up my skirt and climbed onto the back of the bike, reaching round for the spare helmet in the box at the back. As I retrieved it, I looked up at the crowd outside the marquee and realised that we were attracting attention – a mousey middle-aged woman on a Harley Davidson is not the most common of sights, after all. Prof and Lola suspended their row long enough to watch, open-mouthed, and I gave them a happy wave as we pulled away into the road.

Glancing back as the bike picked up speed I saw Millie running unsteadily in her heels along the pavement towards the junction at the top of the road, Kamal standing in wide-armed bewilderment by the marquee where she had left him. As we waited for a break in the traffic so we could turn left, Millie was beside us and we locked eyes for a moment as I lifted my visor. She smiled and blew me a kiss, filling me with a joyous certainty that the time for a reconciliation really is near. But before I could respond, we were away, me holding onto Carrie's leather-clad back, roaring through West London on the most glorious of summer evenings. Back to her father's house which is now *my* house. Back to Igor and Hamish leaping to greet me. Back to looking after hogs and growing vegetables. Back to Crystal sketching in the garden on Sunday afternoons. Back to getting to know Neil and precious days with him and Riki.

Back to life.

My life.

Author's Note

I have always been intrigued and enchanted by the quirky and secretive nature of hedgehogs and when I started thinking about the character of Sylvia who is both spiky yet intensively vulnerable, it seemed the perfect fit that she should volunteer to work in a hedgehog sanctuary.

Even so, I have to admit I knew very little about this curious animal when I began writing *Needlemouse*. My need to find out more so that I could enable Jonas, and to a lesser extent Sylvia, to be hedgehog experts in the book led me on a fascinating journey of discovery about their lives and habits. They really are extraordinary creatures.

Sadly, though, I also found out that hedgehogs are declining rapidly in Britain. In the 1950s it was estimated that there were 36.5 million and yet today there are perhaps just a million hedgehogs left. The reasons for their decline are complex. More and more hedgerows are being lost to intensive farming, and fencing round domestic gardens has become more secure, meaning that hedgehogs are not free to roam for food as they were in the past. The rise of traffic and widespread pesticide use has also been deadly to hedgehogs, as has the increase in the numbers of natural predators such as badgers.

Following recent hedgehog charity campaigns important work is now taking place in the countryside to restore, extend and link key hedgehog habitats. We can also help in our own gardens by putting out wet cat and dog food, leaving wild areas for hedgehogs to nest and hibernate and making holes in fences to enable them to move from garden to garden in their search for food.

If you would like to know more about the plight of Britain's hedgehogs or would like to contribute to the preservation and protection of this increasingly endangered animal, please contact one of the following wonderful charities: Hedgehog Street (www.hedgehogstreet.org) or the British Hedgehog Preservation Society (www.british hedgehogs.org.uk). Alternatively, offer your support for your local hedgehog sanctuary – there are many real life Jonas and Sylvias out there making an enormous difference to the sick and injured hedgehogs who they look after. A wide, although not comprehensive list of rescues can be found here: www.hedgehog-rescue.org.uk.

Thank you!

Jane O'Connor

Acknowledgements

Massive thanks to the judges of Tibor Jones's page turner prize for spotting the potential of *Needlemouse* and to Charlotte Maddox for her brilliant advice and support in getting the book into shape. Huge thanks also to my editor Gillian Green for taking a shine to the hedgehogs, and to the whole Ebury team for their warm professionalism.

I would also like to thank my fantastic colleagues and students at Birmingham City University for their friendship, their constant intellectual inspiration and their enthusiastic response to my fiction writing. I promise none of the characters are based on any of you!

Thanks to Sam and Donna, my best friends through thick and thin, I love you both.

Thanks to my lovely Mum for cheering me on in every endeavour and to Dad for always believing in my abilities. What more could anyone ask from their parents?

Thanks to Mary and Carol for being such great in-laws.

Love and special thanks to my husband Graham for being all round wonderful, and to my gorgeous Toby for his pride in my achievements. Thank you to Adam for teaching me about being brave – I miss you every day.

Finally, none of this would have been possible without the chance to write whilst on maternity leave with my youngest son Billy. Thank you, darling, for being such a good napper! I couldn't have written 1000 words a day any other way.